Get Motivated!

DAILY PSYCH-UPS

KARA LEVERTE FARLEY AND SHEILA M. CURRY

A FIRESIDE BOOK PUBLISHED BY SIMON & SCHUSTER
New York London Toronto Sydney Tokyo Singapore

◆

FIRESIDE
Rockefeller Center
1230 Avenue of the Americas
New York, New York 10020

Designed by Bonni Leon-Berman
Manufactured in the United States of America

10 9 8 7

Library of Congress Cataloging-in-Publication Data

Farley, Kara Leverte.
    Get motivated! : daily psych-ups / Kara Leverte Farley and Sheila M. Curry.
        p.   cm.
    "A Fireside book."
    Includes bibliographical references and index.
    1. Athletes—Prayer-books and devotions—English.   2. Devotional calendars.
I. Curry, Sheila M.   II. Title.
BL625.9.A84F37   1994
796'.01—dc20   93-48850
                                                                              CIP

ISBN: 0-671-88100-0

For D.F.
—KLF

For Jumbos everywhere.
—SMC

◆

A C K N O W L E D G M E N T S

Special thanks to our
families, our friends, and
everyone at Fireside/
Simon & Schuster who
helped *us* get motivated.

◆

You gotta believe!
—*Tug McGraw*

Today, anything is possible. We believe we will start new fitness and diet routines to kick off the new year. We believe we will improve our current exercise programs: pushing a little harder, running a little farther, going a little longer. On this first day of the year we believe we will be happy, healthy, fit, and strong as the days and weeks unfold. We will set realistic goals, practice well, and play hard as we resolve to maintain a workout program in the coming months.

Tug says, "You gotta believe!" But, perhaps more importantly, we *want* to believe. It feels so good to have the self-confidence and desire to want to enhance our health and fitness, our strength and stamina. Nothing makes us feel more accomplished than an extra mile or another set, a winning shot or a personal best.

◆

Today I will believe.

> Whatever you do, don't do it halfway.
> —*Bob Beamon*

Every activity, chore, project, and exercise we attempt deserves our best effort. From a task at the office to our daily workout, we should always aim to give everything we try our best shot. Workouts that we really put ourselves out for are a lot more satisfying and, ultimately, a lot more productive. The harder we work every step of the way, the quicker and more efficiently we'll reach our goals.

By demanding more from ourselves on a regular basis, we'll get more out of ourselves when we really need it. By giving 100 percent when we practice, we'll be able to play to our potential when, and if, we compete. And by giving our all on the field, in the gym, on the court, or in the pool, we'll be setting a good example for others, inspiring them to find activities that are right for them.

We all have days when we just don't seem to have the energy or the interest in working out at peak effort. These are the times to reach inside ourselves and try to find that extra umph that will motivate us to give it a shot.

♦

No matter what I do, I give my best.

The way a team plays as a whole determines its success. You may have the greatest bunch of individual stars in the world, but if they don't play together, the club won't be worth a dime.
—*Babe Ruth*

*T*he company volleyball team, your intramural basketball team, you and your tennis doubles partner, your crew team members—no matter what the makeup of your squad and regardless of what sport you participate in, you've doubtless realized the importance of team cooperation and synergy that the great Babe Ruth suggests. You needn't be a member of a highly competitive team to see that it takes a true group effort to make a winning team. Even the casual golf foursome that plays on Sunday afternoons, or the basketball players that get together informally in the local gym after work, need to perform as a team to be successful.

While we all take the field or the court or the course with the intention of putting in our own best effort, we must be careful not to become wrapped up in our own performance at the expense of the team. Yes, it's important to play our best and try our hardest out there, but it is also vital that we take advantage of, and have confidence in, the skills of our teammates. If we feel good about their play, they'll feel good about ours, and we should be able to work well together.

As members of a team, we must learn to share the work, the glory, and the disappointments. We can't play alone.

◆

Synergy among team members makes for energy for the team.

> You have to set new goals every day.
> —*Julie Krone*

*E*very time we step onto the basketball court; every morning when we lace up our running shoes; every weight-training session we do, bicycle ride we take, and swim workout we attempt, we should have a goal in mind. The goal can be short-term or long-term. It can be modest or challenging. It can be made privately or in consultation with coaches, instructors, or teammates. No matter what we set out to do each day, we should do it with some objective in mind.

A daily goal serves to motivate us and get us to give our best. If we set off on our morning workout wanting to accomplish something in particular, chances are we'll perform better, just as we will if we enter a competition with specific aspirations. The added pressure/exhilaration of a personal challenge is often the jump-start we need to perform at our peaks.

Jockey Julie Krone sets regular goals for herself, which is probably part of the reason she is at the top of her sport. Professional athletes, especially, need to stay motivated and focussed so as not to lose their edge. Part of what keeps them sharp is the constant setting and resetting of personal goals, something athletes at all levels can do as well.

◆

Before I do anything, I will set a new, never-before-attempted goal for the day.

I believe that the day you take complete responsibility for yourself, the day you stop making any excuses, is the day you start to the top.
—O. J. Simpson

I'm too tired. I'm hungry. I've got work to do. It's too late. It's too early. It's too cold. It's too hot. I don't have time. I don't feel well. I don't want to go by myself. The gym's too crowded. I don't really know how to. All my workout clothes are in the wash. I'll go tomorrow, I swear.

Excuses, excuses, excuses. We've all used them and they are all extremely effective in keeping us from our workouts. They've kept us from running, from playing in the tournament, from aerobics class, and from every type of athletic activity you can name. Once in a while an excuse is just our way of buying time and getting a little extra rest. However, if excuses are allowed to accumulate they build a huge insurmountable wall between us and getting in shape. The way to knock down that wall is to see where the excuse is really coming from. Is it fear of failure? Is it lack of commitment or confidence? Is it laziness? It's just as easy to talk ourselves into working out as it is to talk ourselves out of it. And we know we'll feel better once we've done it. Think of getting it done and how happy we'll be—no excuses.

◆

No ifs, ands, or buts, I'm working out today.

Enjoy the successes that you have, and don't be too hard on yourself when you don't do well. Too many times we beat up on ourselves. Just relax and enjoy it. You'll do better.
—*Patty Sheehan*

Chances are there are times when fun is forgotten at the gym, on the tennis court, in the pool, or on a run. Working out seems like drudgery. It's painful, boring, and at times even stressful. Maybe we have not been playing or working out up to par or maybe we're just temporarily burnt out and don't feel like doing anything. It's not important what the source of the discomfort is, it's just important to try to avoid punishing ourselves when we don't perform up to our expectations.

It's too easy to fall into the trap of being constantly disappointed in ourselves and our lack of motivation or success. We need to keep reminding ourselves of the successes we have had—and, frankly, every time we complete a tough work-out or a challenging game we should pat ourselves on the back—and use those to help us through the difficult times. What we'll find is that staying more positive about our all-around performance will only make us do better in the long run.

Every five-mile run, every forty-five minute step class, every goal set and achieved is something to be proud of. If we remember to be as supportive of ourselves as we are of others, we'll learn that it's extremely motivating to be our own number-one fan.

◆

The more I support myself and my endeavors, the more successful I'll be.

If you don't do what's best for your body,
you're the one who comes up on the short end.
—*Julius Erving*

*O*n Saturday, what's best might be a nice long run in the park, followed by a swim. On Sunday, it might be a day off from working out to rest sore muscles and conserve energy for our Monday-evening aerobics class. Tuesday might be circuit training day, followed by another run Wednesday, a day off Thursday, and then a wind-sprints workout on Friday. Finding what works best for each of us individually is the key to staying fit, active, and above all healthy and uninjured. Only we can truly judge whether we're up for a long bike ride or a hot bath.

Forcing another set of tennis when our shoulder is crying for mercy, or pushing another mile when our calves are cramped, is not being tough or aggressive. It's being dumb and careless. An extra mile logged today could be two lost tomorrow as we will inevitably become overtired or injured.

On the other hand, we also know when our bodies can do more. Consistently doing the same workout day after day is simply maintaining our weight and fitness level. Once a workout becomes routine, it's time to add a challenge— more time, weight, distance, or competition. We need to listen to our bodies— responding to their needs in ways that challenge us, but don't hurt us.

◆

My body signals when it's had enough or can do more. I will be aware and respond to these signals appropriately.

> Sweat plus sacrifice equals success.
> —*Charlie Finley*

Success, whether in business, finance, or academics, does not come easily for most people. It usually involves hard work, perseverance, desire, and a certain amount of luck. Success in athletics is no exception.

While our individual goals will vary widely—some of us aspire to drag ourselves to the gym three times a week, others of us want to run a marathon—success within these goals is vital to maintaining motivation. So it stands to reason that no matter how serious an athlete we are, we're going to have to get out there and challenge ourselves and sweat a little. That may mean an extra twenty minutes at the gym, another five miles on the bicycle, or practice-serving another basket of tennis balls—something that pushes us a little farther and makes us work a little harder.

For every extra mile, sit-up, bucket of golf balls, tennis lesson, or session on the StairMaster, we can count on improving our fitness level as well as our skills. Every bead of sweat or aching muscle helps us build healthier, stronger, more fit bodies.

◆

To improve my skills and build my fitness level, I have to challenge myself in each and every workout.

It [racing] is a matter of spirit, not strength. It is a matter of doing your best each little moment. There's never a break. You must have desire,
a very intense desire to keep going.
—*Janet Guthrie*

*I*n a sport that has been dominated by men, auto racer Janet Guthrie has made a name for herself and earned the respect of her peers. And whether we are female trying to make it in a traditionally male sport, a person of average height trying to play a sport that usually calls for more stature, or any other athlete determined to be successful in an activity that we may not be entirely cut out for, we can relate to Guthrie and her challenges.

Many times what makes us achieve in these perceived uphill battles is not size or strength but, as Guthrie says, sheer desire and spirit. The ten-mile race that is our farthest run to date, we finish with aplomb; the advanced step class that is twice as long as the beginning class, we make it through; and the top tennis player whom we meet in a club tournament, we squeak out a narrow victory over. We've all been in situations where we seem to be the underdog, and yet these are the times that call for the most energy and desire. Professional sports are filled with top athletes who might have missed out on great careers if they had listened to conventional wisdom and decided not to pursue their dreams. For us it means sticking with the activities and sports we like and having the urge to be as good as we can be.

♦

I want to be proficient at the sports I participate in, and that should be evident in each and every workout.

It's lack of faith that makes people afraid of meeting challenges,
and I believed in myself.
—Muhammad Ali

We all have voices in our heads that undermine our faith in ourselves and our abilities. We hear them all the time—sometimes they are quiet, sometimes they are loud; they are the ones that say: "You'll never make it up this hill." "She's much better than you." Sometimes we are even harder on ourselves: "I've blown it again." "I'll never get better."

We have to work on trading in those negative voices for supportive, more realistic ones. The voices that cheer us on and celebrate our accomplishments are the ones we should listen to. It is okay to think well of ourselves. If we don't believe in our abilities we will be our own worst enemies. We will back away from challenges instead of meeting them head on. Or we'll give up even before we have really begun. The best way to feed our faith in ourselves is to not dwell on our errors but to pay close attention to what we do right. We can learn from our mistakes, but we can also learn from our accomplishments. It is our accomplishments that fuel our faith and build our belief that we can overcome obstacles and face any challenge.

◆

I'll meet all my challenges fully backed up with belief in myself.

I always felt that I hadn't achieved what I wanted to achieve. I always felt that I could get better. That's the whole incentive. Even today, I still think I can get better. I'll never be satisfied.
—*Virginia Wade*

Complacency doesn't get us anywhere. We have to keep raising our goals a little higher each time we work out. No matter who we are—if we are a beginner or advanced—there is always room for improvement. The trick is not to rest on our laurels. We don't have to be in competitive sports to keep working on improving. We all have certain skills and abilities that are better than others. And we all tend to rely on our strengths and hope that they can compensate for our weak spots. Sooner or later, however, those weaknesses can catch up to us.

The incentive to keep working and practicing isn't just to get a trophy or a win. The point is to get better, and in turn, become more fit. If we keep applying pressure to ourselves we will improve. But be careful. Too much pressure can make us uptight and inhibit our improvement rather than enhance it. It's a fine balance. We don't want to set impossible—and ultimately discouraging—goals. But we shouldn't settle for less than we can achieve. We should always keep our eyes on the next level up.

◆

I won't settle for my minimum performance; I'll keep aiming for my maximum.

For when the One Great Scorer comes to mark against your name,
He writes—not that you won or lost—but how you played the game.
                                    —*Grantland Rice*

No matter how important that club tennis championship may seem; no matter how much is riding on the company golf tournament; no matter how desperate we were to beat our personal record in a 10K, we mustn't lose sight of the main attractions that bring us to athletics: fun and fitness.

So few athletes make a living in sports and even of those who do, most claim a real love for their game. Players who are having fun are usually more successful in the long run. For the nonprofessional, athletics should be about having a good time, challenging ourselves, keeping our bodies—and minds—in shape. Those who play team sports love the social aspect of their games. Those who prefer individual events revel in the peace and solitude of running or swimming or cycling.

While competition is certainly part of athletics, it is just a piece of the complete experience and should not be taken too seriously—by either a winner or a runner-up.

◆

I have fun playing the game—I work hard and I have a good time out there.

It's not necessarily the amount of time you spend at practice that counts; it's what
you put into the practice.
—*Eric Lindros*

We can practice for hours and hours, but if our hearts aren't in it, we're not going to get much out of it. We need to bring focus and concentration to all of our warm-ups. Practice is a time to work out the kinks in our play and prepare for what we might meet in our game. It is a testing ground where we can improve the things we know we can do well and push our limits on things we may be less comfortable with.

If we are not doing an activity that involves team or individual competition we are not exempt from putting our hearts into our "practices." We may be practicing for an ultimate goal of losing weight, getting in top shape, or generally becoming healthy. So, when we go to our class, or take our run, we can think of that as our practice. It's helping us to work toward our goals, which can be our "big game."

◆

Whether I am practicing for the big game or "practicing" for being in better
shape, I will put all I can into my workouts.

Concentration is the ability to think about absolutely nothing
when it is absolutely necessary.
—*Ray Knight*

*S*omething magical happens when we are playing at our optimum ability. Nothing exists except the game. Some people call it playing in "the zone." It doesn't happen all the time, but when it does we feel as if we are in complete control and that we can sense what is going to happen before it does.

Concentration helps us focus and, in effect, turn off our minds. Thinking too much can actually hamper our performance. Instead of just reacting to what's going on in the moment, we start thinking about what we are going to do and what our opponent is going to do, and soon we are so caught up in trying to figure out what is going to happen that we can't respond to the current situation. Concentrating helps to turn off the mental chatter that can distract us. It can also help to eliminate extra babble—when we are focused we are not thinking about what phone calls we have to return or whether or not we'll have time to pick up our dry cleaning. We are completely involved in our game or our workout. We will discover the time passing without our even noticing. When we are concentrating this well, we will not only be performing at our best but we will be getting the best out of our exercise.

◆

When I am exercising I will think about nothing.

Everyone has limits on the time they can devote to exercise, and cross-training simply gives you the best return on your investment—balanced fitness with minimum injury risk and maximum fun.
—*Paula Newby-Fraser*

*C*ross-training, or the combining of two or more activities in an exercise program, is by far the safest and most effective way to reach all-around fitness. By alternating between different types of workouts—running and cycling, swimming and aerobics, tennis and golf—we are giving parts of our bodies a chance to rest while we work out others, and are helping to head off the boredom that can set in when we stick with one sport day after day. Injuries due to overuse are minimized by varying our exercise program, and, if we do happen to get injured, cross-training is a good way to keep in shape while recovering. Even world-class athletes who have to practice one particular sport regularly know the value of cross-training in helping to develop other skills and muscles.

Run. Bike. Swim. Play tennis. Ski. Do StairMaster. Walk. Aerobicize. There are so many choices out there. Exercise should not be a chore. Take your pick from the incredibly varied menu, and enjoy the many ways we can work out our bodies.

◆

Today I will do an activity I have not done lately.

I learned that if you want to make it bad enough, no matter how bad it is,
you can make it.
—*Gale Sayers*

It is true: If we want it enough, we really can make it so. Desire can get us through the toughest workouts or the grimmest of days. Desire can propel us over that last tough hill, or through that challenging mogul run. It can carry us to heights we never thought possible—as long as we have faith in ourselves and believe that when we apply our minds and our bodies with a concentrated effort we will be successful.

There are many people who overcome seemingly insurmountable odds so that they can exercise or compete. There are people who compete in road races in wheelchairs. There are paraplegics who ski. When you overcome odds like that, you don't do it on a whim. You do it because you have the desire to get out there and test your limits and do whatever you can.

Each of us has hurdles or challenges that we need to overcome in order to participate in athletics. No matter what the obstacles, if we want it enough we are capable of achieving a great deal.

◆

I will go after what I want and I know that I will get it.

The pressure makes me more intent about each shot. Pressure on the last few holes makes me play better.

—*Nancy Lopez*

*P*ressure can crush us or it can lift us up and inspire us. Pressure can come from the outside, from coaches, fans, or enthusiastic family members. It can come from a challenging game or match because there is a lot of pressure inherent in competing head to head with an opponent who is pushing us to our limits. There is a lot of anxiety in hearing the footsteps and panting behind us in a race. Pressure can also come from within.

On the upside, pressure can help us rise to the occasion. It can get us working harder than we ever thought possible. Sometimes pressure can contribute to better focus. If we are experiencing a lot of pressure, often the only way to force ourselves to shut it out is to concentrate intensely. Positive stress can help us play or perform at a higher level than we thought possible, and it can be valuable in developing skills, since if we don't feel the urge to improve, we will stay stuck in a rut. When handled appropriately, pressure can get us playing as we never played before.

◆

I will make the pressure work *for* me.

Slumps are like a soft bed. They're easy to get into and hard to get out of.
—*Johnny Bench*

Everyone gets into a slump now and then. It may be a batting slump, where you're just not performing up to your usual for the the company softball team; or it may be a putting slump, where you seem to choke every time the ball hits the green; or it may be a general exercise slump, where every workout seems tough —you can't run as far or as fast, you can't do as many reps, and your usual high-impact class is tougher than ever. Luckily, slumps don't last.

They may seem to go on forever, and the inclination may be to sit out the softball game, pass on a golf game, or skip exercise altogether, but usually the best advice is to continue with the same workout or game schedule as before, because eventually the slump will break. Even the best athletes go through periods of less-than-top performance, lackluster workouts, and waning desire. And tough as it may seem, professional athletes have to go through these performance blahs in front of a huge audience commenting on every missed shot, bad play, or plunging statistic. Fortunately, most of us only have to suffer in front of a minimal crowd. Either way, at times like these it's a challenge to stick with it, but it's the most effective solution in the long run.

◆

Everyone gets the sports blahs once in a while, so, despite wanting to retire my workout wear, I'll stick with my program when I feel this way.

Experience tells you what to do; confidence allows you to do it.
—*Stan Smith*

All the practice and repetition in the world won't guarantee a top performance. We need confidence.

It's a lot easier to drop a ten-foot putt, or get off a three-point jumpshot, or nail a backhand down the line while working out. Without the pressure of competition, and, in some cases, without even the pressure of going head to head with an opponent, these all-star moves are much more doable. But add to the mix the stress of being down in the score, with an opponent all over you, and distractions on the sidelines, and our winning shots and strategies start to teeter outside the realm of possibility. That's when a positive attitude and a confident outlook come into the picture.

If we can step into any athletic situation, competitive or recreational, feeling strongly about our abilities and knowing we have a shot to come out a winner, there's a chance we will put in a good performance. Once we have the physical skills and moves down, it's time for the mind to take over.

◆

I will add a positive, winning outlook to my skills and moves for the best possible performance.

I think the key to life is being yourself. I'd rather be Earl Campbell than anybody else. . . . I don't think it's a good idea to look at somebody else and tell yourself "I'd like to be just like him."
—*Earl Campbell*

As much as we may want to dunk like Michael Jordan, have Steffi Graf's forehand or John Daly's drive, or develop the strength of Arnold Schwarzenegger or the grace of Kristi Yamaguchi, for most of us these are pipe dreams. However, if we decide to be the best golfer, runner, or cyclist we can be ourselves, we stand a much greater chance of reaching our goals.

We all have within us the ability to be competent and successful at any number of activities as long as we are realistic in our choices. A stocky build does not make for the best long-distance runner, just as a tall person is not apt to be a great jockey or coxswain. But once we find a sport or workout that suits us that we can do and enjoy, the sky's the limit. We don't know what our limits are; we don't know how good we can be. However, all of us do know we can be the best at whatever we aspire to. No one can challenge us there—not even Michael, or Steffi, or John, or Arnold, or Kristi.

◆

What's important is not being like some other athlete, but being the best athlete I can be.

Every time you go out on the ice, there are slight flaws. You can always think of something you should have done better. These are the things you must work on.
—*Dorothy Hamill*

No one can turn in a flawless performance every time. However, just because no one is immune to making mistakes doesn't mean we can completely ignore the errors that we make. We just have to be careful about our motives for closely looking at what went wrong. Picking out our flaws isn't done so that we can berate ourselves. We do it in order to rethink our techniques because there is always something that can be improved.

We also have to be selective about when we choose to examine our play. When we are in the middle of a game or working out and we make an error, we need to shake it off or we will lose our concentration. Since we usually can't take a time-out to figure out why a mistake happened and what we can do to prevent it from happening next time we have to leave the analysis for after the game.

The time for evaluation is when we have time to reflect and figure out why things didn't go as planned. When we have targeted our errors we will then know what we need to work on in our next practice. The errors of one day become the workout goals and successes of another day.

◆

I know that I will make mistakes and that I can use them to improve.

I'm a firm believer in the theory that people only do their best at things they truly enjoy. It is difficult to excel at something you don't enjoy.
—*Jack Nicklaus*

One thing is for sure: If it's not fun, we're not going to do it. Because we tie such high expectations to our exercise—I'm going to lose fifteen pounds before the big party, I'm going to win the tournament—working out begins to feel more like a job and less like a joy. Sports and exercise should be fun, not torture. There will be days when we are not having the best of times, but those should be the exception and not the rule. If we think about it, no matter where we are or what we do, there has got to be some form of exercise that will challenge us and allow us to have a good time while we are doing it.

Attitude also plays a role in whether or not we have fun. It's easy to psych ourselves out of having a good time. It can help if we think of exercise as an opportunity rather than an obligation. It's an opportunity to improve our health and tone our bodies. It can get us away from the office and problems at home and it's great for clearing our heads and blowing off steam.

If what we are doing now isn't fun, we need to find another way to exercise or to shake up our current routine.

◆

I'm committed to exercise and I'm committed to making it fun.

I visualize the game. I think about who I am guarding, the things he likes to do.
—*Scottie Pippen*

When preparing to work out, we have to take some time to consider exactly what we are going to do. We can't just go to the gym and switch randomly from one activity to another. We can't start out on a run without first deciding where and how far we are going to go and how long we would like the run to last. If we don't have a plan we won't make any progress. Part of that planning involves actually picturing what we are going to do.

If we play competitive sports we can prepare ourselves for the game by imagining how our opponents play and move and then we can envision how we will respond to their play. When we are visualizing, we have the advantage because we can always imagine ourselves being victorious. (Although your opponent is probably taking some pregame time to imagine himself beating you as well.) This pregame picturing can be applied to noncompetitive workouts, too. For example, if we are working on an aerobics routine we can run through the movement in our heads beforehand and see ourselves doing the steps before we go to the class. Visualization is a dress rehearsal so that we can work out some of the kinks before we actually have to go out and perform.

◆

I will rehearse in my mind before I work out today.

*I just don't feel right unless I have a sport to play or at least
a way to work up a sweat.*
—Hank Aaron

You know that restless feeling that comes when you haven't worked out? It just feels like things are a bit off. You're a little crankier and you just feel out of sorts. That feeling is your body's hint to get back to it and sweat some poisons out of your system.

When you haven't been working out for a while it may seem impossible to get started again. You don't have to pick up exactly where you left off, however; you can do practically anything to get yourself back on track. Even a brisk walk around the block can get your heart going and those old juices flowing again. You'll wake up those muscles that have been idle, and find that when you have reminded your body of what it can do, you'll be ready to start your old routine again.

Exercise isn't just for the benefit of your body—it works for your mind and emotions, too. If you are working hard at the office and don't seem to have time to exercise, that is when you most need to find even a few minutes to work out and clear your head. Exercise can wipe out some of the stress and tension that tend to creep into our lives uninvited.

◆

I will find a way, any way, to work up a sweat and get back on track.

Confidence is a very fragile thing.
—*Joe Montana*

*I*t's easy to lose confidence. It is something that needs to be nurtured and protected. It is vulnerable to attack from the outside by a strong opponent or a difficult goal. It is also vulnerable to attack from the inside. Our own attitude can kill our confidence as quickly as someone else beating us in a bike race or sinking a winning putt. How many times have we seen a professional sporting event where the commentator says, "She just seems to have lost confidence in herself"? Once lost, confidence usually takes time to rebuild. But we can shake off being down on ourselves, regain our confidence, and come on strong.

We can keep our confidence healthy by taking a hard look at our abilities. We need to step back for a moment and assess where we are and where we have been. A quick check of our past triumphs and accomplishments can do wonders for confidence that is shaky. We know that we can achieve what we set our hearts on. We know that we have the skills and abilities to do whatever we want. Confidence is fragile but it doesn't have to be fleeting. We have a right to be confident. We are working hard and striving to meet our goals and are making progress every day. Let's be confident—we've earned it.

◆

I am confident in my abilities and in myself.

> Build up your weaknesses until they become your strong points.
> —*Knute Rockne*

Having trouble with your free throw, backhand, chip shot, breaststroke, or leg lifts? Maybe you're not as confident as you could be in your running pace or your cycling endurance. Is the zing gone from your squash serve? The grace missing from your bowling form? Does your coordination disappear in the middle of a funk class? Is your batting going progressively downhill?

The great coach Knute Rockne would have you isolate that troubling part of your sport and work on making it a positive. Spend extra time visualizing, practicing, and correcting the weakness until little by little improvement is evident. Hit a basket of backhands on the tennis court, swim a few more laps of breaststroke, rent a golf instructional video, or take a lesson.

Coach Rockne would then have you take it one step further. Keep honing that particular skill or move until it becomes smooth and natural. Make that former detriment the strength of your game, your best event. Imagine your opponent's or training partner's surprise when your former Achille's heel is now your ace in the hole.

◆

Today I'll work hardest on my least effective skill.

Despite having played in hundreds of basketball games, I still get butterflies in my stomach before certain games.
—*Isiah Thomas*

No matter who we are or how much competitive experience we might have, chances are there will be times when we will feel nervous before a match, or a game, or even a challenging workout. The key is not to let this feeling distract us or psych us out but to recognize it, accept it, and try to use it to our advantage.

While it can be hard to ward off nervousness once it hits, by acknowledging it and trying to channel this extra energy into our performance we can often make use of this potentially debilitating feeling. Also, by looking ahead to upcoming challenging situations we can best prepare ourselves should the feeling strike. Sometimes we can even head it off completely by practicing positive reinforcement and other self-encouraging exercises as the event approaches.

◆

When I feel nervous about a competition or workout, I will recognize the feeling and try to channel it positively into my performance.

The difference between the possible and the impossible lies
in the man's determination.
—*Tommy Lasorda*

*T*here is a fine line that separates the possible from the impossible. Sometimes we can build that line into a brick wall so that it will take a maximum effort to break through that barrier. At other times we can cross it simply because we really want to. It's amazing to consider what we are capable of achieving. To keep on track we need to remind ourselves of our achievements from time to time. When we look back at where we began, what once seemed totally out of reach now seems so simple. The thing that got us from one perspective to the other is the willingness to "go for it"—giving anything and everything our best effort.

Think about the first time we considered running a race, or the first time we faced a thirty-minute aerobics class. Taking on what seems impossible is the best way to develop our skills and hone our abilities. If we only do the possible we won't get much satisfaction out of what we've done. We'll stay stuck in a rut and not make any progress. When we dig in our heels and put ourselves on the line we can overcome all sorts of obstacles.

◆

Everything is possible if I really work on it.

It is not something I must do but something I want to do.
—*James Fixx*

"*I have* to go to the gym." "I *gotta* run." "I *better* work out today." We all feel driven to exercise, and many of us feel like failures when we don't manage to do it. Our day can be made or broken by whether or not we made our morning visit to the gym or if we did our run. When exercising becomes a burden it is time to rethink why and how we are getting into our workouts—and what kinds of pressure we are putting on ourselves to do them. If we are driven only by obligation and not by desire we won't get very far.

When we find exercise that we love we will not feel as if we are going through torture just to get healthy. When we do something we enjoy, it will not be a chore to get out there and work. It's simple: If we like it, we will do it. If we begin to feel overworked or overobligated it may be time to take a break or vary our routine. We can then rest for a few days or try something else; then, when we begin again, we can start fresh and be reminded of how good exercising makes us feel. We will be able to recapture the fun that probably drew us to exercising in the first place.

◆

I want to exercise and I will exercise.

Rather than viewing a brief relapse back to inactivity as a failure, treat it as a
challenge and try to get back on track as soon as possible.
—*Jimmy Connors*

No one can be perfect all the time. There will be days when we just can't get out there and exercise. Missing a day or two or even a week due to injury, illness, bad weather, bad mood, or for any number of reasons is no reason to throw in the towel. Just because we stopped for a while doesn't mean we have to start all over again at square one. It is surprising to find that results don't evaporate. We can get back to where we left off much quicker than we got there the first time.

Missing exercise is definitely not failing. Sometimes we need to take a break. It's important, however, not to give into stopping for too long. If we do become inactive for a while, instead of thinking, "Well, I've blown it, there's no use starting up again," we should see what it is that made us stop in the first place and what the best way for us to start again is. Maybe we need to change our routine and try something new. Maybe we need to reevaluate our goals. Stopping our activities should be like a brief vacation—don't let it turn into a permanent one.

◆

If I've stopped working out I will begin again today.

When you're prepared, you're more confident. When you have a strategy,
you're more comfortable.
—*Fred Couples*

A plan, whether a workout schedule for the week or a competitive strategy for a basketball game, is something we want to put together for the "fitness" part of our lives. We all have incredibly busy schedules that are filled with business, family, and social obligations, and in order to make fitness a viable component, we have to work it into a particular time frame. We need to set up goals, targets, and plans for our successful performances, especially if we intend to compete regularly. Few of us would arrive at a business meeting without some sort of preparation. The same should be done for athletics.

We shouldn't run without stretching, we shouldn't play a tennis match without warming up, we don't play golf without knowing the rules, nor do we ski without the proper equipment. Preparation is key to enjoying ourselves while working out or competing as well as vital to ultimate success in our endeavors. Just as we wouldn't think of stepping into an academic situation unprepared, or go on a job interview without a strategy, we shouldn't mindlessly perform a workout or compete in a match, game, or tournament without a plan.

◆

I have a plan for my workouts, and a strategy for my fitness goals.

To succeed . . . you need to find something to hold on to, something to motivate you, something to inspire you.
—*Tony Dorsett*

It's hard enough to get out of bed in the morning, let alone rising early to go for a predawn run. Workdays are tiring as it is without trying to squeeze in a lunchtime workout. Free time on the weekend is so precious—can we really fit in the afternoon bike ride? How will we ever find time to exercise?

Somehow we do manage to cram fitness activities into our lives. Whether it's a regular golf game, a daily visit to the gym, or a brisk morning walk, we are able to find some time for sports in our already jam-packed lives. Obviously there's some underlying factor that encourages, almost forces, us to save time each day or week to pump up those endorphins. That something is motivation.

Motivation is different for each of us. For some it may be the dream of being truly great at our sport someday; for others it may be the desire to lose those last five pounds; still others may crave that great postworkout feeling where we're at once calm and pumped up, exhausted and energized. It doesn't matter what motivates us, as long as the force is there—challenging us to lace up our shoes and hit the road, court, course, or field.

◆

Motivation equals results. If I can find motivation, I will see results.

Other people may not have had high expectations for me . . . but I had high
expectations for myself.
—*Shannon Miller*

We can look to other people to set an example that we would like to follow. We can look to people we admire and respect for encouragement and support in what we can hope to accomplish. We can seek others' advice for goals that may be suited to our experience. But for the true measure of what we need to, and can, accomplish we need to look to ourselves.

Ultimately, we must keep our own standards in mind because those are the standards and expectations we need to live up to. We cannot fulfill a dream for someone else and we are the only ones who can make our own dreams come true. We are the only ones who know what we can do. There will always be someone who doesn't think much of our chances or our abilities. But because we are out there working hard and practicing to be better we are the only ones who are completely aware of our strengths and limitations. If we don't think highly of what we can accomplish, who will? All of what we have done and will do rests squarely on our own shoulders. It is usually the person who expects a lot from herself who is able to achieve the most. We need to be courageous enough to ask the most we can from ourselves.

◆

I expect a lot from myself because I know I can achieve a lot.

You only have to bat a thousand in two things—flying and heart transplants.
Everything else—you can go 4 for 5.
—Beano Cook

Ease up. You don't have to play flawlessly in every baseball game. You don't have to make par on every hole on the golf course. You don't have to run a personal best every time you enter a race. And you don't have to win every time you take someone on in one-on-one on the basketball court. You're not perfect. None of us are, and the sooner we can understand that, the happier we'll be, both in our daily workouts and in competition.

Sure, it would be ideal if every time we worked out we showed marked improvement. It would be the greatest if each practice session was considerably more productive than the one before, and every time we beat opponents, we could feel confident that we would beat them every time from then on. But the fact is, it just doesn't work that way, nor does it have to. We can be, and are, perfectly successful if we make the occasional error on the softball field. We can still feel proud of ourselves for finishing, even if we add a minute to our 10K time despite all of our training. And we can still hold our heads up if we miss a few days at the gym. Who hasn't?

Sports are not about being perfect. They're about giving our best, feeling good, and having fun.

◆

I don't have to be perfect, I just have to give my all and hope for the best.

I don't play *small*. You have to go out and play with what you have. I admit
I used to want to be tall. But I made it in high school, college, and now the pros.
So it doesn't matter.
—*Spud Webb*

*F*or anyone who's ever felt she wasn't built for a certain sport or activity, or was given the same message by others, NBA asset Spud Webb is your guy. At five feet seven inches Webb is one of the shortest players in the NBA. However, in a sport dominated by athletes who are, in many cases, pushing seven feet tall, Webb has held his own. He is a tough, aggressive player who has learned to use his diminutive stature to his advantage. He is an inspiration for anyone who has wanted to play basketball or any other sport that seems to demand certain height or weight requirements from its participants.

Throughout history athletes who didn't appear to fit the bill have made it in size-specific sports: football players who were slighter than normal, jockeys taller than usual, long-distance runners built more sturdily than the typical rail-thin track stars. And yet we all find ourselves occasionally paralyzed by these prejudices. But the fact is, virtually anyone can do anything with the right attitude and training.

While, with a muscular, sturdy build, we may not become a world-class long-distance runner, there's certainly no reason for us to pass on the challenge and pleasure long-distance running might bring us.

◆

No matter how I'm built, I'm ready for action in whatever sport I choose.

Success is a journey not a destination. The doing is usually more important than the outcome. Not everyone can be Number 1.
—*Arthur Ashe*

While we all enjoy a certain level of success in our sport, the great Arthur Ashe encouraged us to take a close look at, and learn from, what we experience along the way. Whether we, too, are tennis players, or runners, or golfers, or gym-goers, each workout or competition offers us the chance to grow in ways that go beyond the skills specific to our activity.

From sports we learn concentration—a trait that enables us to focus our minds and ignore distracting stimuli. We learn perseverance as we practice and continue trying to grow. We learn sportsmanship and teamwork, two skills that are transferable to other aspects of our lives. By having a regular fitness program we also recognize the danger of obsession and unrealistic expectations.

Although we may never reach No. 1 in our sport, or be the best at the club, or the top among friends, we should see and appreciate the many gifts athletics does give us, including that innate desire to strive to improve.

◆

Whether or not it's important to me to be tops in my field, I won't lose sight of the incredible learning experience that participation in athletics offers.

You have to have faith and believe in yourself.
—*Gail Deavers*

*O*ne thing that no one can do for you is to get you to believe in yourself. Others can be encouraging or supportive but it is not the same unless you yourself believe. Believing in yourself is a very powerful asset for any tasks that you wish to take on. It is much more effective to think "I believe I can win the club championship" than to think "My friends think I can win the club championship." Faith in yourself is a springboard that you can use to excel to the best of your abilities. No matter what your activity—aerobics, skiing, running, basketball, tennis—or whether you play solo or are part of a team, your success comes down to how, and what, you think about yourself and your skills.

If you are constantly doubting that you can do it, you will soon find that you won't be able to do it. Your mind can convince you one way or another so it's better to get your mind working with you, not against you. Belief in yourself can come long before any technical/physical prowess. Simply believing that you are capable of achieving your goals takes you a few steps closer to making your dream come true.

◆

I only have to convince myself before I can do it.

Learn from the legends: Watch the top players and apply tactics that work for them to your own game.
—Brad Gilbert

One of the best ways to improve in sports is to observe other athletes who are proficient in your activity and try to emulate them. Whether it's a professional tennis player you watch on television, a top class golfer you see at the club, or an ultracoordinated member of your aerobics class, each can offer you the cheapest form of instruction—a model to imitate.

Many times seeing and then remembering a visual picture of how your stroke, form, or technique should look will translate into a better performance. Once your mind records Joe Montana's perfect touchdown pass, or Florence Griffith-Joyner's flawless long jump, or John Daly's powerful drive, it can then rehearse the move over and over, eventually putting you in the picture. You become the MVP passer, Olympic track star, or PGA champion—at least in your mind's eye.

While it's not likely that you will, in fact, mimic exactly the play of your model, your body will have learned a surprising amount from this exercise, and you will see improvement in your performance.

◆

Today I will watch a superior athlete perform and try to imitate his or her skill.

I've always tried to do my best on the ball field. I can't do any more than that. I always give one hundred percent; and if my team loses, I come back and give one hundred percent the next day.
—*Jesse Barfield*

*B*eing part of a team involves not only putting in a good individual performance but also dealing with the ups and downs of teammates and opponents, tough practices, and challenging competitions. It's easy to take the selfish, individualistic approach and be concerned only with our own personal statistics, skills, and performances, and to play hard when we feel like it and lay back in practice when we're not in the mood. However, that's not what team play is about.

It doesn't matter if we're part of a tennis doubles team that plays recreationally once a week, a company volleyball team that plays in a league, or an elite running team that competes nationally, we are still expected to put in 100 percent effort every time we step out on the court, field, or course. We owe it to our teammates and we owe it to ourselves. We expect the same commitment from our colleagues as well.

Being part of a team can be an extremely rewarding experience, especially if the players have similar goals and expectations for themselves and the group.

◆

Being part of a team is a commitment to my sport as well as to my teammates and requires a consistent, all-out effort.

The most important thing is to love your sport. Never do it to please someone else —it has to be yours. That is all that will justify the hard work needed to achieve success. Compete against yourself, not others, for that is who is truly your best competition.
—*Peggy Fleming Jenkins*

We are our own best competition. We can challenge ourselves better than anyone else, and we hold ourselves up to higher standards than anyone else. We are also the only ones who know when we are holding back or when we are pushing ourselves to the limit. No matter what our chosen activity, we are the only ones who know how hard we are working and how much effort we are making. Winning trophies or awards is satisfying and is a tangible symbol of our hard work and achievements, but that's not a real reason to play. We really need to love what we are doing, because if we do we will willingly make sacrifices to do what needs to be done.

If we are working out for someone else, their shadow will be hanging over us no matter what we do. To perform our best we need to break free of everyone else's expectations and let ourselves live up to our own expectations. When we are accountable only to ourselves we may find that we are more successful than we could have imagined and that we will develop a genuine love for our sports.

◆

If I don't love the sport I am playing I will find one that I love and that will challenge me to the best of my abilities.

A winner never whines.
—*Paul Brown*

A winner stays focused and sharp even when the going gets tough.

A winner is humble in victory, and gracious in defeat.

A winner is supportive of teammates and civil to opponents.

A winner doesn't let anger or frustration take the field with him.

A winner plays fair and watches that others do as well.

A winner sets goals and works his hardest to achieve them each and every day.

A winner allows herself to be coached and listens to constructive criticism.

A winner doesn't act bored or arrogant, and a winner rarely complains and never whines.

◆

I can be a winner each and every time I work out or compete.

I learned that the only way you are going to get anywhere in life is to work hard at it. Whether you're a musician, a writer, an athlete or a businessman, there is no getting around it. If you do, you'll win—if you don't you won't.

—*Bruce Jenner*

It's a very simple formula really: hard work = success. No matter what we do —whether we are professional athletes, recreational players, or work out a few times a week—hard work can get us where we want to go.

Olympic decathlete Bruce Jenner also makes another interesting point. Many of us view athletics as recreation and play. It's something we do when we are not engaging in our "real"-life activities. But the dedication and devotion we apply to our racquetball game or our weight training can cross over into other areas of our lives. It can be very subtle, but that planning and goal setting can work off the court and out of the gym as well. If we find that focus and concentration and hard work pay off when applied to our workouts we may also discover that these qualities are soon being applied to figuring out that new computer system at the office. Hard work is as close to a guarantee as we can get to achieving success. We can't work hard all the time, but when we do we will see the rewards.

◆

Hard work is one of my keys to success.

> See the ball; hit the ball.
> —*Pete Rose*

*S*ee the finish line; run the race.
Do ten sit-ups; do ten more.
Set a goal; strive to reach it.

Simplicity. We all have a tendency to complicate our lives. The more elaborate a workout the more we think we are getting out of it. We contort our bodies into painful positions all for the sake of the latest exercise video. We run from one activity to another desperately seeking the exercise program that will work for us. It shouldn't be that complicated. We obsess with figuring out what complex strategies we need to execute just to get ourselves to the gym, or out running, or whatever. We develop elaborate reward systems for when we do get working, or devise elaborate plans so that every minute is filled with "quality" workout time. We set ourselves up for impossible goals and then get bent out of shape when we can't achieve them. It's not that complicated.

The more complicated the workout the more likely we are to quit out of frustration or even confusion. We have to let go of a lot of the complex, timed to the minute schemes and dreams. We have to remember what we are doing this for. We don't need to make ourselves crazy to make ourselves fit. We have to stop obsessing, put on our sneakers, and go.

◆

I will keep it simple.

I'll always be Number 1 to myself.
—*Moses Malone*

*I*f only we could always feel as confident and self-assured as NBA great Moses Malone seems to. If only we could feel that despite our skill level, performance on any given day, or outcome in a competition we are still Number 1 in our own minds for our effort, perseverance, and improvement. While it's hard to maintain this type of self-confidence, especially when we don't perform particularly well, don't show immediate signs of improvement, or seem to be in a slump, if we can try to separate our actual physical performance from the psychological factors, we may find it a bit easier to stay confident.

If we assume that we will always give 100 percent, both on the practice field as well as in competition, then we can take pride in knowing that we have done our very best at any one time. If we can believe that we will stick with our workout schedule no matter how much or how often we may want to quit, then we can feel good about persevering and staying motivated. There is always something to be proud of—there's always a reason to be Number 1 in our own eyes. Sometimes we just have to look closely, beyond the time on the stopwatch or the statistics, because more than just a physical performance, athletics is a healthy combination of body and mind at work together.

◆

To me, I'm Number 1.

In every fat man, the saying goes, there is a thin man struggling to get out. If this is so, then every skinny man must at times find himself surrounded by the ghostly outlines of muscles and heft. And there must somehow exist an ideal physique for every one of us—man, woman, and child. Every body that moves about on this planet, if you look at it that way, may well be inhabited by a strong and graceful athlete, capable of Olympian feats.

—George Leonard, author of The Ultimate Athlete

We are all capable of far more than we can imagine. Every time we take to the field, the court, or the gym we have the potential to surprise ourselves with the skills and strategies we have developed. Athletics is an ongoing process. Every workout or competition is both a learning experience and a practice session. We are constantly striving to realize our potential, to become the best athlete we can be with the talent we've been given and the depth of our desire.

If we look at the improvement in our tennis game, the increased strength in our circuit training, the development of our endurance in running, cycling, and aerobicizing rather than at the occasional setbacks that may occur, we will begin to appreciate and admire the athlete that is within us. Every game we play, every race we run, every workout we complete is something to take note of.

◆

I feel good about myself and my commitment to fitness.

When you lose a couple of times, it makes you realize how difficult it is to win.
—Steffi Graf

Sometimes we take our skills and accomplishments on the athletic field for granted. We expect a certain level of performance from ourselves and are irritated and disappointed when we don't reach our goals. If we consistently shoot a certain score in golf, we assume we'll always play at that level or above. If we are regularly able to ace a certain fitness class, we are sure it will always be that easy. If we are improving our running times at a regular rate, we figure that we will continue to do better and better. It's not until we have a bad day on the court, or course, or field that we realize what we've been acccomplishing so handily.

No matter what our level of sports participation, and no matter how successful we are at what we do, we should never underestimate the importance of our achievements. Just being out there running, smacking the tennis ball, swimming laps, or lifting weights is an accomplishment in itself. Yes, it's good to strive to improve, but we must also remember to credit ourselves for a job well done so far. Sometimes it takes a "bad day" out there to make us realize that our previous workouts and performances are really something to be proud of—they're not easy, and they take a lot of hard work.

◆

I'm proud of my athletic accomplishments.

The main thing is to try to relax, to stay loose. If I start tensing up or try to muscle the ball, I'll be off.
—*George Blanda*

*T*o be at our best, we need to release tension and keep ourselves as flexible as possible—both physically and mentally. If we are all wound up we won't be able to play well and we will make errors. All we will be able to think about is how uptight and uncomfortable we are. The key is to make those pregame, preworkout butterflies work for us. That fluttery feeling in the stomach can be a sign of nerves but it can also mean that we are excited and ready for anything. Being a little nervous can actually be a good sign. It means that we are pumped up and anticipating being challenged.

However, it is important to keep those nerves under control. If we let them take over then our anxiety is dictating how we will perform. What we need to do is channel that nervous energy instead of letting it sap our skills. It may sound silly but jumping up and down or doing some quick calisthenics can help burn off some of that nervous energy. Breathing deeply can be helpful also. To work with our nerves rather than let them work against us it's important to get our focus away from being nervous and back on what we have to do.

◆

I'll take a deep breath and relax when my nerves threaten to take over.

Setting goals for your game is an art. The trick is in setting them at the right level—
neither too low nor too high. A good goal should be lofty enough to inspire hard
work, yet realistic enough to provide solid hope of attainment.
—*Greg Norman*

*H*ow many times have we set overly optimistic goals for workouts or competitions, always with the intention to motivate ourselves, only to be disappointed
by our inability to reach them? By making our targets too rigorous and unrealistic, we are faced with having to fail repeatedly before modifying them—or give
up altogether.

Setting a goal that is "lofty enough to inspire hard work, yet realistic enough
to provide solid hope of attainment" is the cornerstone of improvement in sport.
Getting better is a step-by-step process—whether it's in adding an extra half
mile to a run or an extra five pounds to a weight. Every time we aspire to
something that is beyond our reach in a reasonable period of time, we run the
risk of becoming disheartened, losing faith in our skills and our ability to improve
them. Whereas rigid, "no pain, no gain" goals may seem to inspire hard work,
it's the well-planned day-to-day achievements that really deliver.

◆

Today I will set a goal that will challenge me, yet be reachable in a reasonable
period of time.

The concentration and dedication—the intangibles—are the deciding factors . . .
between who won and who lost.
—*Tom Seaver*

Concentration and dedication can't be measured or quantified. But we can see clear evidence of them in individual behavior and in who is likely to be the winner in any competition. The person who is enthusiastic about sports shows up regularly at the track or at the gym. He has made the commitment and is following through consistently. The athlete who is truly dedicated, however, does more than just show up. He comes prepared to work and to put in some extra concentrated time and effort. The dedicated athlete puts in more practice time or seeks advice or coaches or new trainers. He is constantly working to improve his game.

Part of that improvement will come with better concentration. Concentration is harder to evaluate or measure. It is the ability to stay focused and to keep our minds solidly on what we are doing. If we are concentrating, we can put ourselves, mentally and physically, into our workouts. It also means keeping our focus at 100 percent for the duration of our workouts and not letting our minds wander to other events or activities. The more we concentrate, the better we will be able to work.

◆

Concentration. Dedication.

Do not let what you cannot do interfere with what you can do.
—*John Wooden*

I could never run a marathon.
I could never swim a mile.
I could never bench-press my own weight.
I could never do twenty minutes on the StairMaster.
I could never play softball.
I could never win at golf.

Maybe we can't do any of these things. But, then again, maybe we can. If we have already shut the door on these possibilities we will never know if we really could do those things or if we are just standing in our own way.

Denying ourselves certain achievements belittles what we *can* do. By saying we could never do something we are setting that up as the ultimate achievement. Every time we don't do it we are reminding ourselves that we didn't hit the top. We may never run a marathon, but who's to say that we won't be able to run five or ten or even fifteen miles? Ultimately, each and every mile is a great accomplishment and deserving of credit. We shouldn't be sidetracked by what we can't do. We should celebrate and improve on what we can do. Instead of focusing on the things we can't do, we should make an inventory of what we can do.

◆

I will work with a can-do attitude and leave the can't-do's behind.

I will always be someone who wants to do better than others. I love competition.
—Jean-Claude Killy

Many people thrive on competition. They are not happy unless they are working hard to beat someone else. Competition keeps them going and keeps their practices and workouts intense. Loving competition isn't necessary to being a successful athlete, but it certainly gives some players an edge as well as heightening their enjoyment of the game.

Competition can be great. It can bring our play up to a new level. There is a big difference in the way we focus and try when we are just volleying or doing our usual run than when we are keeping score or running in a race. Competition is a way of concentrating our efforts toward a single goal. We don't have to be cutthroat or over the top about competing, but some healthy competition can shake up our usual routine.

◆

I will compete wholeheartedly with my opponent, whether it's the clock, myself, or another person.

I used to store my anger and it affected my play. Now I get it out. I'm never rude to
my playing partner. I'm very focused on the ball. Then it's over.
—*Helen Alfredsson*

It's never a good idea to hide or ignore emotions as volatile as anger, and this is especially true on the sports field. Suppressing anger is not only uncomfortable and anxiety-producing, in athletics it's a detriment to our game as well. How many times have we become irritated either at ourselves or at our partners or teammates and tried to hold it in and continue playing? If we are mad at ourselves, we become tense and spend the next few points or minutes of the game thinking about an error we committed or a move we should have made. If we are angry at teammates, we become distracted, waiting for them to blow it again, until we, too, are not playing well.

While there is no place on the tennis court, golf course, track, or anywhere else for unsportsmanlike displays of anger or frustration, it is important to have a way to vent frustrations so that they do not interfere with the rest of the competition. A deep breath, a time-out, and a silent self psych-up session are all effective ways to get back on track on the heels of a minor breakdown in our game. Dealing with emotions in competitive and noncompetitive situations is a very personal thing and every athlete has to find what works best for him or her. It's a must, however, to be able to blow off steam in an acceptable, nonoffensive manner.

◆

In order to keep my head cool and my game hot, I will find a way
to vent my anger.

Athletics should reduce stress, not increase it.
—*Mark Allen*

Whether we compete regularly or exercise on weekends, whether we run races or take aerobics classes, the overall athletic experience for us should be positive. Participation in sports is a terrific way to blow off steam, use up nervous energy , and otherwise reduce stress. The beating of our hearts, the pumping endorphins, and the heavy breathing all combine to create a state of euphoria and calm. This feeling is the reason we should continue getting up at 6 A.M. to row, keep up our swim workouts, and stick with our tennis lessons.

However, on those occasions when the pressure of competition becomes too intense, the guilt over a missed workout becomes overbearing, and the anxiety over a less than perfect performance takes over, we have lost sight of the goal of our exercise program: to limit, even reduce, stress in our lives.

Most of us are so bombarded with stresses at work, tension at home, financial pressures, and personal conflicts that the last thing we need is additional weight thrown on. The reason we lace up our athletic shoes and hit the road, court, or course in the first place is to alleviate some of life's hassles. We need to maintain the proper balanced attitude about sports, and use its invigorating and calming powers to our advantage.

◆

Athletics is what I use to quell anxieties, not create them.

I think we now come to the park expecting to win instead of playing not to lose.
—*Eric Davis*

*T*here is a big difference between confidently playing to win and frantically playing to avoid losing. It sounds like merely two different ways to say the same thing, but they are worlds apart in attitude and inspiration. It is much harder to try to *not* do something than it is to try to *do* something. When we play only in order not to lose we are playing from a position of fear. We will always be looking over our shoulders and wondering and worrying if we are doing enough to keep that loss at bay. Any time we make an error we will panic because it will feel as if we are getting one step closer to losing. Eventually when losing becomes big enough and scary enough it can keep us from winning.

If we have confidence and expect to win, we are going into our competition or exercise routine from a position of strength. Positive expectations can give us the strength we need to achieve our goals.

◆

Confidence, not fear, will be my motivation.

My concentration was at such a high level. My mind was right there. I felt fresh, like I could stop everything.
—*Patrick Roy, after his team won the Stanley Cup*

Have you ever had one of those days when you felt you could do anything? When not only what you have to do but how you will do it is perfectly clear? Everything clicks into place; everything seems effortless. The weights that felt so heavy yesterday almost lift by themselves. That hill that's been giving you so much trouble on your bike suddenly seems like a piece of cake. Sometimes there is no explanation for why you find yourself "on." Usually it's the result of practice and hard work combined with being in a situation that is inspiring you to draw on all of your resources. It's wonderful if it happens when a championship or trophy is on the line, but even if there is no competitive payoff the feeling can help you sail through your exercise.

Unfortunately, we don't have a switch that can be flipped to create that focused, invincible feeling. Being prepared and willing to put your heart into your workouts can help to achieve that feeling. Once you have experienced this euphoria, you will know what it feels like and be able to grasp it more often.

◆

I will concentrate and work hard, and I know that I will always
be prepared to be "on."

> Preparing mentally [for competition] takes more out of you
> than the physical aspect of it.
> —*Summer Sanders*

*F*ew of us compete at the level of Olympic swimming medalist Summer Sanders, but we've all been in situations where we want or need to perform at a certain level in our sport. It may be in the local 10K race, or the tournament at the club, or even in a challenging fitness class. And we all know that, in addition to the challenging physical preparation we must undergo, we have to maintain a level of mental fitness as well.

For some it's best to psych *up:*
—with a high-energy drink or food
—by listening to loud music
—by doing calisthenics or other heart-pumping warm-ups

For others it's best to psych *down:*
—by meditating
—by visualizing the match or activity unfold
—by listening to quiet, relaxing music

The method itself doesn't really matter—its effectiveness does. Because much of athletic success is attributed to mental fitness skills, it's important that every athlete, of every level, find the way to best prepare his or her mind as well as body to perform.

◆

Today I'll work on improving my mental as well as my physical skills.

When you are out there sailing for two hours, it helps to visualize things. When it is windy I hike really hard and imagine myself with legs of steel that would help me hang off the boat forever. In light wind I think about the words patience, smooth, *and* calm.
—*Julia Trotman*

Visualization can help us see ourselves the way we want to be by creating a mood that gets us more focused and concentrated on what we are doing. The more creative we are the more likely it is that the visualization will work for us. Engaging our imaginations in our workouts is especially helpful if we are performing in some form of endurance sport where there is a danger of losing concentration or of becoming bored. When we are slaving away on the StairMaster we can help ourselves get through the workout if we imagine that we have the legs of a marathoner and that they will never get tired.

Visualization and positive self-talk are closely related. If we *imagine* ourselves as undefeatable, we can also *tell* ourselves that we are undefeatable. Along with our image we can create words that can be repeated as a mantra to enhance our performance. We see it, say it, and become it.

◆

I will *see* myself as strong and powerful. I will *tell* myself that
I am strong and powerful.

There's no substitute for guts.
—*Paul ("Bear") Bryant*

*H*aving intense determination can get us through almost anything—injuries, poor playing conditions, a bad day. Fortitude can be an excellent ally in a rough time—it can get us to stay in the battle when it looks like we might be losing. When we've got intensity and perseverance we can overcome many obstacles. We know we have what it takes because we need courage to start an exercise program in the first place. Any new endeavor involves risk, and if we are taking risks there is always a chance that we might fail. But if we have the guts we will get through it.

Intensity isn't exactly something that we can just go out and acquire. It's something that develops over time. We have to train ourselves to pay attention to what our minds and bodies are telling us. Sometimes it's that little voice inside that says, "C'mon, you can do it, don't give up." Other times it's just a feeling that comes over us that lifts our level of play and gets us to refocus on the job at hand. It can power us through whatever training walls we are up against and carry us to the other side—often to victory. We can have all the skills and training possible, but it's often guts—determination—that enables us to succeed.

◆

I will dig deep and let my guts take me as far as I can go.

> I don't feel any pressure . . . I just try to stay calm, follow my game plan and
> try not to overthrow.
> —*Dwight Gooden*

Pressure can make us feel as if we can't do anything. It can bear down on us and make us panic—working out and competing then seem nearly impossible.

When we are under pressure the best thing we can do is to maintain our equilibrium. In tough situations, a well-thought-out and developed plan can be a stabilizing influence. When we can fall back on a trusted plan we can breathe a little easier and relax and allow ourselves to do our best. A strategy like this is something we can develop over time. As we gain experience, we can develop alternative plans to cope with particular situations. Sometimes the best approach is to go all out. Sometimes doing our best means holding back a little and keeping ourselves under control. We may need to hold a little back so that we have something left for later in the game or later in the season.

◆

I have no doubt that I can play under pressure because I have a good game plan.

In concentrating you have to wipe everything out of your mind but . . . the ball.
Nothing but the ball. Glue your eyes to it. Marry it. Don't let it get out of your sight.
Never mind your opponent, the weather, or anything.
Nothing but the ball. Make that ball an obsession. If you can get yourself into that
trance, pressure won't intrude. It's just you and the ball.
—*Rod Laver*

*I*ntensity, focus, and concentration. We need to home in on the job that needs to
get done. It's not beating our opponent that's the most important—it's getting
our racquet to meet that ball. We can be pumped up and totally mentally prepared, but if we can't execute the basics of our sport we won't get anywhere.
Single-minded focus will help us make the most successful moves.

We will also discover that when we reach that level of concentration we can
shut out all other intrusions. There is a kind of quiet that comes with that kind of
intensity. Time actually seems to slow down, and we may feel that we have more
time to move and play. We won't hear the yelling on the sidelines or the traffic or
other people around us. We will feel as though we have been hypnotized and are
in some sort of sport-induced trance. It can happen in the gym or running or
rollerblading. It's just us and whatever we have chosen to do that day.

◆

I will completely concentrate on the most important aspect of my game.

The man who can drive himself further once the effort gets painful
is the man who will win.
—*Roger Bannister*

In other words, when the going gets tough, the tough get going. As America's first four-minute miler, Roger Bannister knows about pushing the body hard—up to and beyond previous limitations. And yet had he not had the incredible drive to do so, he would not have been one of the greatest runners who ever lived.

Amateur and professional athletes alike are faced with their own personal limitations as they work out and compete. All of us, no matter what our level of involvement in sports, think we know the far reaches of our potential. We have a certain time we have never beaten in our usual bike ride, a person we have never dominated on the tennis ladder, a crew we have never passed in a regatta, and a weight we have never lifted at the gym. We strive to reach these points.

Those among us who can reach a little farther and push the limits a little more are the ones who will enjoy improvement and ultimate success in sport. If every time we hit five miles in our run we tire and then stop, how can we expect to add to our mileage? If we never challenge tennis players who are better than we are, how will we ever improve our game? Athletics is about constantly setting, reaching, and pushing limits as we move forward.

◆

Today I will push myself a little farther as I approach the limits in my workout.

Everybody keeps telling me how surprised they are with what I've done. But I'm telling you honestly that it doesn't surprise me. I knew I could do it.
—*Patrick Ewing*

Knowing what we can accomplish is all the ammunition we will need against the naysayers that come our way. We should ignore anyone who tells us that we can't do something. But also consider why they are saying that we can't. Is it really that they don't believe in us or are we poised to do something that they could only dream of doing? Or are they making a misguided attempt at protecting us and not letting us get our hopes up too high? No matter what their motives, if they can't support our program we don't have to pay any attention to them.

There is nothing wrong with having high hopes. There is actually nothing better, especially if we are going to be able to get what we want. If we don't match our belief in ourselves with those high hopes we will not excel. Hopes of any level won't do us any good if we don't have the mental stamina to get behind them and work for them. When we believe in ourselves we can accomplish anything, from losing weight to winning championships. Don't listen to other people telling you what you can't do—listen to yourself telling you what you can do.

◆

I am never surprised by what I can achieve.

> Talent is God-given, be humble; fame is man-given, be thankful;
> conceit is self-given, be careful.
> —*Anonymous*

If we have talent, and with that talent achieve some success in a sport, then we have to be mindful that we keep a good, positive attitude that does not turn into conceit. It's okay to be confident, and it's all right to feel good about our skills and athletic potential, but the way we conduct ourselves around others is also part of being a well-rounded, successful athlete.

An athlete of any level who is cocky and obnoxious is one whom few people like to have around. No matter how highly ranked we are on the tennis ladder, or how well-respected we are on the golf course, or how valuable we are on the ball field, we will be thought of much more highly if we are humble and gracious both on the field and off.

It's possible to be sure of our skills and talent and still project humility. It's possible to be at once confident and modest. If we're lucky enough to have been blessed with the ability to participate in athletics, we should respond with professionalism and poise, regardless of how good we are.

◆

I will exhibit grace under pressure and handle success with poise.

Setting a goal is not the main thing. It is deciding how you will go about achieving
it and staying with that plan.
—*Tom Landry*

We can set all the goals we want, but we also need to figure out how we are
going to get from point A to point B. No matter what our level of fitness, there
are a lot of little steps we can take that can carry us forward from where we are
to where we want to be. Once we have decided what we would like to achieve
(run farther, lose weight, tone muscles) we can break those larger goals into
smaller parts or mini goals (get around the track once without stopping, add
healthy foods to our diet, increase the amount of weights we lift). After all,
fitness and health are cumulative—what we do each day can take us closer and
closer to our goals.

We need to develop a game plan that will give us a number of accomplishments
along the way as we are working toward our main objective. It can help to write
down, each week, what we hope to accomplish and be aware of how that takes us
to our ultimate goal. Once we have a plan we *will* get there step by step.

◆

I will keep my goal in sight, but I will keep an even closer watch
on how I plan to get there.

> You must accept your disappointments and triumphs equally.
> —*Harvey Penick*

*W*e win some; we lose some. We reach some goals; sometimes we fall short. And yet, because winning and losing, reaching and falling short, are all part of the learning process, we must accept both while striving to improve and grow.

Consider most of the top athletes in the world—they don't always have great games, hit winning shots, or run their best races. Sports involve ups and downs, ebb and flow. Taking a weak performance too hard or a strong performance too seriously is almost always unnecessary, at times unappealing, and typically ineffective. But accepting successes and disappointments equally makes for a balanced, healthy approach to sports and fitness.

◆

Athletics is not all trophies and personal bests but a mix of hitting a peak and falling short, both of which I can understand and handle.

Racing takes everything you've got—intellectually, emotionally, physically—and then you have to find about 10 percent more and use that too.
—*Janet Guthrie*

We have all heard stories about people digging in and giving that extra effort that put them over the top. Sometimes it comes from adrenaline, sometimes it is psych and sometimes it is just sheer determination. We also have that extra potential. Everyone is capable of going hard and coming up with just one more burst of energy. It is that extra rush that helps us accomplish a tricky skill or maneuver or gets us past a tough opponent.

Unless we consistently challenge ourselves we won't know just what we can do. That little bit extra is there, we just have to let it out by fully extending ourselves physically, mentally, and emotionally.

◆

I will give my all plus 10 percent.

Do *you* believe you're a starter or a benchwarmer? Do *you* believe you're an all-star or an also-ran? If the answers to these questions are the latter, your play on the field will reflect it. But when you've learned to shut off outside influences and believe in yourself, there's no telling how good a player you can be. That's because you have the mental edge.

—*Rod Carew*

When it comes to athletics, there's a lot to be said for self-fulfilling prophecy. So much of success in sports is mental, so believing in yourself is half the battle. There's no room for self-doubt on the tennis court, the golf course, or the baseball field. To have the mental edge that former Major League batting champion Rod Carew is speaking of, we have to step out onto the field or court or track feeling like a winner, whether we're there to compete, or just to workout.

We all get into funks where we feel inadequate, incapable, or just plain spastic. But we all have the power to get out of the dumps with the help of a little positive thinking—whether it's visualizing ourselves playing a great game, remembering a previous win, or recalling a helpful affirmation. And that positive outlook will do wonders to improve our performance, not to mention our mood. As Carew says, once we are able to really believe in ourselves and our ability, the sky's the limit.

◆

Today I will think like a winner.

I don't believe in playing hurt, in taking injections to cover the pain.
—*Monica Seles*

Playing hurt is one of the biggest mistakes an athlete can make. There isn't much that is worth risking permanent damage to our bodies. Most professional athletes who have taken the risk to play one last game often find themselves playing their last game ever or, at the very least, not playing up to their potential. When we are injured, the pain is a sign to stop. If we continue to play in pain we run the risk of injuring ourselves to the point that we may be unable to play again. There are also a lot of people who will tell us to suck it up and to be tough and keep on going. It's very tempting to listen to such gung-ho advice, but it's not worth it in the long run.

It's definitely frustrating to be injured. Sometimes all those good motivators like desire and mental toughness can make us want to jump back in too soon. We have to remember to transfer that motivation into getting better and taking care of the injury. Sitting out and watching isn't fun, but playing with pain can leave us sidelined permanently.

◆

If I'm injured, I will give my body the time it needs to heal.

The only way a kid is going to practice is if it's total fun for him—and it was for me.
—*Wayne Gretzky*

Excellent advice for a future hockey star from ice hockey's "The Great One," but it's also good advice for the weekend, nonprofessional athlete as well. We've got to have fun when we are working out or competing or we will lose interest and stop. Having fun doesn't mean fooling around. We can have a serious, goal-oriented, and productive workout, but we can give it our own special fun-loving twist. All it takes is a little imagination. We can set up games for ourselves that will take our minds off sweating our buns off and bring smiles to our faces.

If we have determined to hit a certain number of tennis balls, we can imagine that they have the face of someone who has been causing us some trouble lately—the boss, for example. It may bring a little zest into our stroke and vent a little aggravation at the same time. If we're out running, we can count all the people who are wearing green. It may seem silly, but inventing some little distraction can give us a fun goal that is separate from our more serious workout goals.

♦

I will find a way to make my workouts fun and that will keep me working.

I just have to be myself and not worry about everyone looking at me and watching.
—*Frank Thomas*

Everyone gets self-conscious once in a while. Whether we're getting down in funk class or trying to pump up on the tennis court, whether we've just a made an error on the ball field or a great shot on the golf course, we all have moments where we become much too aware of possible spectators and what they might think about our performance. Professional athletes have it tough. They, as baseball player Frank Thomas implies, have to play under the scrutiny of thousands of fans. They have to learn to keep praise and criticism in perspective. However, unless you're a professional athlete competing in front of an audience, chances are there are few people paying much attention to you as you sweat and strain.

Even if we do find ourselves working out or competing in front of others who appear to be watching we have to remind ourselves that we are out there not to entertain others but to have fun and get in shape—in other words, we're doing it for ourselves. And we can be fairly sure that those who are watching are doing so in support of us, or because they wish they were out there themselves. We have to be very careful not to assume the worst about what others think—"She runs funny," "His legs are so skinny," "They don't make a very good team"—but rather to assume the best—"She's really playing well," "He's getting better and better at swinging the golf club."

◆

Today I will concentrate on not being self-conscious while I work out.

It's not the size of the dog in the fight, but the size of the fight in the dog.
—*Archie Griffin*

As a two-time Heisman trophy winner, and with the relatively small stature of five feet nine inches, Archie Griffin had to call on other qualities besides size for his success. In a sport dominated by athletes both tall and large, Griffin used his incredible moves and smarts to dazzle fans and outwit opponents. For a football player, he was not a "big dog," but he did have a lot of fight in him.

We all have the potential to participate in any sport we choose, as long as we have the desire and develop the appropriate skills. Size or body type does not have to be a determining factor. While the average basketball player is not so average in height, we occasionally see outstanding players who are quite regular in size. Just as the typical long-distance runner is very slight, there have been quite successful runners who don't fit this prototype.

It's all about spirit and desire. It's about the power of the underdog. When we set our hearts and minds on something, chances are our bodies will cooperate. We are truly our own best motivators.

◆

My only limitations are the ones I set for myself.

I love to win, dude. I love to win.
—*Manute Bol*

Winning is fun. The lure of winning is what draws many people to sports in the first place. There is an adrenaline rush that comes with victory that is unlike any other experience. Even if we're not playing on a team or in one-on-one competition, we can bring that spirit of wanting to win to our workouts. It's just that the opponent is different. For some of us, it might be those fifteen, ten, or five pounds that we are trying to shed. For others it's that tenth mile we want to run. And for yet others it's the snooze alarm that lets us sleep in instead of working out. A victory, of whatever variety, is sweet no matter if the opponent is another person, an obstacle, or ourselves.

Winning loses its fun when it becomes the only acceptable outcome. Winning isn't just about beating the other guy. When we go out with the intention of creaming our opponent we may be the winner on paper but we may have lost a valuable experience. It's difficult to enjoy playing if we are always expecting to win or if we are the one who is expected to win. When we do come out on top the triumph loses some of its magic and it won't seem as if we've done anything unusual. If we reach beyond ourselves to win, it will be that much sweeter.

◆

I will find the joy that is in winning and in giving my best effort to win.

I've never run into the guy who could win at the top level in anything today and didn't have the right attitude, didn't give it everything he had, at least while he was doing it; wasn't prepared and didn't have the whole program worked out.
—*Ted Turner*

It takes a lot to be at the top. We not only have to be willing to work hard for it, we also have to be ready and willing to put in quantity and quality time. And that's not just physical practice time. It means we have to make the effort to focus and concentrate on what our goals are and how we are going to realize them. It means putting mental time into the planning and execution of our workouts and practices as well. We can have the perfect program carefully tooled to help us to be our best, but if we don't put ourselves into it 100 percent we'll go nowhere.

Attitude is key. It influences not only what we aspire to but how quickly we can get there without alienating our opponents or making ourselves crazy. A positive attitude will take us a long way if it is coupled with working out consistently and believing in ourselves while we are doing it. Positive attitude breeds confidence, which in turn helps us to turn in our best possible performance.

◆

Attitude, effort, preparation, and planning are my watchwords.

A man has to have goals—for a day, for a lifetime—and that was mine, to have people say, "There goes Ted Williams, the greatest hitter who ever lived."
—*Ted Williams*

You can't become the greatest hitter who ever lived or the greatest anything that ever lived without deciding exactly what it is that you want to accomplish. Goals are very important. And it's not just the long-term ones that count. Your goals don't have to be very elaborate, or even very lofty; they can actually be quite simple. In fact, the simpler the goals the more likely you are to keep working on them. It also helps to break those big goals into smaller steps. Goals are cumulative—those little short-term goals lead you toward achieving your long-term goals.

Sometimes a goal can be as simple as getting to the gym on a regular basis. You'll be surprised at how achieving one goal so easily leads to mastering others. You will also find that when you set your sights on smaller, manageable goals you *will* achieve them. And when you've made one goal happen that will fuel your confidence and help you to move on to the next goal, and the next, and on to your ultimate goal.

◆

Today I will set my sights on an attainable goal.

The moment of enlightenment is when a person's dreams of possibilities become images of probabilities.
—*Vic Braden*

*I*t is terrifically exciting to have worked and worked at honing a skill and to be standing on the edge of achieving a personal best—be it in running, tennis, golf, or racquetball. The moment when we realize that practice has paid off, that our triumphs and frustrations have not been in vain, that we, too, can set a goal and reach it, like a professional ball player or an Olympic gold medalist, is the moment that makes participation in sports the incredible high it can be.

Every athlete, from the twice-a-week LifeCycler to the competitive swimmer, can reach this peak—where, as tennis guru Vic Braden says, possibility becomes probability. It's the moment when we stop saying we can't run a marathon and start training instead; when we take our devastating forehand and unreturnable serve onto the tennis court to challenge a previously unbeatable opponent; when our thigh muscles are on fire, but we continue pedaling up the killer hill we've yet to conquer.

These achievements are so important and encouraging to us as we develop and grow in skills, strength, and stamina. We should relish these moments and lean on them when the challenges seem tougher and the goals harder to reach.

◆

Anything is possible and many things are probable
if I stick with my fitness program.

> Once you are physically capable of winning a gold medal,
> the rest is 90 percent mental.
> —*Patti Johnson*

*O*nce we are physically capable of doing *anything*, the rest is mostly mental. If we've cycled thirty miles several times, and we're now set to compete in a twenty-mile bikeathon, we know we can do the distance, it's just a matter of how well we will do it. The same is true for playing in a squash tournament. If we've beaten a certain opponent on a number of occasions and are now set to meet him in the quarterfinals, we've got to be mentally psyched for the win— we know we can beat him because we've done it before.

Mental preparation can be as simple as taking a few moments before stepping on the field, track, or court to meditate, focus, and visualize our performance. It can be as involved as taking part in a regular ritual that we set up to get us ready to play. It's up to us to find a mental tune-up routine that works best for our game.

◆

> My workout involves not only physical fitness, but mental fitness as well. My
> mind needs as much preparation as my body.

The principle [is] competing against yourself. It's about self-improvement, about being better than you were the day before.
—*Steve Young*

Each new day brings a new opportunity to work out and get fit. And each day presents us with a chance to improve. If we are not happy with what happened the last time we worked out—we didn't reach our goal time on the exercise bike or lost our squash match—we have today to make changes. We don't have to rely on anyone else to tell us that we're getting better. We are the best judge of how well we have done each time out. We know how much we have pushed ourselves, how far we have gone, and how much better we have done than the time before. We can' t change our bodies overnight, but our daily efforts at improvement add up, over time, to big changes.

Competing against yesterday's efforts can mean a lot of different things. Sometimes it means doing one more rep on the Nautilus machine than we did yesterday, or trying out a new machine, or making one less mistake. Sometimes being better than we were yesterday simply means getting to the gym today. Improvement comes slowly, but surely, and when we keep at it we will notice that we can make changes from one day to the next.

◆

I am getting better and better every day.

Set your goals high, and don't stop till you get there.
—Bo Jackson

Bo Jackson certainly knows what he's talking about. A very successful college athlete, he was drafted by two professional leagues, the NFL and Major League Baseball, and played two professional sports until a debilitating hip injury and later hip replacement forced him to give up football. After others had their doubts, he came back to continue his career in professional baseball.

Most of us may not have the lofty aspirations that Jackson does, but we do have goals and expectations for ourselves that we work toward. Even if we never enter any sort of competition, we do compete against ourselves as we try to better each earlier performance, and race against the clock as we look to knock seconds off our time. Setting goals is invaluable in mastering any sort of athletic endeavor, and adjusting them higher and higher as we reach them is the way we continue to improve.

Whether we do aim to compete on the professional or semiprofessional level, or we're simply looking to improve our time in the 10K, be more of an asset on our company softball team, or master two-putt greens on the golf course, we should always be striving toward a goal that is just out of reach. It should be rigorous enough to motivate but obtainable within a reasonable amount of time so as not to frustrate.

◆

Before I work out or compete today, I will set a goal for the day, as well as a long-term goal to work toward in the future.

No one man is superior to the game.
—*A. Bartlett Giamatti*

We have all seen incredible individual performances: Michael Jordan, Bo Jackson, Martina Navratilova, the list could go on and on. It may seem as though these players have exceeded the bounds of the games they play, but they have actually just taken their games to another level. They couldn't have done it without the competition they have experienced or the personal drive and desire that they have devoted to getting ahead. The game, their game, has taken them to superstardom and they may have influenced the way the game has been played, but the same game is played in high school gyms, on sand lots, and community tennis courts, across the country.

No matter what game we take on, as an individual or a team player, it will be the game that will help us to excel: learning the rules, practicing the moves, playing our hearts out in the last few minutes of the quarter or the half or the period. Without the game we wouldn't be able to test our limits and take our risks and become a better, more aggressive winning player. Without the game we wouldn't be able to realize fully what we are made of or what we are capable of achieving. It may only be a game, but it is always worth playing.

◆

I will play my heart out for the game.

> I don't psych myself up. I psych myself down. I think clearer
> when I'm not psyched up.
> —*Steve Cauthen*

Different strokes for different folks. We all use different techniques to get ourselves ready to work out or compete. Some of us need to get really pumped and hyper so as to transfer that energy onto the field, court, or course. Others may need to find a peaceful corner in which to meditate before taking on an opponent or a tough workout. We may need to concentrate exclusively on the task at hand, or we may be better off trying to put it out of our minds until it's time to begin.

No one can tell us how to prepare for working out or competing; it's something we have to get a feel for on our own. If we try to fire ourselves up with lots of adrenaline before we begin and then find that halfway through our exercise we're completely wiped out, then that's probably not the best technique for us. If, on the other hand, we try the quiet, meditative approach and then take the field and feel like we're half asleep, then we probably aren't good candidates for Zen and the art of exercise.

Professional athletes all have different methods of preparing for taking on opponents. We, too, should find the mode of preparation that works best for us.

◆

Today I will concentrate on how I prepare for my workout or competition,
making sure it's the best method for me.

Every athletic career, no matter how modest or lofty, is a journey.
—*Dan Millman, author of* The Warrior Athlete

Whether we're competitive professional or semiprofessional athletes or week-end sports enthusiasts our participation in athletics contributes greatly toward our balanced, healthy lives. Playing sports teaches us a lot that we can use in other parts of our lives, and we don't need to be tops in our field to take advantage of it. Everyone can benefit from the lessons learned on the court, in the pool, at an aerobics class, or during a race. While our daily jog or weekly golf game or regular workout may not seem to be on a par with the feats of sports greats like Michael Jordan, Steffi Graf, or Joe Montana, you can bet that they deal with the same issues that we do every day.

From our first struggling strokes in the shallow end of a pool to our competent 1,500-meter individual medley; from our initial lack of control of our junior size tennis racket to our club championship trophy; and from our unbearable insecurity in our beginning high-impact class to our mastering the advanced workout, we have all traveled far, both physically and psychologically. Accomplishment in sport is more than just improving our game, or stroke, or time. It's also about learning confidence, perseverance, control, and motivation. It's about handling loss as well as handling victory; staying focused when the inclination is to give up.

◆

My participation in sports is important, and is a constant learning process. I feel confident that what I get out of my workout is valuable.

I never underestimate an opponent. . . . A guy might be small in stature,
but he can be very tough inside.
—Carl Banks

It doesn't matter at what level we compete, chances are we've all made the mistake of underestimating an opponent, and then suffered the consequences. It may have been the frail-looking, knobby-kneed tennis opponent who took us in straight sets, the disorganized-looking softball team that pulled it all together on the field, or the golfer we'd seen play once and had poorly prejudged. Underestimating our opponents is all about overconfidence and not taking a match or game as seriously as we probably should, only to be sorry later.

Even if the situation doesn't involve underestimating an opponent, it can still be detrimental. Maybe we need to swim a certain time or distance to qualify for an event. We dismiss the goal as easy and obtainable and find after the starter's gun goes off that it's not quite as simple as we had thought. We all know the feeling: "Oops, I guess I'm not as prepared as I thought I was." No matter what our level of skill, or frequency of participation, preparation is paramount, and overconfidence is the kiss of death.

◆

I will enter every competition with respect for the opponent—
be it a fellow competitor, or a ticking time clock.

> I don't think I can play any other way but all out . . . I enjoy the game so much
> because I'm putting so much into it.
> —*George Brett*

Sure, it's a lot of fun to win or to be our best, but when we put all we have into what we are doing it heightens our pleasure, as well as our physical accomplishments.

The best exercising happens when our minds, our bodies, and our hearts are all in sync. It is at those times that we'll find ourselves with a smile on our faces even though we are working really hard. That smile isn't just from endorphins, either. It's from the pure pleasure exercising can give us. And if it's not fun, why do it?

◆

Going all out will get you more than winning, it will get you to have a good time.

When you are winning too much, sometimes you think you should never lose again.
I am learning to lose.
—*Goran Ivanisevic*

Every winning streak comes to an end sooner or later. We should definitely enjoy it while it lasts and try to do everything possible to keep it going; however, the streak will end. Losing is no picnic, but it is an essential part of the game. And it doesn't just tell us that there is someone better than we are. We can learn a lot more from losing than from winning. Being graceful in the face of defeat is a valuable ability, and any true winner knows how to lose.

Losing can also teach us about the way we play. When we lose we may discover a weakness we didn't know we had. By winning so often we may be relying too heavily on one aspect of the way we play. Losing can teach us to look for ways to improve our play by becoming more dimensional. A loss can teach us not only that we are not invincible but that we can pick up a few tricks from our opponents. Notice what our opponents do in certain situations. Can we take a few pages from their book and use those lessons on them the next time we meet? We should walk away from a loss thinking about why we lost and what we can do about it. If we don't win, we should be sure to learn something from losing.

◆

I can learn to lose without giving up on winning.

We didn't get great goals. We just scored no-fear goals. Heart goals.
—*Rich Pilon*

Sometimes winning doesn't come from picture-perfect scoring or playing. There are many wins that would never make it into a textbook on how to do it. Perfection is not a realistic aspiration because there just isn't such a thing in sports. We don't have to be perfect to be victorious. Although we can't be flawless in what we do, anything else is possible if we have the guts to go out and fight hard for what we want. We may also find that we need to adapt our play from the standard. There are no two professional golfers who swing or putt exactly alike, nor are there any two professional tennis players who serve identically. Are any of these players less perfect than another? The one thing that they all have in common is putting 100 percent of themselves into their play.

As hockey star Rich Pilon implies, a lot of heart can drive in more points than all the perfection in the world. Solid teamwork can help create perfection out of a lot of less than perfect individual efforts. Bravely entering into a contest and standing up to an opponent or taking on a strenuous fitness program is a victory in and of itself. With heart and bravery we can take it all the way to the top.

◆

I'll have perfect heart, even if I can't have perfect play.

I'm trying not to look too far ahead. All I'm thinking is one shot at a time, one hole at a time, and that's what I want to keep doing.
—Michelle McGann

One shot at a time, one step at a time, one thing at a time. We've all heard this advice, yet how many times do we find ourselves thinking ahead in a match or a game, and not focusing on the task at hand? How many times do we anticipate our next opponent or upcoming challenge when what we really should be doing is concentrating on the job in front of us?

If we're about to tee off on the seventh hole of a tough golf course, should we be fretting about the awesome trap that awaits us on the ninth hole? Probably not. If we're battling the fourth seed in a tennis tournament, should we be anxiously considering how we'll play the first seed if we meet her? Don't think so. If we're battling "the wall" in the marathon at mile 18, should we be worrying about how we'll be feeling at mile 25? No, actually we should probably be more concerned with reaching mile 19. And even while we're in the throes of a tough workout, we should be concentrating on our present activity and not anticipating what's to come. No matter what our game, it takes a lot of energy and focus to perform well, so we have to learn to get the most we can out of ourselves moment by moment.

◆

Today I will focus exclusively on the task at hand and not anticipate the challenges to come.

> You don't run twenty-six miles at five minutes a mile on good looks
> and a secret recipe.
> —*Frank Shorter*

*I*f there is any secret, it is simply called *work*. We can't succeed at anything with only a flashy smile, the ability to talk a good game, and a shortcut. There are no shortcuts to success. We will encounter many people who believe that if they look the part (wear the right gear, spout the correct terminology) they somehow have an edge over the average guy. We can't rely on that kind of posturing for too long because sooner or later we will get found out.

Being able to perform at the level of someone like superstar runner Frank Shorter takes many hours of training, and many hours of mental planning and all-around dedication. We may not need to invest the training time a professional does, but we won't do well without being consistent about the amount of time that we do work out. An on-again, off-again athlete will never truly succeed because consistency is what helps us to get ahead. Consistent hard work will also help us to build our confidence. Confidence is more than the belief that we can do whatever it takes to carry us through. Confidence is our reward for all the hard work that we do.

◆

I know the secret to success is hard work.

If I would be happy, I would be a very bad ballplayer. With me, when I get mad,
it puts energy in my body.
—Roberto Clemente

*A*s athletes, we all need to find our own technique for motivating ourselves and pumping ourselves up when the situation demands it. For some of us, getting angry is just the motivation we need to get the job done. When things aren't going as planned—our workout is weak or our performance is poor—we use anger, at ourselves or our opponents, to get a little jump-start. Consider tennis professional John McEnroe. He is notorious for using his temper to fire himself up and perhaps psych his opponents out.

Experience will help find the method that works best for us in the heat of competition or during a tough workout. Whether it's anger or positive self-talk, singing to ourselves or meditating—if it brings results, we should use it.

◆

I need to find the technique that motivates me best when I'm playing my worst.

> Everybody pulls for David, nobody roots for Goliath.
> —*Wilt Chamberlain*

Sometimes it feels as if the better we get at a sport, the more we find others cheering for our opponents. While we work feverishly on our tennis game taking on and handling more and more opponents, or our basketball team practices regularly, gradually winning more and more games, we discover, to our dismay, that the folks who had been so supportive of us in the past now are putting their hands together for the other guys. It's almost as if in our quest to get to the top of the ladder at the club, or to win the league championships, or to be the best, we have given up the welcome fans we had had.

It seems that way because it may, in fact, be true. People, athletic and otherwise, gravitate naturally toward the underdog. And while we enjoy and flourish with their support as we are getting better and better, we must stay motivated when we find ourselves winning games and losing backers. Whether we find ourselves all of a sudden no longer the "crowd favorite" at our regular golf round-robin, or we have gotten the reputation as the killers in the corporate softball league and feel hurt/offended by the lack of support, we need to remember that others are only doing what comes naturally. As Wilt Chamberlain says, they are cheering, not for Goliath, but for David.

◆

If others seem less than supportive of me or my team, I must remember not to take it personally and never give up.

Part of being a champ is acting like a champ. You have to learn how to win and not run away when you lose. . . . Everyone has bad stretches and real successes. Either way, you have to be careful not to lose your confidence or get too confident.
—*Nancy Kerrigan*

*E*veryone, no matter how accomplished she may be at her sport, has good days and bad days. The avid runner, the weekend golfer, and the competitive sailor all have days where they perform to or beyond expectations, running a personal best, shooting a low score, or sailing a great race. These athletes also have days where nothing seems to go right—their coordination is off, their skills aren't up to par, and their hearts and heads just aren't into it. It's during these somewhat unusual highs and lows that we must try hardest to maintain a level of confidence that is, itself, neither too high nor too low.

After an exceptionally good workout or win it's easy to get carried away with the excitement of a job well done (and we *should* be proud of ourselves), yet not at the expense of others' feelings or our concept of reality. On the other hand, a less than glowing performance can be upsetting and frustrating, but it is an isolated experience that we can learn from and improve upon and should not knock down our sense of self. If we can maintain a steady level of confidence while going through the expected ups and downs of working out and competing, we will perform better and more consistently, not to mention feel better about ourselves.

◆

Each success and disappointment is a learning experience, none of which should affect my consistent feeling of self-confidence.

You learn how to be a gracious winner and an outstanding loser.
—*Joe Namath*

*I*t's hard to lose. When we lose it feels as if all of our hard work has gone to waste. It's very easy to get down on ourselves and give into feeling anger and despair. But for our sake, we need to acknowledge the achievements of our opponents, as well as the fact that we made them work for their victory. Just because we didn't win this time doesn't mean we are losers. So we shouldn't act like one.

By the same token, a win isn't an excuse to gloat or to rub the loss in our opponent's face. Celebrating is fine—after all, we have won and we deserve to be happy about it. It is a confirmation of our efforts that lead up to the competition. We lose everything if we put down our opponent because he fell short. Undoubtedly, we will meet the same player again, and he may be even more psyched to win the next time.

It's a lot harder to be an outstanding loser, but if we maintain our composure we will be able to see what went right and capitalize on that the next time. Once we have lost, we need to leave it behind and move on. If we dwell on our disappointments, we will bury our chances for victory on another day.

◆

A loss doesn't make me a loser.

It ain't braggin' if you can do it.
—*Dizzy Dean*

*T*here's a fine line between self-confidence in our skills and pride in our performance and an over-the-line arrogance. While self-confidence is important in motivating us to keep up the good work, we must be careful to maintain a healthy ego—one that encourages us, yet is not overly aggressive or obnoxious that will put off our colleagues or fellow competitors.

Our egos should be on a par with our skills, but we should keep them in check no matter how accomplished we may be. We should use our egos to give us the confidence to step onto the tennis court with a tough opponent, push ourselves in a challenging bike race, or really go for it in an advanced workout class. We should not use our egos to intimidate opponents, boast about our skills, or especially to show up others. When managed properly, egos can work for us in bolstering our self-esteem and therefore improving our performance. When mismanaged, strong egos can offend others, and, at times, even backfire on us, if we fail to live up to our boasts.

◆

A healthy ego, used properly, can be a real asset. Overconfidence can be a real detriment to us and a turnoff to others. I will keep my ego strong but in check.

Tennis can be a grind and there's always the danger of going stale if you think about it too much. You can get embittered if you train too hard and have nothing else on your mind. You have to be able to relax between matches and between tournaments.
—*Maureen Connolly*

When we are trying our best to improve our golf swing or perfect our serve or master a step aerobics routine it is very easy to become single-minded about our activity. Sometimes people become so obsessed with their workouts that they ignore everything else in their lives. Obviously, this is not a healthy attitude.

As important as it is to keep working, it is equally important to take a break and give ourselves a breather. This doesn't mean that we should turn into couch potatoes, but if we have been working hard on one specific activity we may need to take some time out and give ourselves a well-deserved rest. No matter what our exercise of choice, if we take some time off, when we return we will feel refreshed and may find ourselves playing better and stronger because of the break.

◆

I will take a break and relax so that when I play again
I will be refreshed and renewed.

I've always made a total effort, even when the odds seemed entirely against me. I never quit trying; I never felt that I didn't have a chance to win.
—*Arnold Palmer*

No matter what the odds, there is always a chance that we can win. (Well, maybe not if we're going one-on-one with Michael Jordan, but in our everyday athletic endeavors we do have a chance.) It may look bleak at times, but there is always a possibility that we can pull it out at the end. However, if we don't make a total effort we will never know if we lost because we gave up, and basically beat ourselves, or if it was because we were beaten by the other guy.

The odds may be stacked so heavily against us that we will be considered the underdog. While it may be disheartening to be undervalued, there actually are some advantages to not being the favorite. No one will expect us to win, so some of the pressure will be off us. Without that undue pressure we can relax and play our own game. Sometimes the underdog, through perseverance and heart, can emerge victorious. The only way to know the real outcome of our game is to keep on trying to the bitter end.

◆

Even if the odds seem stacked against me I will keep on going and know that I always have a chance.

> You have no control over what the other guy does.
> You only have control over what you do.
> —A J Kitt

*U*ltimately you are the only one who can get you to exercise. Trainers, coaches, workout buddies can all help, but *you* are the one who makes the difference, because when it comes down to it, you are the one who has to lace up your sneakers and get started on your exercise routine. No one else can do it for you.

If you're in competition with someone else, you can't control how he plays or responds to the way you play. You can try to influence them, but you're not pulling their strings and they're not pulling yours. Sometimes it can be discouraging to see how the other guy does. Getting passed on the track by someone isn't the greatest feeling in the world. You have to remember that everyone has his own agenda. The person passing you may be in training for the run of a lifetime, he may be a professional, or maybe he's just been working longer or harder than you. It's easy to compare yourself to another person unfavorably and lose faith in yourself and your abilities. But he isn't making you fall behind, and you can't change the way he performs. When it comes down to it, you and only you have the ultimate responsibility for your performance.

◆

I can't control all the factors that influence my performance
but I can control myself.

> Just do what you do best.
> —*Red Auerbach*

*I*t feels good to do something we're adept at. It's extremely satisfying to play a game or participate in an exercise that we have a talent for. And what better way to keep up an active, consistent training program than to have it made up of things we like to do and are good at. All of a sudden, workouts in the gym don't seem so tedious, getting up early for a run doesn't seem so unpleasant, and practicing a move or skill for hours isn't as exhausting.

There are so many choices of sports, workouts, and fitness classes—finding something that's just right for us should not be difficult. We just need to get out there and sample the many athletic activities available and appealing to us. If running is a bore and hard on the knees, try swimming. If swimming's not our event, take up cycling. If tennis isn't our game, pick up a golf club; golf's too slow, try downhill skiing. Find your activity and work on developing it to the fullest. You'll see greater results if you just do something that's doable and enjoyable.

◆

Today I'll pick my best and favorite workout and enjoy the challenge and
satisfaction it offers me.

*Before I go out on the field every day, I tell myself, "You are having fun,
and you want to set a good example to those who are watching."*
—*Cory Snyder*

When we take to the streets in our running shoes or on our bikes; when we hit the StairMaster or the LifeCycle or the weights at the gym; when we tee off in golf, tip off in basketball, or take off on a power walk, we should do so with the goal of having fun. Top athletes profess a love for their sports and confess there is a "fun factor" in playing games for a living. And athletes of other skill levels are allowed to have fun also.

The more positive our approach to working out, the more pleasant the experience will be and the better our chances of performing well. Positive energy can do wonders for turning around a lackluster workout. And when we are truly enjoying ourselves in step class, on the tennis court, and during a ball game, it is evident because we often perform at a top level.

Another bonus of having a good time is that others will sense our upbeat energy and find it infectious. As we pass other joggers, we'll encourage more smiles, praise among teammates, camaraderie in the clubhouse, and friendly conversation at the gym.

◆

Before and during my workout today, I'll remind myself to have fun.

> The truth is that most busy people cannot sustain a seven-day-a-week [training] schedule. There are too many other stresses and responsibilities in their lives.
> —*PattiSue Plumer*

*F*or those of us who feel it necessary to squeeze in a workout every day, regardless of its quality or duration, we've just been let off the hook by Olympic runner PattiSue Plumer. While it seems commitment to a sport or fitness level would mean practicing or competing as close to every day as possible, for most of us who are amateur athletes, it is just not viable nor is it mandatory.

Even professional athletes have other interests and responsibilities—family, hobbies, even other sports interests. So it stands to reason that those of us who do not make our living in athletics would have as many, if not more, outside distractions and obligations. The busier our schedules, the harder it may seem to get in a good workout on a daily basis. However, the good news is that we can still maintain our fitness levels without being on the seven-day-a-week plan.

By simply keeping up a regular and consistent workout schedule we can stay fit, and even improve, yet also sustain a balanced, well-rounded life. We can also avoid feeling guilty about not training long or hard enough.

◆

Athletics is only one part of my balanced life. If I miss a day of working out,
I will simply catch up tomorrow.

I found out that if you are going to win games, you had better be ready to adapt.
—Scotty Bowman

Rigid plans are very susceptible to breaking apart. The more inflexible we are the more likely we are to run into disappointment. Adapting to a game situation can mean the difference between winning and losing. Set plays are great because they give us a plan to follow and can point us in the right direction. But stubbornly sticking to a plan when it isn't working is a recipe for defeat. We'll find that if we are willing to adapt our play we will be more successful.

Flexibility can also help us to become more well rounded. Cross-training has become very popular because it is a very sensible way to get in shape. It allows us to work different parts of our bodies so that we can achieve overall fitness. If we do only one thing, we may soon find ourselves out of balance. If we want to become better athletes, we need to adapt ourselves to new routines and even to new sports. Combining aerobics and weightlifting, for example, can enhance our performances in both areas. Being able to do more than one sport or type of workout keeps our exercising interesting and fresh. If we switch things around and keep it interesting, we are more likely to keep on going.

◆

Flexibility keeps you fresh and competitive.

If you train hard, you'll not only be hard, you'll be hard to beat.
—Hershel Walker

We've all been fed the "hard work pays off" line. It's usually recited to us by a coach or instructor right when we're about to throw in the towel. Sometimes, while running on a cold and blustery morning we challenge ourselves by saying, "Faster, farther, faster, farther"; while our exhausted legs and frozen hands say "You've got to be kidding." While serving tennis ball after tennis ball from a seemingly bottomless basket, our minds say "Concentrate, focus." Our aching shoulder says, "Enough already."

Sometimes it seems as if all of our hard work does not, in fact, pay off. What it does is make us sore, tired, and downright sick of working out. These are the times we have to remember the adage, or at least Herschel Walker's spin on it.

While days and days of workouts may not seem to be yielding the results we had hoped for, and the goals we are aiming for are seeming more and more out of reach, we have to feel confident that there will be a breakthrough, and that it's just around the next corner, or over the next hill, or in the next practice.

◆

Hard work does pay off. It may not be today, and it may not be tomorrow, but it will happen, so I need to feel confident and keep up my workout schedule.

To go beyond is as wrong as to fall short.
—*Confucius*

We all overdo once in a while. We eagerly go out and push ourselves too far and too hard and we suffer the painful consequences. We've all experienced something like hitting the slopes the first weekend of the season and not being able to ski the next day because of various aches and pains, running on the first warm day of spring and limping for days afterward or energetically starting that New Year's resolution and getting so sore that we can't follow up the next day.

Overdoing it can lead to injuries and disappointment. When we push ourselves over our limit we can easily lose valuable momentum and time. What seemed like a big accomplishment quickly becomes a huge setback. It can be hard to keep our enthusiasm in check sometimes. But it will help to pay close attention to our bodies as we exercise. There is such a thing as taking the whole "no-pain, no-gain" theory too far. We don't need to take on the world the first day out, and frankly, there is no way to accomplish everything you want to in one day or even one week. Moderation is the best approach while we are starting out. It's much more important to keep on working than to make what may seem to be huge strides all at once.

◆

I will not overdo.

I'm not trying to prove anybody wrong, I'm just trying to prove something to myself.
—*Mike Piazza*

Fitness and exercise are not about proving anything to anybody but ourselves. The fact that we run thirty miles a week, or take aerobics classes every day, or play two rounds of golf every Saturday, or can bench-press our own weight, is important only in what it means to us. We shouldn't be training for a marathon just to show someone how wonderful we are. Nor should we overdo it at the gym to keep up with those who we're trying to impress. The beauty of participating in sports is that it is so personally satisfying. What we do, we do because we want to do it, not because we've been challenged, or put down, or feel the need to prove something to someone.

Athletes of all levels are constantly challenged by colleagues, coaches, teachers, and opponents to show their stuff. We're bombarded by advertisers who try to encourage us to get out there and do something by threatening us with gaining weight, being out of shape, and just not being good enough. When taken the right way, all of these outside factors can be great motivators. They can mobilize us to take to the court, gym, and track. However, for us to really benefit from our exercise program, we have to be doing it for the right reason and person—to prove something to ourselves. No amount of working out to impress others is ever going to be as effective as working out to impress ourselves.

◆

I work out for me, and me alone.

I go into the locker room and find a corner by myself and just sit there. I try to achieve a peaceful state of nothingness that will carry over onto the golf course. If I get that feeling of quiet and obliviousness within myself, I feel I can't lose.
—*Jane Blalock*

Everyone has her own way of preparing for a competition. For some of us it's the moment of quiet meditation PGA champion Jane Blalock describes. For others it's cranking music, eating and drinking high-energy foods, and distracting ourselves with conversation, warm-up, or watching others play or perform. It doesn't matter what helps us prepare to compete as long as it's effective and we're comfortable with the process.

While most professional athletes will sing the praises of one precompetition technique or another, it's important to find something that works best for us. Although we may be encouraged to try various ways to prepare, ultimately we're looking for the way to make our own performance better. The peaceful, contemplative method of psyching up may not be exactly right for the athlete who really needs to get pumped up before a tennis match or a volleyball game. On the other hand, getting fired up and hyper before a round of golf or a 10K run may be a misuse of energy. It's a personal choice, and one that has a prominent effect on how we run, play, shoot, and swim.

◆

I will find my own personal psych-up method so that I'll be best prepared for tough workouts and competition.

I'll never think that there's something I can't do, whether it's beating my opponent one-on-one or practicing another hour because something about my game is just not right.
—*Earvin ("Magic") Johnson*

This can-do, do-whatever-it-takes attitude is the attitude of champions. If we approach our sports and fitness with a positive outlook we will be successful. A positive attitude doesn't just count when the chips are down or when we are going for a championship or a trophy. That attitude should be with us every day so that we can take on opponents or workouts or practice with the same level of focus and intensity. A can-do attitude means a willingness to put ourselves on the line and give a maximum effort at all times. It means not giving in to thinking that we can't make changes either in our fitness level or in how we play. It means working hard and earning our successes. When we don't try our best, regardless of the circumstances, we are taking away an opportunity to learn.

Confidence in ourselves is key, not only in executing a well-tuned performance, but also in helping us to know that we can improve. We need to believe in what we can do already and have faith in our potential and in our ability to grow and learn. A positive attitude can carry us through the learning experiences and help us to be our best.

◆

I can do whatever I think I can do.

A 100 percent concern with a game to the exclusion of all else is surely tinged with
obsession. The single-mindedness necessary to fight one's way to the top, in no
matter what sport, is something not shared by the majority of mortals.
—*Paul Gallico*

Commitment to a sport is good. Perseverance is also good. But obsession, the
undying need to work out more and more, get better and better, is often dangerous, and never worthwhile in the long run. To concentrate so intensely on a single
goal or activity to the exclusion of all else is to become too one dimensional and
risk potential burnout. It is also a recipe for illness or injury.

By staying well rounded, despite how competitive we may be, we are giving
ourselves a better chance for success. We are keeping our goals in perspective
while striving to reach them. We are staying in top physical shape, yet still
maintaining other interests by cross-training. We can still be competitive if we
choose to, yet we can avoid the obsession that plagues some athletes.

◆

Today while working out, I'll think of all the other activities I enjoy and that
make me a well-rounded person.

Enjoying success requires the ability to adapt. You shouldn't outline a program and etch it in stone. We all have different physical limitations and skills that make us unique individuals. Try to make modifications in your program to enhance it. . . .
Only by being open to change will you have a true opportunity to get
the most from your talent.
—*Nolan Ryan*

Now here's a guy who knows whereof he speaks. A pitcher for twenty-seven years in Major League Baseball, Ryan pitched six no-hitters while playing for a total of four teams. Talk about having the ability to adapt.

A workout program set in stone is an invitation to failure. While setting up goals and a schedule is a good idea, the ability to be flexible is an even better one. By modifying and enhancing the way we exercise, we are zeroing in on the system that works best for us—and, frankly, gives us the most impressive results and the most pleasure. If we've hit the wall with a certain workout, maybe it's time for a little variety. If we're bored with our training, maybe it's time to add more of a challenge. No one said we had to stay with the same program day in and day out. In fact, the more we change and vary our program, the stronger and more effective we'll be all around. A career like Nolan Ryan's is the stuff of dreams, but we certainly can benefit from taking some of his suggestions.

◆

I will develop and work with a flexible fitness program.

If you can believe it, the mind can achieve it.
—Ronnie Lott

—A personal best in the 10K
—A higher ranking on the tennis ladder
—Acing the advanced high-impact class
—More reps on the Cybex machine at the gym
—Nonstop to the top of the killer hill in mile 9 of my bike ride
—Two-putt greens on every hole
—Ten more minutes on the StairMaster—at the next higher level
—Another 100-meter individual medley—only faster
—A great run through fresh powder on an advanced trail
—More sit-ups; more push-ups; more leg lifts
—A more consistent free throw; a meaner curveball; an untouchable serve

◆

If I can believe it, I can achieve it.

Tactics, fitness, stroke ability, adaptability, experience, and sportsmanship all are
necessary for winning.
—*Fred Perry*

*O*verall health and fitness come together like pieces in a puzzle. And while
tennis great Fred Perry is talking about the skills that can take a player to the
top at Wimbledon, no matter what exercise we do we can adapt his advice to
ourselves. What he is really talking about is finding the smaller parts of the big
picture:

—Tactics = setting realistic goals
—Fitness = making the commitment to getting in shape
—Stroke ability = knowing the techniques of our sport or routine
—Adaptability = adjusting workouts to our ability and energy
—Experience = devoting time to exercise and getting better
—Sportsmanship = always being fair to ourselves and others

No one aspect is more important than any other. When they all come together
they can help us to be the best that we can be.

◆

I will concentrate on putting all the pieces together.

> As long as I can concentrate and remain somewhat calm,
> I can normally do very well.
> —Al Oerter

While it may seem that remaining calm is not exactly the psych-up technique that would lead to a great workout or performance, oftentimes it is the perfect antidote to an overanxious, unfocused mind. We've all been in situations where our brains become our own worst enemies. Whether it's in trying to complete a workout or in the throes of competition, we've all had days when we just can't seem to concentrate and execute the task at hand.

Sometimes in order to psych up, we have to psych down. We need to relax and focus on the workout ahead of us. What do we want to accomplish? Is this a reasonable expectation? How do we go about getting this done?

A calm, focused mind is often a valuable asset, both in practice and competition. If we steer our minds into this state of centered relaxation, it just may help us better our golf swing, smooth out our backstroke, and take on the StairMaster. Who knows? We may find the last mile in a 10K comes a lot easier, our batting average improves, we're more efficient on the ski slopes, and we're playing a mean tennis game.

◆

Before today's workout, I will try and reach a state of
total mind relaxation and concentration.

There is no doubt in my mind that there are many ways to be a winner but there is really only one way to be a loser and that is to fail and not look beyond the failure.
—*Kyle Rote, Jr.*

A loss isn't the end of the world. It may feel like it at the time, but it really isn't. A loss is bad only if we accept it and consequently believe that we are losers. A loser can never win. Once we are convinced that we are easily defeated we will be. We won't be able to stand up to anyone or anything.

A winner suffers defeat once in a while—and a winner knows that it is simply part of the game, no more, no less. We have to swing, and miss, a lot of balls to be a .500 hitter. We have to slip and fall and get up and try again to become a good skier. We have to miss a lot of putts before we can consistently get the ball in the hole. If we give up because of a loss, we are missing an opportunity to improve. What can we learn from it? What can we do next time to avoid it? By accepting failure we deny ourselves the chance to move beyond the failure. A loss isn't the end; it can be the source of inspiration for a new beginning.

◆

If I lose, I will know that it's part of the game and that there is life after losing.

I'm a good baseball player. But I can be a *great* baseball player.
A *star* baseball player.
—Deion Sanders

Never settle. If we reach one goal then we need to lift our heads up and see what our next goal will be. Don't be satisfied with achieving one goal; always ask, "What's next?" If we can get to one level then we can certainly get to the next. The time to start planning our next goal is when we are close to achieving our first goal. That way, we can keep moving ahead without losing momentum. We need to keep feeding ourselves new goals to maintain our edge. If we are hungry, we won't be satisfied and we will keep on improving.

We don't ever have to tell or show or prove to anyone what we have done. It will be enough to know for ourselves that we have continually reached for our best. Confidence can carry us along as we strive for higher and higher goals. We have to approach our goals with the attitude that says, "I can do this. I am capable of achieving this goal and I will not fail." It means that we know just what our potential is and that we are willing to test that potential. We will not settle for anything less than the best.

◆

I won't be satisfied until I have reached the top.

I don't think anyone can perform as an athlete if they can't be themselves. . . .
The only way to reach your potential is to be free.
—*Nancy Reno*

*T*he more in control we are of any aspect of our lives, the happier and more successful we tend to be with that part. Whether it's a job that we are confident in and are performing up to our potential, or a sport we participate in and are very adept at, if we're playing the game our way, chances are it'll be a good experience. We gain this personal control of the situation by being ourselves out there—playing our game, acting the way we feel comfortable, talking our talk, and walking our walk.

If we need evidence of this, we just need to take a look at some of the biggest characters in professional sports, and then at their records of success. Andre Agassi is certainly not the most conventional tennis player around—he's hyper, he's mediagenic, he wears nontraditional tennis garb, he's a teen heartthrob . . . and he's one of the top players in the world. In basketball there's Charles Barkley —he's manic, he's funny, he's a real character . . . and he, too, is at the top of his sport. Throughout the years there have been dozens of athletes who have marched to a different drummer and, at the same time, been some of the best competitors out there.

We should feel comfortable doing whatever it takes to motivate ourselves to work out, and if that means wild outfits, unusual training regimens, or oddball strategies, then so be it.

◆

I can be who I want to be and do what I want to do.

In certain situations we'd be down and the competitor in me would want to get it all back in one play. That impatience makes for bad plays, mistakes, and turnarounds.
—*Browning Nagle*

We can't do everything at once, in one play or in one day. We will discover that if we overcompensate we will not accomplish what we had hoped. Rushing ahead usually forces us to fall even farther behind. Impatience needs to be kept firmly in check. As eager as we are to do well or to get through our routine we have to take the time to pay attention to what we are doing. If we haphazardly fly through our workouts we won't get the full benefit of our exercise. Any shortcut will shortchange us in the long run. We also need to exercise patience with ourselves and our progress—especially when we are starting out on a new program. Exercise is a cumulative activity. We won't be able to accomplish all we want to achieve in one workout. It will take time for those workouts to translate into lost pounds, better muscle tone, or victories on the court.

It is great to be competitive, but controlled competitive instincts are what will get us ahead. When we rush, we will make errors. Be psyched and competitive but don't go too far overboard.

◆

I will be patient with myself and my progress.

I know you've heard it a thousand times before. But it's true—hard work pays off.
If you want to be good, you have to practice, practice, practice.
—*A. J. English*

It's true. We have probably heard it a thousand times before. But a professional athlete should know as well as anyone about the benefits of practice. A pro should also know and admit to the hours of agonizing drills, the boredom, the frustration, the occasional toying with the idea of quitting, and the temptation to get by with less than 100 percent effort. And while it does, in the long run, usually pay off—especially for a professional—we, too, often suffer these ills in our daily workouts.

Let's face it, exercise can be grueling. It can be monotonous. It can be a source of frustration. What we have to remember, though, is the reason we do it to begin with. If our goal is to maintain or improve our fitness level, we can be assured that our perseverance will be worth it. If we're trying to lose weight or shape our bodies, we can be confident that a regular workout is an effective way to meet that end. If we participate in sports for the competition and exhilaration, we should know that there is no substitute for a pumping heart and pumped up endorphins. And if all this means we have to suffer through another seemingly endless aerobics class, hang in there for one more mile, or power through one more drill, we can do it because we know it will pay off in the long run, and we'll be mighty proud of ourselves.

◆

Practice may not make perfect, but it will make me better, and today I will approach my workout as an invaluable means to a valuable end.

A positive attitude can really make dreams come true—it did for me.
—*Zina Garrison*

*A*chieving a world-class ranking as a professional tennis player was the ultimate goal for Zina Garrison, and she suggests a good deal of her success can be attributed to having a positive outlook and a confident attitude. While many of us will never reach the uppermost echelons of our sports, we, too, have the capacity to boost our achievements by maintaining an upbeat state of mind.

Staying up when we are feeling down—after a tough loss or a slump or an apparent stall in noticeable improvement—or looking forward to future challenges with enthusiasm—instead of dread or anxiety or boredom—may be difficult, but it will be worth it in the long run. The energy spent on anger, frustration, nervousness, self-doubt, or putting down opponents is better spent on concentration, perseverance, visualization, and affirmation.

While there are obviously no promises when it comes to athletic achievement at any level, the experts and professionals give an upbeat attitude a thumbs up.

◆

Today I will use all of my energy *positively* as I work out or compete.

> I used to get out there and have a hundred swing thoughts.
> Now I try not to have any.
> —*Davis Love III*

When we start to play a sport we inevitably think about every move we make. Is my racquet at the right angle? Am I doing these sit-ups correctly? How's my follow-through? Am I lifting these weights the right way? We are constantly evaluating and checking how we are doing. What we have to work toward is making those moves unconsciously. When we have internalized our lessons and memorized the techniques then we can do them when we need them automatically. For example, when you tie your shoes you probably do it without a second thought. Next time you do it, think about what you are doing; you may be surprised to find that you do it a lot slower than normally.

There is danger in thinking too much. Unfortunately there usually isn't any one way to approach every athletic situation. There are always options that we can exercise. The problem is, if we run through all of those choices mentally we may miss our opportunity and not be able to do what we want or what is best for the situation. We need to relax and let our instincts take over. Trust our natural responses and reflexes. We should have the confidence that we will "know" what to do without thinking about it.

◆

I don't have to think about it—I just have to do it.

Perhaps the single most important element in mastering the techniques and tactics of racing is experience. But once you have the fundamentals, acquiring the experience is a matter of time.
—Greg LeMond

*T*here is no such thing as an instant, overnight expert. Cycling expert Greg LeMond has certainly put in many hours on the road to becoming one of the biggest names in his sport. In getting ourselves in shape, or when we are learning a new sport, time will definitely be on our side if we use it well. At first we will need to spend time working on the basics. No matter how tedious this may seem this will be time well spent. The basics create a solid foundation on which we can build the rest of our exercise program. Once we have acquired the basics we will be able to fine-tune them by putting in as much practice time as we can.

Testing our skills in different arenas and ways can also make us more experienced athletes. An experienced athlete is one who knows what to expect under certain circumstances and under certain conditions. She also knows how to deal with any situation that arises—she is always prepared. As her experience grows, with time, she will know better and better how to cope with whatever she encounters.

◆

I will put in the time and reap the rewards of experience.

I feel very comfortable at the plate and capable of doing something every time I'm up, but I'm only trying to hit the ball hard and do the things I need to do. I don't want to put any pressure on myself. I'm not thinking about .400.
—*Andres Galarraga*

There's a fine line between having the confidence to accomplish something and putting too much pressure on ourselves to achieve. Yes, we want to, and think we can, run five miles in under thirty-five minutes, beat a tough opponent at racquetball, go four for four in the softball game, or ace the most advanced aerobics class, but we have to be careful not to let our confidence translate into what becomes a do-or-die situation. The more keyed up we get over winning, hitting, scoring, or performing, the more we chance choking in the heat of competition or working out.

Overconfidence is like overtraining—it is taking a good thing way too far. The fact is, more is not necessarily better, and by keeping from overthinking the situation we give ourselves more of a chance to achieve our goals. Professional baseball player Andres Galarraga had to keep his head in check as he approached the outstanding batting average of .400. If he thought too much about it, he feared it would affect his game. His strategy was to just give his best at each and every game, in hopes that he would, eventually, reach this peak. We, too, need to practice feeling confident about our goals while maintaining a well-balanced attitude toward the situation.

◆

I have goals to reach, but must be careful not to put unnecessary pressure on myself in an effort to reach them.

As simple as it sounds, we all must try to be the best person we can: by making the best choices, by making the most of the talents we've been given.
—*Mary Lou Retton*

When we are working an exercise program we always have a lot of choices. The first choice we usually confront is, "Am I going to work out today?" We should do our best to answer that question in the affirmative. Most of us are lucky enough to be able to participate in some form of exercise, whether it is walking or tennis or swimming or skiing or running or whatever. We may not have the abilities or the desire to participate in team or competitive sports, and that is our choice to make. We may be much more comfortable working out alone in a gym or at home with videos or an exercise bike. We can also make the choice to not exercise in any formal way but to incorporate healthy habits into our life-style. We can walk instead of using the car or go out and ride our bikes or hike recreationally without the express intention of improving our aerobic conditioning or muscle tone.

We should make the commitment to being as healthy as we can possibly be, and if we don't have specific "athletic" talents we can focus on developing our other abilities. We owe it to ourselves and our bodies to do something to get our muscles moving and our hearts pumping.

◆

I will make the most of what I have and not take my health for granted.

Sports do not build character. They reveal it.
—*Heywood Hale Broun*

Sports can bring out the best in us. And not just our best physical performance. Sports can inspire us to dig deep and reveal the qualities of integrity and leadership. Character doesn't come out of nowhere. Those traits may be lying dormant inside us, and what it takes to bring them out is the competition or challenge. It may also take a particularly difficult loss to test how we react to what could be a very disappointing situation. How we react to an unsuccessful endeavor is just as revealing of our integrity as how we react to a success.

We don't have to have been the captain of the varsity squad to have found these qualities in ourselves. It can be the hardworking example we set in step aerobics class or our willingness to help someone else learn how to improve his backhand. Remember, it takes a certain amount of character to make the commitment to work on our health and fitness in the first place. Character is what allows us to be true to our ideals and to keep going no matter what obstacles we need to overcome. Character keeps us going at those times when it's hard to maintain our intensity. We really don't know what we are capable of until we give it a shot. Character allows us to give it the best shot possible.

◆

I won't know my depth of character unless I test it.

We all have dreams. But in order to make dreams into reality, it takes an awful lot
of determination, dedication, self-discipline, and effort.
—*Jesse Owens*

We all need dreams to keep ourselves going. But to keep dreams alive we have to work on them. If we neglect them they will fade away. It's not enough just to have dreams or to work at them haphazardly. Putting real effort into making our dreams come true will make the achievement more meaningful. We have to commit ourselves to making them come true. We can do this by developing a plan, setting aside time to work on that plan, and working on it with focused attention.

Dreams don't have to be lofty pie-in-the-sky wishes. The size of the dream doesn't matter—it's the amount of effort that we put into achieving them that counts. One person's dream of finishing a marathon is just as important and worthy as another person's dream of winning a gold medal at the Olympics. The important thing is that the dream has special significance for the individual. We need to be willing to dare to dream and dare to make those dreams come true.

◆

I will feed my dreams a steady diet of hard work and determination.

A full mind is an empty bat.
—*Branch Rickey*

... **O**r a missed basket, or a double fault, or a poor time, or a fumble, or a bogie, or any other subpar performance in any sport or during any type of workout. We've all had moments when we feel utterly helpless, spastic, and ineffective, when we can't seem to play our game because we're so distracted by other matters.

The more cluttered our minds are with problems at the office, family issues, headlines, dates, numbers, or other information gobbledy-gook, the less focus, attention, and energy we can give to our workout or competition. A clean, clear mind can be tuned in to the task at hand, helping us get the most from our twenty-five minutes on the LifeCycle, fifteen-mile bike ride, or Saturday tennis game. Not only will we perform better, we will get into the flow of the exercise a lot faster, making it a more enjoyable experience all around.

It's not always easy to check our problems at the door of the gym, on the side of the court, or in the locker room, but it's certainly worth a try. Chances are our athletic performances will improve, and the problems, too, might seem a bit more manageable.

◆

Today I'll leave any sort of brain clutter I may have on the sidelines as I try to
work out with a clear and focused mind.

> I think everyone should experience defeat at least once during their career.
> You learn a lot from it.
> —Lou Holtz

*F*ormer professional and college coach Lou Holtz felt he could learn a lot from a single defeat. What about the rest of us, who, over the course of our athletic lifetimes, will suffer defeat dozens, if not hundreds, of times? Does it stand to reason that we will learn that much more?

While sometimes it seems that the only lessons learned from defeat are painful ones, if we look deep enough there is really a lot more to it than that. Losing teaches lessons of a physical nature that are specific to our sport—a missed scoring opportunity, a bad defensive decision, inadequate preparation. We recognize and understand our errors and work to avoid them in the future.

Perhaps more important, though, are the lessons that are more psychological in nature. A loss or missed goal can elicit all sorts of unwanted and unhelpful feelings. Often our confidence is hurt and our pride wounded. We feel inept, or at the very least disappointed in our performance. Identifying these feelings and moving on from them is the best recovery strategy. Dwelling on errors or bad calls or poor performances will only hurt in future outings and delay the learning process. Even professional athletes and coaches get hung up on losses. What they are coached to do, however, is to study them, understand how they happened, and use that information to prepare for the next event.

◆

Everyone wins and everyone loses. When I lose, I will learn from the experience and not make myself suffer over it.

Concentrate, play your game, and don't be afraid to win.
—Amy Alcott

It seems unlikely that anyone might be "afraid" to win, but, in fact, many athletes have trouble "going in for the kill, " for a variety of reasons. It may be that we're competing against an underdog, feel guilty about playing too aggressively, and switch to a less-effective strategy which eventually costs us the win. Or maybe we are the underdog and are not expected to win, and therefore suffer from lack of motivation and low expectations. Women may feel uneasy about defeating men, just as top-ranked teams may ease up when they play inferior squads. Whatever the reason, we sometimes find ourselves underperforming, particularly in competition.

PGA professional Amy Alcott's suggestion—to keep our concentration and continue to play our own game—makes a lot of sense. The less distracted we are by our opponents, be they other players in our golf foursome or other runners in a race, the more we will be able to perform consistently and successfully. While it sometimes seems impossible to keep other people's opinions and expectations out of our minds, it's important to stay on track regardless of the score or the time. An underdog probably does not want to be treated as less than competitive, just as the club champion would probably love the challenge of an unexpectedly tough match. No one will think any less of us if we win unexpectedly, or in a big way, as long as we do it graciously and with aplomb.

◆

A match or game or race is played to win. I will give every competition my all, despite the expectations of others.

It's very, very dangerous to have your self-worth riding on your results as an athlete.
—Jim Courier

*T*here's more to life than sports. No matter if we are professional athletes, competitive amateurs, or enthusiastic recreational players, athletics are only a portion of what makes us who we are. We have other responsibilities, interests, commitments, and pleasures; from our careers to our children, our stamp collections to our volunteer work, we are complete, well-rounded individuals with a lot to do.

While there certainly are benefits, both physical and psychological, to participation in sports and fitness activities, it's important to keep a healthy balance between these and all other aspects of our lives. Athletics cannot take up a disproportionate amount of time, or other parts of our lives will suffer. Too much time in the gym might mean not enough time handling personal business. Too much concentration on improving our golf game might mean not enough focus on our families.

And when we do suffer a bad day on the court, or field, or course, or track we must remind ourselves that it is simply that. It's not a personal failing, nor is it anything that time, practice, and concentration can't remedy.

◆

Athletic participation is important to me, but it's only part of the complete, well-rounded person I am.

Mental toughness is to physical as four is to one.
—*Bobby Knight*

Mental toughness is essential for any type of physical activity. The mind is a powerful ally in competition and overall fitness. It can help us overcome any physical opponent, no matter how strong. There are a lot of contributions the mind makes to play. Our minds can help us to be prepared for any challenge. We can watch and analyze our opponents, plan our approach, think out our counterattack. If we've been knocked down, it's our minds that can get us right up and back into it. We can be in excellent physical condition, but if our heads aren't in gear we are candidates for defeat.

If we are mentally tough, we can come out on top even if we may be physically overmatched. Our mental attitude and grasp of just what we need to do can compensate for a lack of strength and even a lack of skill. Mental acuity can't completely overcome physical shortcomings, but a mind and body working together can make for a tough opponent.

The athlete who comes out on top is the one who mentally prepares before his game, thinks on his feet, and when it's all over thinks about what has happened to be even better prepared the next time.

◆

My mental outlook is an indispensable ally. I will make a solid partnership with my mind and body.

You find that you have peace of mind and can enjoy yourself, get more sleep, and rest when you know that it was a 100 percent effort that you gave—win or lose.
—*Gordie Howe*

It's hard to give 100 percent all the time. There are days when we just can't seem to give everything we have. We may feel like we just don't have it in ourselves to go all out. We may be overtired or have just played our hearts out in an important tournament. Sometimes we may need to pick and choose the times that we will give everything we've got. However, when we do decide to go for it, win or lose, we will never be able to fault ourselves.

Going all out is the best way to get what we want. If we can go home after working out or playing a game in which we have given our all, we will find ourselves content. We won't be second-guessing ourselves or beating ourselves up for what we did didn't do or wondering "what if?" We have to have the will to succeed and the courage to fail, and the only way we can find that will and courage is to put ourselves on the line—completely. No compromises are allowed if we are going to be able to be our best and be happy with the outcome.

◆

If I have truly given 100 percent I can't be unhappy with the outcome.

I knew I could be a big man in baseball, a little man in basketball and a broken man in football. I made the right choice.
—*Dave Winfield*

Not every sport is right for everybody, and not everybody is right for every sport. Yet there is something out there for all of us, no matter what our skills, body type, interests, or time factors, and it's up to us to find it.

While it's great to be proficient at several sports, not everyone is so blessed. And because regular participation in one activity is commendable, we should all strive to have at least one sport or fitness activity that we consider ourselves good at and that we do on a regular basis. It's fine to mix it up a little, but the satisfaction that can be had from concentrating on, practicing, and improving in one area is worth the hard work. It gives us skills, both mental and physical, that are valuable in all aspects of our lives. It teaches us perseverance, motivation, and discipline; gives us self-confidence and poise. It also becomes part of our identity: "He is an excellent skier." "She has really become a consistent tennis player." Being accomplished at anything feels good, especially when it's as good for you as athletics are.

◆

Today I will concentrate on my best event or exercise.

When anyone tells me I can't do anything . . . I'm just not listening any more.
—*Florence Griffith Joyner*

Negative talk. It's probably the most destructive thing that can happen to us and our exercise. We have to beware of it coming from others. We have to know that it will happen—sometimes it will be an opponent who is trying to psych us out, sometimes it may come from a well-meaning friend who questions our abilities ("Are you sure you can run a marathon?" "Do you really think it's a good idea to try the intermediate slope?") or even from a coach or instructor ("I don't think you are quite ready for this class"). It's usually easy to counter these naysayers. We can look them in the eye and say, "Yes, I can." In fact, when someone tells us that we can't do something it can inspire us to go right out and do it.

It's harder to deal with that negative talk when it's our own voice we hear. We all do it. We criticize ourselves mercilessly and we are often the only one standing in the way of our progress or success. Knocking down that wall of negative words isn't easy, but it can be done. We have to listen carefully to what we tell ourselves, and when those negatives creep in we have to stand up for ourselves and say, "Yes, I can!"

◆

I am not listening to the negatives—I am creating my own positives.

Chance can allow you to accomplish a goal every once in a while, but consistent
achievement happens only if you love what you are doing.
—*Bart Conner*

Anything we truly enjoy doing, we're going to be better at. Whether it's the
career we've chosen, our hobbies like gardening, cooking, and painting, or the
sports we choose to play. When talent combines with a love of what we're doing
it makes for an athlete whose commitment to the game is evident in each and
every performance.

We've all had the feeling ourselves when we are out there playing the games,
doing the workouts, and practicing the skills we so enjoy. That is why we tend to
gravitate to one sport or activity over others—we get pleasure from our regular
tennis game, our weekly round of golf, our Saturday-afternoon sail, and our
early-morning run. We're really having fun out there, and we're pretty darn good
too.

Love of the sport also gives us that extra edge that we need to excel. Skills
and practice alone won't do it. Those who are truly great at their sport have a
love for the game that gives them an added advantage—an advantage that can
often translate to success.

◆

The more I enjoy myself in my workouts, the better I'll do.

Get the job done.
—*Don Shula*

*T*he simplest directions are usually the best. Cut to the chase, no excuses. We have to decide what we want to do and then go out and do it. Unfortunately, "simple" can be a little deceptive. A lot of planning and effort goes into "simply" getting the job done. We have to think and work and decide exactly what that job is. The bigger the job, the more we need to clear up before we can get to it.

—Run three miles.
—Go to the gym after work.
—Increase time on the StairMaster.
—Practice backhand.
—Swim laps.

◆

I will make a workable plan and get the job done today.

When you're a winner you're always happy, but if you're happy as a loser you'll always be a loser.
—*Mark Fidrych*

Sometimes it seems easier to settle for less than our best effort than to really put in that extra push to reach our potential—whether in competition or practice. We talk ourselves into being satisfied with our performances even though we know we can do better, run farther, cycle faster, or handle more of a challenge. While we can't help occasionally putting out a less than 100 percent effort—we may be overtired, or sore, or distracted—it's not something we want to get in the habit of doing. It can only lead to poor practices later.

No matter what our skill level or experience, we all know what our potential is and what our limits are, and striving to reach these heights (while not overdoing it) is how we grow and improve. When we may be tempted to slack off, cut a workout short, throw a tennis match that we may be struggling in, or dog it on the basketball court, we have to dig in and keep up our top effort. We want to make it a habit to play and practice our best.

◆

Every time I take to the field, court, course, or gym, I'll put forth the best effort I can at that moment.

If we could give every individual the right amount of nourishment and exercise, not too little and not too much, we would have found the safest way to health.

—*Hippocrates*

For thousands of years, scientists and medical experts have been looking for the perfect balance between diet and exercise for optimum health. What seems to come up time and again as far as exercise is concerned is consistency.

The jogger who is out there year round, stomping through puddles and bearing up under heat and cold, or the person who works out at the gym several times a week, is infinitely better off than the tennis player or golfer or cyclist who dusts off his equipment at the beginning of the season, only to store it away again when the conditions become unfavorable and not do anything until next season.

It's not necessary to be obsessive about working out, just conscientious. If the weather turns and our regular softball league ends, we should look for another activity to fill our time and get our bodies moving. Exercise shouldn't be for the weekends or summer months only. It should be a year-round and important part of our schedules.

◆

Today I'll think ahead to the next few months and plan workouts that I can do during inclement weather, shorter daylight hours, or a busier schedule.

I build confidence when I practice a variety of shots—hitting it high or low, working the ball. A lot of golfers go to the range and just hit full shots. That doesn't build on-course confidence, because you won't always hit full shots out there. My confidence is built on knowing I can effectively work the ball in any circumstance.
—*JoAnne Carner*

Professional golfer JoAnne Carner builds her confidence by practicing her entire game, not focusing on specific parts but working on the complete picture. When we are feeling a lull in self-confidence, it is often helpful to go back to the basics. We can reestablish our confidence by working on all of our moves and strategies so as to be well prepared to take to the field or court or course again.

Too many times we find ourselves obsessing on small components of our workouts that may not be up to par. Perhaps our squash backhand has been off lately, or maybe we've had trouble with chip shots on the golf course. The deficit has detracted from our performance, causing us to feel less than positive. We then take our workout to the extreme, working almost exclusively on the ailing move, only to let the rest of our game suffer. A better approach is to give some extra attention to the part that needs help, while going back to a basic workout of our entire game. Sometimes this remedial practice helps us get our entire game back into the groove—including the problem area. We then are still in top form and feeling confident about our overall performance.

◆

I will not obsess on areas of my workout I think are lacking but work instead on the basics, knowing that this, too, will help me return to top form.

> Desire! That's the one secret of every man's career. Not education.
> Not being born with hidden talents. Desire.
> —*Bobby Unser*

We've got to want it. No one can give it to us on a silver platter. There are plenty of people with talent and abilities who never use them to their full extent. They don't take their skills to the maximum because they are not fueled with the desire to pursue and develop them. It is also easy to learn a lot about your sport and know the technical aspects of the game. There are books, videos, lessons, etc., that can give you a step in the right direction. None of these technical skills, however, will get you anywhere if you don't add desire into the mix.

It is also possible to have average abilities that can be taken to an entirely different level when we are striving for something that we really want. There are many athletes, professional or otherwise, who may not have been given as much talent as other players, but they are impressive players because they have given more than the next guy. Desire is a secret weapon—and it's a potent one. It is the key that can turn our game around from a poor performance to an excellent one.

◆

I can do it and I will do it, no matter what.

My goal in sailing isn't to be brilliant or flashy in individual races,
just to be consistent over the long run.
—Dennis Conner

*T*his philosophy can pay off in any sport, not just yacht racing. It can also be a valuable standard to apply to our individual fitness efforts. We don't have to be amazing and fantastic every time out. We just have to be as consistent as possible. There are definitely times when we surprise ourselves with an out-of-the-ordinary performance. But it's not something that we can rely on happening. In fact, in many Olympic competitions the low and the high scores are thrown out in an effort to avoid these aberrations.

Consistency is developed over time with effort and concentration. Consistency is also important in preparing for any competition. We can't just pick up and be at our best without putting in our hours beforehand. Working consistently can get us to a certain level of performance. It can also help to keep us there. As a matter of fact, the only way to maintain a standard of performance is to keep on putting in our time to working out. If we practice consistently and are consistent in our preparation and execution, we'll definitely come out on top.

◆

I will strive for consistency, not flashiness.

> I let my racket do the talking. That's what I am all about, really.
> I just go out and win tennis matches.
> —*Pete Sampras*

Pete Sampras keeps it simple. He has a goal, and he goes for it. He is the embodiment of focus and intensity. Nothing can deter him from winning his match. He doesn't engage in any fancy fanfare or histrionics. In fact, he doesn't need to elaborate on his serve, his groundstrokes, or his play. He lets his performance say all that has to be said. We can all take a lesson from the manner in which he performs.

There are a lot of people who talk a good game but when it comes down to it they can't turn in the performance they have been bragging about. What we say about how we work out isn't half as important as what we do when we work out . The proof is in our mileage, or score, or completed class, not in what we say we can or are going to do. Words do play a role in performance and there is nothing wrong with a little psych talk. We need to be sure that it is for the purpose of getting ourselves up rather than talking down our opponents. Remember, however, no matter what we say or how we say it we have got to let our skills do the talking.

◆

My abilities will have the last word.

I try not to get too caught up thinking about the task ahead. I just do what
has to be done. I have the belief in myself that what I'm doing is right.
Then I let the rest happen.
—*Eamonn Coghlan*

Oftentimes our best workouts or performances are done when we approach the task with a completely clear and relaxed mind. We know what we want to do and how well we want to do it, so we simply let our bodies run on "automatic pilot." We may have a goal in mind: a seven-minute mile, a set of twenty-five reps, a home run, service ace, or a twenty-rebound game, but these targets slip unobtrusively into the backs of our minds as we start our exercise. However, the good news is that many times these goals become realities the less we obsess on them.

We know that in work issues or personal conflicts we can get tied up by "overthinking" a problem. We spend too much time "what if-ing" instead of simply tackling the task at hand. The same can be true for workouts. The more we agonize over performance or goals or scores or opponents, the more distracted and less effective we become. When we put on our sweats and running shoes, we know what has to be done. At that point the best we can do for ourselves is to jump right in and do it.

◆

Today I will try and put distracting thoughts out of my mind
as I work out or compete.

> I remember when I was in college, people told me I couldn't play in the
> NBA. There's always somebody saying you can't do it, and
> those people have to be ignored.
> —*Bill Cartwright*

*I*t's sad, but it's true. There's always someone who will say, "You'll never do it." "It will never happen." These people don't know what they are talking about. They don't know us or our abilities or our aspirations. But because there is always someone who will have nothing but discouraging things to say, we have to create a wall of confidence and faith in ourselves that blocks out those negative thoughts.

We also have to be aware of what we are telling ourselves. Sometimes it's more subtle than a simple "I can't do this." Have you ever noticed that you feel the need to stop at the same place in your run or exercise routine? Usually it's not because you have reached your physical limit. It just may be the place where you have stopped before. Now, we are good enough to keep going, but if we listen carefully we may hear ourselves saying, "This is the place I usually stop." It's not quite the same as saying, "I can't," but it will have the same effect. Negatives can come from any source, but to get to our goals we have to push through the negatives and keep on striving.

◆

Today I will ignore the negatives whether they are from the outside or the inside.

> You hit home runs not by chance but by preparation.
> —*Roger Maris*

Home runs, miles, time, reps, matches won. Goals aren't miraculously achieved out of nowhere. Nobody wakes up one morning and runs a marathon and wins. It's just not possible. For every home run that has been hit there have been hundreds of strikes, hundreds of errors, and, most important, hundreds of hours in batting practice. We have all experienced the mistakes and losses that pave the way for future successes. We just have to get ourselves ready for those victories. Preparation involves a commitment on a number of levels. We need to prepare ourselves both physically and mentally for whatever we may face.

Long-term preparation involves conditioning and training and maintaining a healthy body. Short-term preparation can be as simple as stretching or making sure we've had enough water and the right foods before we go out and exercise. Preparation can get us used to doing things the way they work best for us. Chance and luck are an absolute factor in sports, but we can maximize our luck by thinking ahead and getting ready and not being taken by surprise. We may even find that we are better prepared than we thought.

◆

I'll create my own luck and chances by being as prepared as I possibly can.

If you aren't playing well, the game isn't as much fun. When that happens I tell myself just to go out and play the game as I did when I was a kid.
—Tom Watson

As kids we played sports for the pure fun of it, for the excitement, exhilaration, and camaraderie it offered us. We liked to win, we enjoyed practice and improving our skills, but didn't become obsessed over playing up to other people's expectations or achieving unrealistic goals.

Now, when the pressure of an upcoming race or tournament is getting too much, or we find ourselves dragging our bodies to work out with little energy and less enthusiasm, we need to look back at how we used to play. We should remember the exuberance with which we donned our soccer uniform or hustled in basketball practice; the way we ran just for the fun of it, and could have played tennis all day had not we been called off the court.

Sports should be fun, first and foremost. Even those athletes who make a living at their sports must try to keep the competition in perspective. The more loose and relaxed we are, and the happier we are to be there, the better we'll play—it's as simple as that.

◆

Today's workout will be a good time.

On the field you're quite reserved. You have to have fantastic concentration. You must be aggressive, but you can't go completely nuts because you'll just make a lot of mistakes. It's a difficult balance.

—*Bob Lilly*

Controlled exuberance. We have to walk that fine line between being too psyched and being in control. If we go too far one way or another, we run the risk of limiting our performance. Finding that balance is mainly about pacing ourselves and understanding our limits and how much we can push ourselves. If we go totally all out too soon we'll burn out very quickly. If we hold back we may never play at our best. It is a hard balance to maintain, but we will discover that the more intense we are, the easier it will be to keep the forces of psych and cool equal.

We don't have to be playing team sports for this to apply. Balance is equally as important on the ski slopes or the squash court or the track or the gym. We should remember the times we have gone for a run or began an aerobics class and started out a little too quickly. We were probably anxious to get up to speed, but we can't go our hardest right from the very start; we have to work up to it. Balance.

◆

I'll find that fine balance between being psyched and remaining in control.

I am willing to put myself through anything; temporary pain or discomfort means nothing to me as long as I can see that the experience will take me to a new level. I am interested in the unknown, and the only path to the unknown is through breaking barriers, an often-painful process.
—*Diana Nyad*

Sometimes we have to suffer to get what we want—especially when we are trying to get to another level of performance or excellence. Be careful, however, because the philosophy of "no pain, no gain" can be taken too far. When we are working out we have to keep things in perspective. Going so hard that we injure ourselves permanently isn't the point of exercising. The point is, however, to challenge ourselves. Pushing ourselves beyond what we've been able to do in the past is extremely satisfying. Making our legs pump harder or our arms lift more weight may result in a little pain the next morning, but if we haven't overdone it, the pain will be just a little reminder that we are getting the most out of our fitness program. If we can't walk the day after a tough run we have clearly overdone it. A twinge or two indicates progress. Anytime we try anything new or put more effort into our old routine we will be a little sore. As our muscles adjust, the soreness will go away until we challenge ourselves again.

◆

I will accept a little discomfort as part of the package
of working toward my goals.

I never gave up, even when people told me I'd never make it.
—Bob Wickman

As athletes, we come up against all sorts of challenges every day. Some are challenges we create for ourselves—a targeted time for a 10K run, the number of days a week we want to work out, a batting average—and some are given to us by others. Both are invaluable to us as we try to improve and become more and more proficient in our sports, and both are important to stick with despite what may appear to be long odds.

Challenges we give ourselves are basically goals we set and expect to reach by a certain time. Because we are in control of these challenges, we have every chance to make them tough, but realistic; not easy, but not impossible, either. We can put pressure on ourselves, but not undo pressure. While it is sometimes difficult to stick with these goals as they start to seem more and more out of reach, we must encourage ourselves to hang in there and not give up. The same can be said for goals that others have for us.

Many times the most difficult thing of all, though, is trying to stick with a goal when others have given up on us. It's hard enough to stay confident in ourselves and our skills without having our supporters lose faith. These are the times to really dig in and stay focused. It's rewarding to achieve a goal at any time, but when the odds seem to be against us, it's even more exhilarating to succeed. Run a marathon. Win a golf tournament. Do something that really takes guts.

◆

I believe in the power of me.

Make short-term goals more important than long term. While long-term goals are important, the short-term ones provide the success opportunities to keep you moving forward. Short-term objectives bring immediate focus and direction to your efforts.

—*Jim Loehr*

*E*very time we set a goal for ourselves, be it to go to the gym on a fairly regular basis or to run a marathon, we are challenging ourselves to accomplish something that is out of reach. The satisfaction of finally reaching that goal is exhilarating. No matter what the size of the achievement, the result is the same—we are proud of ourselves. And, while it's good to keep motivating ourselves with more and more targets to aim for, it's important to set goals that are within reach and can be achieved in a reasonable amount of time. It is a lot more encouraging to reach many short-term goals than it is to strive for weeks toward a long-term goal that seems to be farther away. The end result may be the same, but by taking baby steps there, we will feel like the progress is coming fast and furious.

Short-term goals can be set daily or weekly, giving us focus and direction as we work out and hone our skills. Maybe we want to work on the various components of our tennis game individually so that ultimately we can beat the person on the top of the club ladder. Perhaps we want to do a triathlon so we gradually work on the swimming, cycling, and running that make up the event. So much of motivation in sport is about desire to reach a particular level, so it's only natural that pursuing these short-range plans will do wonders for our fitness program.

◆

Today I will set a short-term goal that I will achieve within the next week.

Training gives us an outlet for suppressed energies created by stress and thus tones the spirit just as exercise conditions the body.
—*Arnold Schwarzenegger*

Stress is all around us. So much so that it's almost impossible to avoid it. We all have to deal with hassles at work, problems at home, or general demands on ourselves and our time. While we can't eliminate stress from our lives we can work on eliminating the effects of that stress on our bodies and our attitudes. There's nothing like a good sweaty workout to clean out our systems and clear our heads. No matter what burdens we carry around with us from our day we can throw them off, or at least put them on the back burner, by exercising.

Exercising can also help us to burn off steam. Instead of screaming, yelling, or throwing things, getting physical, positively, can be a very constructive way to vent our anger or frustration. Just getting out there and doing something physical can change our perspective and give us a real boost. Exercising is great for getting our bodies toned and our hearts and lungs healthy. It's much more difficult to measure, but the lift exercising can give to our spirits is sometimes more valuable than the physical benefits.

◆

If I'm feeling stressed or overwhelmed, I'll try to exercise because I know that it can help me get over a bad spell.

I am a winner each and every time I go into the ring.
—*George Foreman*

If every time we step onto the tennis court we feel confident in our ability to win the match, and every time we run a race we are enthusiastic about our chances of running a personal best, and every time we start a workout of any sort we know it will be valuable and successful, then we, like heavyweight champion George Foreman, have the positive attitude we need to be the best. Unfortunately, it's not easy to always be so sure about our abilities and chances for success. Most of the time we feel unsure of where we stand and not completely confident in our ability to perform.

We should feel that each and every game, match, or challenge is ours for the taking. We should take the field with positive energy and attitude that we will transfer into our performance. We will keep our chins up should things not be going our way, and later turn it all around.

Approaching a workout or competitive event with an upbeat, confident attitude is good strategy. We should all make it part of our game plan.

◆

Before I lace up my athletic shoes, I'm confident of my chances of success.

You have to be able to center yourself, to let all of your emotions go. . . . Don't ever forget that you play with your soul as well as your body.
—*Kareem Abdul-Jabbar*

*M*any professional athletes insist on the importance of mental as well as physical fitness. While their arduous workouts and full schedules of competition demand extremely fit and strong bodies, most pro athletes will agree that a clear and focused mind and a positive attitude are also invaluable for ultimate success.

Basketball legend Kareem Abdul-Jabbar played in the NBA for more than twenty years in one of the most rigorous and demanding of pro sports. While he kept his body in great shape, his skills honed, and his energy high, he never forgot the value of a healthy head, heart, and soul. Semiprofessionals, amateur athletes, and weekend warriors alike can all benefit from Kareem's advice. Despite hours of workouts and hundreds of dollars in lessons and equipment, we can still miss our marks if we don't practice good inner fitness.

Every workout, every round of golf, set of tennis, or game of hoops should begin with a clear head. Leave office problems, personal issues, and other distractions in your locker and take the field, course, or court with a mind that is focused simply on the task at hand. Enjoy fully the experience of the practice or competition, and let the emotions of the game be the ones that propel you.

◆

Every game is played with body and mind. Today I'll concentrate on good mental fitness as I work out or compete.

*There's no such thing as natural touch. Touch is something you create
by hitting millions of golf balls.*
—*Lee Trevino*

It's very easy to watch the Olympics or a professional tournament and think, "Oh they're such natural athletes." They always make it look so easy, don't they? Michael Jordan effortlessly sinks another basket; Nancy Kerrigan executes a flawless triple jump; or Andre Agassi serves up yet another ace. But even these "natural" athletes spend hours and hours working on every aspect of their performance. We can't go out and win a marathon in our first try. Even the most natural athlete in the world can't be perfect in every sport. Or perfect the first time she plays.

It's also very easy to think, "They're naturals and I could never do what they do." Maybe not, but this is largely because making the commitment to be a professional athlete has to happen at a very early age. We can't all strive to be professionals, nor would we want to devote our lives to sports. We can, however, make the commitment to pursue our own level of excellence and create our own natural touch.

◆

Instead of wishing I were born with natural abilities, I will focus on the skills I
have and make them work for me.

All of us get knocked down, but it's the resiliency that really matters. All of us do well when things are going well, but the thing that distinguishes athletes is the ability to do well in times of great stress, urgency, and pressure.
—*Roger Staubach*

When work or family pressures are intense, it is hard to go out and swim laps or lift weights. But that's precisely when we may need to exercise the most. A solid workout can help us to sweat some of the stress out of our systems. It can also allow us to do something for ourselves just when others are making demands on us and our time.

The type of determination that keeps us going when life is a little rough can also keep us going when a game or a workout runs into some snags. It is also the type of resiliency that helps us to come back after being knocked down. A knock-down can come from illness, injury, or any other source. We have to know that we can, and will, recover. A defeat or a loss shouldn't keep us down forever. Being a fair-weather athlete won't help us to improve; it will keep us stuck in a rut. It may be very hard to climb out of that rut or to pick ourselves up after a fall, but we need to put ourselves on solid ground again so that we can get moving once more.

◆

When it seems too hard to work out I will know it is time to work harder.

In order to excel, you must be completely dedicated to your chosen sport. You must also be prepared to work hard and be willing to accept constructive criticism. Without a total 100 percent dedication, you won't be able to do this.

—*Willie Mays*

*T*here is no doubt about it. When we devote our time and energy to exercise—or anything, for that matter—we will see results. It's inevitable. When we have dedicated ourselves to being healthy or being in better shape or lowering our golf score or raising our weekend running mileage we need to follow up that dedication with some action.

Hard work is beneficial, but we need to have some checkpoints to be sure that all of our hard work is propelling us in the right direction. We shouldn't be afraid to ask for help or advice from someone who can teach us something. Whether it's the local tennis pro or our friends or trainers at our gym, we can learn something from their perspective and viewpoint. Be prepared. They may find something about our performance that needs criticizing. Our form or our approach may need some refining. Be open to hearing their advice. If we are not dedicated to improving and getting the most we can out of our exercise then their input will never become our improved output.

◆

I am dedicated to exercising and to learning how to perform better.

If you want to achieve a high goal, you're going to have to take some chances. . . .
Is taking the risk worth it? That depends on your philosophy of life. You realize that
striving and giving it your all, but falling a bit short, is going to help you
more than never having taken that risk.
—Alberto Salazar

If we had never picked up a baseball bat for the first time as preteen Little
Leaguers we never would have had the chance to experience the excitement of
being part of, and contributing to, a team. If we had never signed up for golf
lessons, we would have never have gotten into the sport that makes our Satur-
days so pleasurable. And if we had never joined a gym, entered a running race,
or joined the company volleyball team we would never have had the fun, camaraderie, competition, and personal satisfaction that those activities afforded us.
The bottom line is: If we don't try, we don't know.

The same can be said for our daily workouts. If we don't try a harder step
class, we won't know if we can do it. If we never cycle farther than ten miles,
how will we see what our limits are? And if we don't get out of bed, put on our
running shoes and hit the pavement in the morning, how will we ever start our
day with that postexercise high that at once relaxes and exhilarates us? We've
got to give it a try.

◆

Exercise is about going for it—and today I'm going to.

I don't ever look back. I look forward.
—*Steffi Graf*

Whether you won or lost yesterday doesn't really matter. What happened at the gym last Tuesday is ancient history. We can't go back and change it or relive it. If it is a victory or a milestone workout we can remember it and savor it, but that is about what we have done, not what we can do. If we have been disappointed by a loss or a bad day, we can learn from it, but win or lose we have to move on.

Making progress is what athletics and exercising are all about and we can't move ahead if we are constantly looking over our shoulders. We can't be looking back to see who is gaining on us or remaining focused on old losses or wins. Looking ahead is as much about attitude as it is about not staying stuck. The attitude that keeps us moving is the one that keeps our chins up and our eyes intent and firmly focused on our goals. Looking forward means moving past the little errors that we all make and letting them slide. As soon as we begin to obsess about a little slip we will soon be making more and more mistakes. Looking forward helps us to figure out how to make sure some of those errors don't happen again. By looking forward and moving forward we will get to our goals.

◆

I will keep moving forward and I won't look back.

You have to expect things of yourself before you can do them.
—*Michael Jordan*

Expectations, like goals, are important in sports. They give us something to strive for, something to push toward. Expectations, unlike goals, can be more demanding since we "expect" to reach, if not exceed, them. By expecting something of ourselves, be it a workout of a certain length or caliber, a free-throw shooting percentage, or a golf score, we are setting a minimum at which we believe we can perform. We are saying to ourselves, "I expect to run three miles in under twenty-seven minutes," or, "I expect myself to spend twenty minutes on the StairMaster," or, "I expect to make par on a certain number of holes."

We are thinking, "I have done *that* well in the past, I've been working hard, and I expect to perform at *this* level now." While it's important to keep expectations in check—not too high, and therefore unreachable—it is helpful to keep adjusting them to encourage improvement and avoid boredom.

◆

I expect myself to perform at a certain level, which is on a par
with my skills and training.

*The opponents and I are really one. My strength and skills are only half of the
equation. The other half is theirs. . . . An opponent is someone whose strength
joined to yours creates a certain result.*
—*Sadaharu Oh*

Every time we compete, whether in an informal tennis round robin, or the playoffs of our softball league, our weekly golf game, or a national rowing regatta,
we are coming head to head with athletes just like us—athletes who are at our
level, giving their best to try to come out on top. Even though at times it feels
like it is us against the world in some of these competitive events, we can rest
assured that our opponents are feeling the same anxieties and having the same
aspirations we are. It is what we both bring to the table that dictates the final
outcome. Our having a good day, combined with our opponent being slightly off
his game, makes for one result. Maybe another day it would be different. We
cannot take all the blame, nor can we take all the credit when we win, for it is
the combined efforts of both sides that create the circumstances we face and the
results we achieve.

Professional athletes scout their opponents to get a preview of what they might
come up against. We might do the same before a big tennis match or softball
game; however, we'll never know for sure what will happen once that first ball is
in play or the starting gun goes off.

◆

Competition is a combination of my game today and my opponent's game today,
and no amount of anticipation will ever fully prepare me
for what will actually happen.

The mind messes up more shots than the body. So watch it!
—*Tommy Bolt*

No matter what sport we participate in, how experienced we are, how much we practice, how confident we are, and how well we've been playing, there will always be times when our minds suddenly seem to take over, to the dismay of our bodies. And whether it's choking under pressure, being psyched out by an opponent or a situation, or just not being able to focus, no amount of self-talk seems to get us back on track.

The mental aspect of sport is vital and influential to athletes at every level. If our heads are not in the game, we may be in trouble. How many times have we been ahead in a racquetball game only to have our opponent catch us and eventually win? How many times have we virtually talked ourselves into double faulting on the tennis court, despite hours of successful practice serves the day before? Seemingly simple workouts become nearly impossible on days when we just can't concentrate and get the job done.

The good news is, everyone suffers from this every once in a while. Our heads take over and it's all downhill from there. We basically need to ride out the bad spell and simply give it another shot tomorrow.

◆

When my head takes over, and my body falls apart, I just need
to be patient and try again.

Sports should always be fun.
—*Charles Mann*

When all is said and done, when our mileage has been totaled, the score tallied, our calories counted, and our improvement noted, what we really want to say about our exercise program is that we had fun out there. Let's face it, ultimately we will do the best we can each and every time we work out, trying to build strength and stamina, while at the same time losing weight or shaping our bodies. Does our final batting average on the company softball team really matter? Will anyone remember how much we dominated in the club tennis tournament or how badly we lost in a friendly round of golf? It's doubtful. However, what will remain with us is the feeling, be it positive or negative, we have toward a sport or race or tournament.

We've all found ourselves working out with or competing against someone who is taking the whole situation far more seriously than we are. It makes us uncomfortable, not to mention inadequate and ineffective. We may have wished we were anywhere but on that court or course or field. It's especially during these times that we want to remember what National Football League All-Pro Charles Mann says. Sports *should* always be fun. It's something we do just for us—to improve our physical and emotional selves as well as to enjoy the social benefits it may bring.

◆

No matter how frustrating a workout may be, or how intense a competition may get, I will remind myself that athletics should be a positive experience.

The most important factor for motivation is goal setting.
You should always have a goal.
—*Francie Larrieu Smith*

A goal can be to get up in the morning to go running or to win a local 10K race; to improve your tennis serve or to win the club tournament; to go to the gym at least three times a week or to master the advanced high-impact class. A goal can be something to strive for in the future or it can be for tomorrow. It can be very ambitious or it can be a more moderate, reachable target. Details aside, every athlete of every level should have some sort of a fitness goal to motivate, mobilize, and otherwise get her moving.

A goal of being able to do thirty minutes on the StairMaster will challenge you to go to the gym and keep working at it until you make it. A goal of being able to run a marathon in six months will force you to keep up your running and cross-training. Lowering your golf score, walking twenty minutes a day, improving your free-throw percentage, and entering a triathlon are all goals that will encourage keeping up a regular workout regimen. Motivation to work out is hard enough to come by at times, so a target is one effective way of keeping the desire alive and the challenge fresh.

◆

I have a goal for today's workout, as well as a long-term one
that I am aiming for.

I really lack the words to compliment myself today.
—*Alberto Tomba*

Outstanding. Peerless. Perfection.
Excellent. Fantastic. Marvelous.
Magnificent. Superb. Exquisite.
Astounding. Exceptional. Unequaled.
Matchless. Unsurpassed. Unrivaled.
Incredible. Unique. Stellar.
Notable. Amazing. Fabulous.
Impressive. Grand. Beautiful.
Dazzling. Gorgeous. Spectacular.
Remarkable. Wonderful. Extraordinary.
Phenomenal. Astounding. Indescribable.
Wondrous. Sensational. Thrilling.
Astonishing. Breathtaking. Impressive.
Striking. Splendid. Unbelievable.

Go ahead, be a one-person cheering squad.

◆

Today I will find the words to compliment myself.

When you get in a slump on the road, the best thing to do is get home. When you
get in a slump at home, the best thing is to get on the road.
—*Ralph Houk*

*S*ometimes things just don't go our way. We run into problems at the office. We are frustrated in our relationships. Our athletic skills just aren't up to par. Basically, we get into slumps. And while we may have less control in working issues out at work or with partners, we can take charge of our fitness program if it starts to falter.

Many times we hit a plateau that we can't seem to get off of. For weeks we may be swimming the same times despite repeated efforts to pick up the pace. Other times we have trouble even reaching our norm. Our baseball batting average is slipping, our golf score is climbing, our running is slowing. We can't seem to do anything right. We feel uncoordinated, heavy, slow, and unmotivated. Our timing is off, and our talent is out to lunch. Often the best solution at times like these is to take a break and make a change in our workout.

Try a new running route. Cross-train. Take a lesson. Take the day off. Lengthen the workout. Shorten the workout. Sample new equipment. Exercise with a friend. Exercise alone. Wear your lucky T-shirt. Dump your lucky T-shirt. Whatever you do on a regular basis, do it a little differently now.

◆

If I've hit the wall in my training, it may be time for a new approach.

The ones who want to achieve and win championships motivate themselves.
—Mike Ditka

We look for motivation in all sorts of places. We engage personal trainers, read books, make solemn oaths, and enlist the aid of friends, family and coworkers, but the only one who can really get us working is ourselves. It may seem as though having a coach yelling at us during our workouts would be great motivation, but it only takes us halfway. No amount of coaching or persuasion will get us going or achieving if we don't make a commitment by ourselves and for ourselves.

The motivation that comes from within is actually more powerful than the motivation that comes from outside sources. Our cheering squad may not be able to make it to the away tournament, our coaches may be preoccupied with other players and not available exactly when we need them, or our workout partners may be sick on the day that we had been about to take on a new fitness exercise. When we are our own prime inspiration we can always rely on that source of motivation. A coach or trainer or friend can help keep us on the right track or pointed in the right direction. But we have to be willing to be our own best coach/trainer/motivator and keep ourselves moving. After all, the best exercise and work doesn't come from doing for anyone else; it comes from doing it for ourselves.

◆

I am the strongest and most reliable source for my own motivation.

I train myself mentally with visualization. The morning of a tournament, before I put
my feet on the floor, I visualize myself making perfect runs with emphasis on
technique, all the way through to what my personal best is in practice. . . .
The more you work with this type of visualization, especially when you do it
on a day-to-day basis, you'll actually begin to feel your muscles contracting
at the appropriate times.
—*Camille Duvall*

Professional athletes from all sports use visualization as a training tool in preparing for competition or even just a regular workout. By seeing ourselves in our
"mind's eyes" performing an exercise, stroke, shot, or move, we are in effect
practicing our event without even stepping out onto the floor, course, field, or,
as is the case with professional water-skier Camille Duvall, the water.

Oftentimes visualization can be used if we're in a slump—if our times are not
as fast, we can't do as many reps, our game is not as on. Mental imagery can help
by having us rehearse various components of our sport in our heads, like the
forehand that seems to have a slight hitch, the pitch that has lost its accuracy, or
the final kick in our run that seems to have fizzled. We can correct these faults in
our mind's eye by repeatedly visualizing these strokes and strategies until our
minds have virtually trained our bodies. And, as Duvall says, our muscles even
begin to contract as we go through the motions in our heads.

◆

Before I work out today, I will visualize myself
successfully performing my activity.

I like to be against the odds. I'm not afraid to be lonely at the top. With me, it's just the satisfaction of the game. Just performance.
—*Barry Bonds*

It's a lot of fun to play against the odds. When we come out on top it feels sweeter somehow if we've played against, and overcome, outstanding opposition. It seems odd to say, "Don't be afraid to win," but sometimes that fear is what stands in the way of an excellent performance. We may just be afraid of making that all-out effort or we may fear suddenly being the one to beat. We have to leave fear behind us if we are going to do well, because we need to be fearless on the field and fearless about what we want to achieve.

There is another benefit from playing fearlessly. If we play without fear, we will be uninhibited and unencumbered and will find that fearless play will bring out our best performance. For many people just the fact that they can get out there and move and sweat and play is reward enough. They're not worried about stats or miles or reps or minutes. Surprisingly enough, when we forget about all the numbers and the pressure we will not only play better we will have fun too. We can take all the risks we want and be as creative as we can be. We shouldn't be afraid to take our performance to the top.

◆

I will play without fear of winning.

I work on a certain move constantly, then, finally, it doesn't seem so risky to me. The move stays dangerous and looks dangerous to my foes, but not to me. Hard work has made it easy. That is my secret. That is why I win.
—Nadia Comaneci

*T*here's nothing more satisfying than finally mastering a skill or move that has been difficult for us in the past. All of a sudden we can do a double axel on skates, bench-press our own weight, run ten miles, or hit a successful approach shot on the tennis court. All of the practice, concentration, and visualization has paid off. The move is still as tough and impressive to others as it always was, only now we can do it—so it doesn't seem nearly as overwhelming to us.

Sometimes it's worth the extra effort it takes to learn and become adept at a more challenging skill. The dunk on the basketball court, the splits at the gym, the chip shot on the golf course—any move that takes more time and energy to master is a move worth having. Having an extaordinary talent under our belts gives us added confidence both in working out and competing. It reminds us how skilled and accomplished we are, and can intimidate opponents who may come up against us. More than anything, however, it signifies setting and reaching a goal, which is always of value.

◆

Today I concentrate on one of the tougher aspects of my workout, in hopes of getting closer to mastering it.

People say I'm still around because I have a lot of heart, but I know all the heart in
the world couldn't have helped me if I wasn't physically fit.
—*Jimmy Connors*

We can be completely on top of our game mentally and emotionally, but it
won't do us any good if we are not physically up to par. Wanting something badly
enough won't make it happen. We have to back up that desire with some action.
And that action usually involves some time at the gym, on the court, or on the
track. Our bodies have to be able to back up what our minds and spirits want to
do. It is important to have heart and desire, but they cannot take the place of
being physically prepared.

Heart can get us out of a rut or make some compensation for being a bit
physically overmatched, but it can't make up for poor conditioning. We can't rely
on heart to win our games or make our fitness programs a success. However,
heart can be the thing that gets us working in the first place and keeps us working
when we may be inclined to give up. Guts and fortitude are the key ingredients
to hanging in when the odds are against us, but that desire has to be matched
with physical training.

◆

Have a lot of heart, but remember to back it up with being in shape.

If you're not making mistakes, then you're not doing anything. I'm positive that a doer makes mistakes.
—John Wooden

When we were kids learning a sport we knew that not doing it perfectly the first time was part of the package and was an important part of the learning process. By doing things over and over again we were able to learn from our misthrows, missteps, and missed hits. Back then we knew we were making mistakes because we hadn't had a chance to develop our abilities.

Now, as adults, if we are learning a new sport or trying a new workout routine we also have to allow for some slipups. We have to be as forgiving of ourselves as we were when we were kids. Remember that when we make mistakes it means we are taking risks. It is unpleasant to feel awkward and unskilled, but if we keep at it we will master the new stroke or sport or skill. If we are turning in a flawless performance every time, then we are probably only operating within our safety zone and not challenging ourselves. Without taking a risk, pushing a little harder, we won't improve. Making errors can only help us to be better at our game.

◆

I will accept that I will make mistakes; I will know that I will learn from them.

My thoughts before a big race are usually pretty simple. I tell myself: "Get out of
the blocks, run your race, stay relaxed. If you run your race,
you'll win. . . . Channel your energy. Focus."
—*Carl Lewis*

When it comes time for competition, we often go from the steady, reliable
athlete we've been all week in practice to someone obsessed with beating the
opponent. We lose track of the hard work that's gone into training for a specific
event and think only of ending up Number 1 at the end of the day. Unfortunately,
this single-minded pursuit often railroads the honed athlete who is truly prepared
for the competition and replaces him with an athlete whose performance can
become sloppy and ineffective.

The athlete who has been working hard all week in practice is the athlete who
should show up at the starting line or tip-off or first serve. You know your game.
You know what makes you proficient at your sport. All of your energy should be
focused on performing to your potential—the way you've done hundreds of times
in practice sessions. Let your energy take you surging forward, leaving harmful
distractions sidelined.

◆

I will show up for a competition, whether it's against an opponent or a stopwatch,
and perform just as I have practiced all week—only today I'll push it
that much harder and reap the rewards that may bring.

I go to the plate thinking, "This pitcher isn't better than I am." Last year I did what everyone wanted me to do instead of what I'm best at. Now I don't care if the pitch is over my head or in the dirt, if I think I can hit it, I'm swinging.

—*Brian McRae*

We have to know, for ourselves, what we do best. We can't let anyone else tell us what or how to do something. Sure, a coach or trainer can show us the mechanics of certain techniques or give us the principles behind the moves, but once we know the basics we have to make the rest our own. We need to be able to trust ourselves.

We know better than anyone else what we are capable of doing. We know better than anyone else what we truly want to do. If we think we can do something, or want to try something new, we must not hold back. We will give it our best shot because our best shot can be outstanding. We shouldn't let anyone tell us that we can't, or even that we shouldn't try. We need to be able to trust ourselves. It is important to take the time to build our confidence and learn what we can do. We shouldn't rely on others to tell us if we are good or not. We should show them. In our heart of hearts we know that we are great. If we trust ourselves, we can't go wrong.

◆

If I think I can, I can.

How many times have you started the season, or, after a long layoff from the game, resumed golfing by shooting a score that was better than expected?
Shortly after, however, you find your score mounting. A good score early in the season can be attributed to the correct mental attitude. Your first "surprise" round probably was played completely relaxed and with the thought in mind that a score quite a few strokes above normal would be satisfactory.
—*Sam Snead*

*A*ttitude is everything. If we feel positive, have reasonable expectations for ourselves, and stay focused, the potential for greatness is there, as golf legend Sam Snead explains. On the other hand, if we lack confidence and set unrealistic goals, we are bound to be disappointed.

Sometimes our best performances occur when we simply approach the workout or game just happy to be there, expecting little but concentrating all the same. We have nothing to lose. We are not overly confident, not intimidated by unobtainable goals, and not feeling undue pressure to achieve the impossible. We are simply there—on the court, field, track, or course—letting ourselves play, trusting that our minds and bodies will know what to do. Even top athletes fall victim to overly elevated expectations—either their own or their teammates', coaches', or fans'—which can lead to subpar performances. It's important for all athletes to remember those wonderful moments that Snead talks about when we are, in fact, overachievers and are pleasantly surprised.

◆

Today I'll keep my expectations in check and my attitude up
as I work out or compete.

Before I was ever in my teens, I knew exactly what I wanted to be when I grew up.
My goal was to be the greatest athlete that ever lived.
—*Babe Didrikson Zaharias*

Being "the greatest athlete that ever lived" is a very high aspiration. Babe Didrikson Zaharias was able to reach amazing heights in a number of sports. She fulfilled her dreams. We, however, may not entertain such lofty thoughts. Our goals may be as simple as running around the block without stopping or even just getting to the gym three times a week. The important thing is to have goals— what they are depends entirely on what we want to accomplish and what we are capable of doing. When we determine what goal we are shooting for, that in turn determines what we are going to do to get there.

While there may be any number of approaches to fulfilling our goals, all goals have one thing in common. They are clearly defined and are something that requires us to stretch our abilities. An unfocused goal like "I want to get better" won't carry us as far as a specific goal like "I want to increase the amount of time I spend on the StairMaster." The latter goal not only gives us something specific to work toward, it also has the seed of what we need to do to achieve that goal. In this case, adding more time by day or by week to our StairMaster workout. We don't have to try to be the greatest athlete in the world, but we can make our own dreams come true.

◆

I will create specific goals to work toward.

There is a difference between conceit and confidence. . . . Conceit is bragging
about yourself. Confidence means you believe you can get the job done.
—*Johnny Unitas*

*I*t's great to be confident; in fact, being confident is one of the most important
keys to success. To understand the difference between conceit and confidence
think back to your high school days. The jock who strutted around bragging
about his accomplishments usually made everyone else feel uncomfortable and
inadequate. The athlete who provided quiet inspiration by excelling without a lot
of talk not only exemplified confidence but inspired it in others as well.

You deserve to have confidence in yourself. You work hard, you put in your
time, and if you don't believe in your abilities, who will? Saying to yourself, "I
can do this" isn't acting like a conceited braggart, it's giving yourself credit where
credit is due. It is owning up to your accomplishments. You don't have to go
around letting everybody and his brother know that you have infallible faith in
your abilities, but you can make certain that you let yourself know. If you try to
win a race or a competition without confidence you are setting yourself up for a
loss. Trusting yourself and your abilities is a big step toward success.

◆

I believe that I can get the job done.

> Pressure? I don't mind the pressure. The only pressure I'm under is
> the pressure I've put on myself.
> —*Mark Messier*

Some of the most intense pressure we experience comes from ourselves. Because we are usually our own harshest critics we are also the most demanding about our performance. A little pressure can be great for testing our limits and improving our performance. It can really bring out our best, but putting unreasonable demands on ourselves will only set us up for a fall. We can really crumble under the pressure, especially if it is of our own making. When someone caves in under pressure the failing is usually attributed to the pressure of the event or situation or the high skill of the opponent. What is really happening is that the individual is internalizing the pressure coming from the outside and letting it keep him from performing at his best.

Pressure can actually help us perform better. Pressure can give us a little extra dose of inspiration rather than making us choke. The footsteps behind us in a race can get us moving a little faster. If bathing-suit season is fast approaching, that can be just the right amount of pressure we need to keep hard at work at the gym. A little judiciously applied pressure can be an asset, not a liability, to our workouts.

◆

I won't crumble under pressure—I will use it to my advantage.

If you make every game a life-and-death proposition, you're going to have problems. For one thing, you'll be dead a lot.
—Dean Smith

No basketball game, golf match, tennis tournament, or running race is a live-or-die situation, no matter how much it may feel like it at the time. When it feels like a loss would be the end of the world and a win will change your whole life, you can be sure that, no matter how bad the outcome, you will recover, and no matter how good the outcome, you'll eventually come down to earth. The anxious anticipation and overreaction you feel is only a useless distraction and a misuse of energy. The sooner we learn to evaluate competitive situations realistically and react appropriately, the better and more focused our performances will be.

The same can be said for noncompetitive situations. If we miss a workout, don't achieve a goaled time, or cut short a run, it is not a big deal. It's one day when we did not perform up to our expectations or aspirations. We'll make it up tomorrow—no problem. But if we torture ourselves about the situation, or force ourselves to work out when we're not up to it, we'll be worse off—both physically and mentally. Fitness is important to us, but we must keep it in perspective and have confidence that if we miss a day we'll simply make it up tomorrow.

◆

Working out is important to me, but I must keep its importance in perspective.

Most people miss the great part mental outlook plays in this game.
—Billy Martin

Missing the mental part of our game is a common error that we all make. Our mental outlook is key both in the way we approach our workouts and the way we execute them. We need to have the right mental attitude to prepare ourselves fully for exercising or competing. We have to think out carefully what we want to do and how we want to do it. The right mental attitude encourages and supports our efforts. If we engage our minds before we get our bodies moving, we can tap into our strengths and overcome our weaknesses.

It's easy to overlook the role our minds plays in exercise. We spend so much time and energy focused on our bodies—are we losing weight? are we toned? are we working harder, better, faster? And while our minds are always working when we exercise, it's important, and helpful, to get our minds actively involved in our workouts. Our minds are pretty powerful—mental outlook can get us psyched up or it can tear us down. We've all had the experience of thinking, "I don't want to do this—I am not psyched" and, lo and behold, we don't have a successful or even pleasant workout. Mentally we can set the tone for how our workouts will feel and how much we are able to accomplish.

◆

I'll tone up my mental outlook while I tone my body.

I know a lot of people think it's monotonous, down the black lines over and over, but it's not if you're enjoying what you're doing. I love to swim and I love to train.
—*Tracy Caulkins*

If we enjoy what we are doing we will do it more often and get more out of it. But because most sports involve repeating an activity over and over again, we need to find something that we really enjoy so that we are absorbed in it completely. That repetition is essential for reinforcing how we should move and the most efficient way to do our exercise. Unfortunately, it can also become quite tedious.

Training should be fun. Some people can just zone out and move effortlessly through a workout. Others get into a rhythm that helps to carry them along. Still others will never do the same routine two days in a row. They know that they are susceptible to being bored and will shake things up to keep them going. Music is a great way to keep your workouts fun. Finding someone to work with is also helpful. You can motivate each other, exchange tips on training and keep one another moving. If you have been doing the same old workout day in and day out, it's time to try something new and find the fun again.

◆

I have made the commitment to work out, and I have made the commitment to enjoy myself while I am doing it.

You become a champion by fighting one more round. When things are tough you fight one more round.
—James J. Corbett

If you give up when things are getting tough you will never know what you could have accomplished if you hadn't quit. No matter what the circumstances, there is always a little left that you can give. And you won't be disappointed if you make the decision to stick with it. In any exercise program you will hit some rough spots. They may feel insurmountable, but you will get beyond them. You may feel you aren't making any progress or that it just doesn't seem worth it to continue. This is just the time to get yourself psyched up to keep plugging away. Many times when you begin to feel discouraged it will be just before you are able to make some notable progress. Everyone who works out is familiar with hitting plateaus where she just doesn't feel as if she is getting anywhere. A plateau can be a sign that you are really getting ready to go to the next level, and you may just need to give yourself a firm push to get there.

It can be frustrating to keep working out when you are not seeing noticeable improvement. You *are* changing and improving, and it is important to keep working beyond the point when you are frustrated. If you hang in, you will meet your goals.

♦

I am always willing to keep working to reach my goals.

For every finish-line tape a runner breaks—complete with the cheers of the crowd and the clicking of hundreds of cameras—there are the hours of hard and often lonely work that rarely gets talked about.
—*Grete Waitz*

Exercise is hard work. Sometimes it seems very hard to just get out of bed in the morning to go work out. But it is usually well worth the effort. We may not have as ambitious a goal as a marathon to work toward, but our personal goals are just as big and just as important. It takes hard work to run that extra mile, burn off an extra pound, or get our serve in. It's important to realize, however, that what seems hard to do one day may seem easy the next. As we keep working diligently and consistently we can see our dreams realized. But we have to remember to look not only at the moment of glory but at all the moments that lead up to our success.

We all have a tendency to measure our hard work by the minutes, the miles, or the final score. But we are the best judge of when we are working hard. It is important to give ourselves a pat on the back and celebrate our little victories. Achieving our goals may not be accompanied by flashbulbs and fanfare, but we need to recognize our own efforts.

◆

I will give myself credit for the hard work that I do.

Sometimes when I start a play, I never know if I will be able to do what I would like. But I always go ahead and try. I have confidence in my ability as a basketball player. I guess deep down inside I know it will work.
—*Julius Erving*

Faith in our abilities is an important thing to foster. When we believe in what we can do, and know that we can trust in ourselves, we will be able to accomplish a great deal. Confidence allows us to take risks and be creative in ways that we cannot if we are always questioning or second-guessing our abilities.

Building confidence isn't easy, but it does come with time. The first time we return an excellent serve on the squash court might not give a huge lift to our confidence, but the tenth and twentieth time we do, it will. The great thing about confidence is that it grows along with our skills. The more we work, the better we get, and the stronger our confidence will be. There is an important distinction that should be made between being confident and overconfident. Overconfidence can lead to careless mistakes. When we overestimate what we think we can do we are cheating ourselves out of an opportunity to develop our skills fully. We will be successful if we match our abilities with our faith in them.

◆

I have confidence in my abilities.

The only discipline that lasts is self-discipline.
—*Bum Phillips*

We needn't have been members of professional sports teams under the strict discipline of coaches and trainers to realize the truth in former NFL coach Bum Phillips's comment. For even in the best of exercise classes, or the most reliable of workout partnerships, we still may find ourselves losing motivation and discipline, despite the best efforts of our instructors or exercise partners. And what we find is that no matter how charismatic the class teacher or how persistent our friends, it is ultimately ourselves who must self-motivate, self-discipline, and self-affirm.

The desire to get up at six A.M. for a pre-work jog, to serve a basket of tennis balls until our shoulders ache, to do fifty sit-ups and then do twenty more can be achieved only when we find the energy and perseverance within to reach for and finally attain our goals.

Encouragement from coaches, friends, and family is all helpful, but we must look within for that little extra umph.

◆

I am a disciplined athlete—I can motivate and encourage myself.

The only way to prove you're a good sport is to lose.
—*Ernie Banks*

We spend so much time worrying about who is Number 1, or who was the victor, that it's easy to lose sight of the other things that go on in any competition. Because of this overemphasis on winning it's tough to feel good about losing. However, a loss is an opportunity to see what we are really made of. Being a good sport doesn't mean brushing a defeat off with an "Oh, well, that's the way it goes." Every loss has its lesson. If we lost because we made a mistake that's just a fact of life—it's not something to beat ourselves up about. In every contest someone has to come in second, and most people, including professionals, do a lot of losing before they are capable of winning. If we failed because we didn't try hard enough or weren't prepared, we probably deserved to lose.

The person who throws a tantrum when things don't go her way, or bad mouths the referee, her equipment, or her teammates will never be a winner no matter how many championships she subsequently wins. A good sport can face a loss gamely because she knows that she gave her all and worked hard. She just didn't happen to win—this time. A good sport always accepts full responsibility for her loss and then goes home and figures out how to win the next time.

◆

Losing comes with the territory; I will accept my losses graciously.

I just hit some shots that I'll probably never hit again.
—*Lauri Merten*

Have you ever done something so well that you surprised even yourself? Sometimes we can have an outstanding performance when everything seems to go our way. The conditions are perfect, we are on, and we seem to be unbeatable. We can spend the rest of our lives trying to recapture the moment. It becomes a superstitious thing, and many athletes will go to such lengths as eating the same breakfast or wearing the same socks they had on that fateful day. Because our play was so great it can almost seem like magic is the only way it could have happened. And the only way we think we can be sure that it will happen again is to create rituals. Keep in mind, however, that we create our own magical moments. Success is a spell built from our sweat and tears and dreams and hard practices. It may seem as if we could never recapture that beautiful line drive or that amazing putt that clinched the title. We may not be able to do it every time on command, but we will know that we have it in us. Once we have successfully hit the ball, or completed a run, or aced a workout class we will be able to do it again. We may not do it beautifully every time. But we *will* do it again and again and again.

◆

If I have done it once, I can do it again.

My strongest point is my persistence. I never give up in a match. However down I am, I fight until the last ball. My list of matches shows that I have turned a great many so-called irretrievable defeats into victories.
—*Bjorn Borg*

*H*ow many of us wish we have the persistence and perseverance that so characterized the great tennis player Bjorn Borg? We'd stay tough even if we were down in our weekly squash game. We'd dig in and really go for it in the last mile of a challenging road race. We'd stick with our exercise/weight-loss program even if we weren't seeing the immediate and satisfying results we had hoped for. Basically, the tougher the challenge, the more we'd hunker down to meet it.

Most of us, however, don't have this incredible stick-to-itiveness. We are more apt to lose confidence when we're being beaten or get discouraged by lack of results. It's not that there's anything wrong with us; it's just human nature. It takes a special person to stay focused and positive even in the most challenging of circumstances.

We can all work on this skill, though. We can practice affirming our performances and praising ourselves for our motivation. The more supportive we are of ourselves, the more we'll stay strong when the going gets tough. When our goals seem out of reach, and we're floundering around, we need to be our own biggest fans.

◆

I will always hang in there no matter how tough my workout or competition gets.

You must sacrifice, train, do everything possible to put yourself in a position to win.
But if you consider second or third a failure, I feel sorry for you.
—*Joe Falcon*

Wanting to be in great physical shape, lose weight, compete professionally or semiprofessionally, or achieve any other fitness goal is a major commitment. We must decide on our goal—be it to become proficient in figure skating, compete in a marathon, play on a baseball team, lose fifteen pounds, or build up some muscle tone—and then make plans on how to get there. It takes time, desire, perseverance, motivation, skill, practice, and a little luck.

If we want to learn to ski, we take lessons, watch videos, and spend time on the slopes. If we want to run races, we build up our mileage, cross-train, and improve on our minutes per mile. Every goal has steps we need to take to reach it. However, the road might not always be smooth, and the end might not always be what we had hoped. It is at these times that we have to be careful not to be hard on ourselves for falling a bit short.

If we have put forth our best effort in trying to reach our goal, we should be proud of our achievements. We can't always end up on top, but if we can feel confident that we gave it our best shot, we can be pleased about what we have accomplished and optimistic about future tries.

◆

I can be proud each and every time I give my best effort to achieve a goal.

Heart in champions has to do with the depth of your motivation and how well your mind and body react to pressure—that is, being able to do what you do best under maximum pain and stress.
—*Bill Russell*

*P*ressure is often a true test of our commitment and motivation. Those who throw in the towel at the first sign of a little opposition or difficulty won't get very far. A little bit of pressure can help us to bring out our best. This challenge can come from a new competitor, a new exercise routine, or anything that adds some inspiration, pressure, or stress. The depth of our motivation can also be tested by how well we overcome the obstacles that may stand in the way of our working out at all. We should take a look at how we respond to difficulty: Do we give in easily? How quick do we blow off our workout for whatever reason? When we give in to pressure that prevents us from working out, we will never improve.

Heart is the ability to rise to any occasion no matter what the circumstances. Pain, fear, or expectations can put undue pressure on us and it can be hard to handle. Resist giving in, hang tough, and keep on fighting. Sometimes when we have a lot of resistance to overcome we will find ourselves pushing harder and turning in a better performance than we have in the past.

◆

Pressure will enhance my performance, not crush it.

I never stay away from workouts. I work hard. I've tried to take care of my body. I'll never look back and say that I could have done more. I've paid the price in practice, but I know I get the most out of my ability.

—*Carl Yastrzemski*

When it comes down to it, the only sure way to get ahead is to work hard. That doesn't mean that the work can't be fun—after all, we are "playing." Pushing ourselves to the edge constantly can be exhausting, and it is smart to pay attention to how much we are working. Working hard isn't a license to beat our bodies into the ground. Knowing how much we can take will help us to build our abilities—it's not for beating ourselves up. A big part of working hard is knowing when we can't. We need to respect our bodies and listen to injuries or illness and not just plow mindlessly ahead.

Hard work can be overdone, so be careful. We don't want to burn ourselves out in practice or warming up and have nothing left to give when it really counts. But when we are in that clutch situation, no matter how it turns out, we want to be able to say that we were fully prepared and gave everything that we could. When we have played full out and we have done our best we can rest easy in knowing that we worked our hardest.

◆

I will work hard, but I won't overdo it in the process.

The greatest efforts in sports . . . come when the mind is as still as a glass lake.
—*Timothy Gallwey*

Often we hear about athletes playing in the "zone," or experiencing runner's high—achieving a state of peak performance and perfect calmness—while working out or competing at the top of their ability. It's as if the body and mind are one, running or swimming or playing on sort of flawless automatic pilot.

While this heightened state is not always achievable on demand, it is most likely to occur when the mind, as Gallwey states, is "as still as a glass lake." That means no hostile anger toward the opponent, no distractions from problems at work, no self-criticism. We know our sport and have done it dozens, if not hundreds, of times. Why not relax and "go with the flow," letting mind and body get in sync as we serve an ace or ace a workout.

Negative or unfocused thoughts take an incredible amount of energy—energy that is being taken away from your physical actions. The calmer and less cluttered your brain is, the more you can channel that unused energy toward peak performance.

◆

Keeping a calm and uncluttered mind is important to peak performance. Today before I work out, I will clear my mind of any unnecessary and energy-depleting thoughts.

Never change a winning game; always change a losing one.
—*Bill Tilden*

*I*f it ain't broke, don't fix it. If our tennis serve is giving us one ace after another, or our putts are always in the hole, or the way we kick in during our last mile is bringing in personal bests, then by all means leave well enough alone. While the tendency may be to do a bit more tinkering, just make a few minor adjustments, the results may make for a big disappointment. Sometimes when we get into the flow of peak performance it's best to just go with it—enjoying the success while it lasts.

If, on the other hand, your backhand looks like a bad fly swat, your chip shot is a long way from its mark, and your breaststroke seems to self-distruct after a while, then perhaps it is time to evaluate your skills and make a few changes. Everyone's game falls apart every once in a while. Even the top athletes suffer temporary slumps when they are forced to return to square one in order to get back on track. Take a close look at what skills are ailing. Maybe it would help to watch a professional and practice visualization skills. Or maybe a lesson from a trusted instructor is called for. Perhaps it's just a matter of taking a bucket of balls out to the court or course, or swimming a few extra laps. There's no need to panic if it seems your skills have gone south and your enthusiasm for working out has gone with them—it's just time for a bit of reevaluation, and a lot more practice.

◆

If my skills need a tune-up or my enthusiasm needs a jump-start, I'll just take a positive, proactive approach to getting everything back on track.

You go for it. All the stops are out. Caution is to the wind, and you're battling with
everything you have. That's the real fun of the game.
—*Dan Dierdorf*

*T*here is nothing like playing at our maximum ability and concentration. Nothing
exists except our game and our goal. When we are putting our all into our
workouts it can feel as if we are the only one in the gym or out on the track. All
outside distractions fade away into the background. It can feel as if it is just our
exercise and us. Completely pouring every ounce of physical and mental ability
into what we are doing can give us a feeling of exhilaration and joy that is
hard to describe. That buoyant feeling (sometimes called the endorphin rush or
"runner's high") is also the payoff for every morning workout, every exercise
routine. There just isn't anything like taking everything that comes our way in
stride.

Giving our all can compensate for small errors, being a little off, or for luck not
being on our side. Sometimes our enthusiasm can take us farther than our abilities might indicate. That totally psyched feeling and effort is the secret weapon
for success. Putting everything into our game will help us get everything we can
out of it.

◆

If I give 100 percent of myself I will get much more back in return and get the
extra bonus of having a great time doing it.

A competitor will find a way to win. Competitors take bad breaks and use them to drive themselves just that much harder. Quitters take bad breaks and use them as reasons to give up. It's all a matter of pride.
—*Nancy Lopez*

*E*very time we fall into an athletic slump—when we can't seem to run as far or as fast, we don't feel as coordinated in step class or on the tennis court, our softball batting average begins to slip, our golf score begins to inflate, and we have the all-around blahs—we run the risk of throwing in the towel, giving up, losing confidence. However, the true competitors among us will use these opportunities to help motivate ourselves to work a little harder and hang in there a little longer.

No slump ever lasts forever. We will always be able to return to form, sometimes it just takes a while. If we lose faith during these periods and give up, we are going to miss out on the chance to reach the fitness goals we have set for ourselves. If, on the other hand, we stay tough when it seems as if our abilities have deserted us, we will feel especially proud when we finally regain our form. Whether or not we ever formally compete, we should always have the heart of a competitor and never give up.

◆

In good times and in bad, I believe in my skills and will always make the best of any situation.

I'm careful not to give into theatrics when times are tough, I don't like it when
somebody gives into outside pressure and puts on a show for others.
—*Tony La Russa*

Sometimes we all feel the need to express anger or frustration on the playing field or in a workout. Perhaps we've made a careless error, aren't performing up to par, can't seem to hit our stride, or are disappointed in the actions of a teammate. We want to show our discontent and are tempted to engage in theatrics, like throwing a racket or cursing. It's at these times that we have to control ourselves, because these emotional outbursts are rarely helpful and, in fact, are usually detrimental to our performance.

The energy spent in worrying about a missed shot, arguing over a close call, stressing out over a less than perfect performance, or fretting over a teammate's mistakes is energy we should be devoting to our game or workout. It's okay to be dissatisfied with the way we are performing, but it's almost always more effective to put our anger aside and try and learn from our errors. We stand less of a chance of distracting ourselves and offending others and will most likely get a better performance out of ourselves in the end.

◆

I will keep my emotions in check and will put any anxious energy toward
a better workout or performance.

It's amazing how much of this is mental. Everybody's in good shape. Everybody knows how to ski. Everybody has good equipment. When it really boils down to it, it's who wants it the most, and who's the most confident on his skis.
—*Reggie Crist*

When we are performing at a high competitive level there isn't a lot of difference between the players. If our heads aren't in the game, we will soon find ourselves out of it. Mentally we have to be completely tuned in to cope with any and all situations. Confidence comes from challenging ourselves and successfully completing our workout routine. Every time we complete our run, or our Nautilus circuit, or get in our second serve we are adding to our confidence.

We won't be able to build our confidence by being inactive or by doing the same old routine every day. We need to be sure that we are reaching for higher goals every time out. In order to strive for these goals we really have to want to improve and get ahead. Without that desire we will find ourselves running in place and going nowhere.

◆

Every time I work out it's an opportunity to build my confidence.

I consider myself one of a very small handful of drivers in the world that are top drivers. The best one? I don't think anybody can say they're the best one because, from one week to the next, you can be on form or off form a little bit.
—*Nigel Mansell*

It's great to feel confident about our athletic skills. Whether we seem to be working out really well, playing our best racquetball, feeling great while running, or actually winning in competition, when we're feeling good about ourselves and our skills, it seems to make the hard work worthwhile.

But remember, no matter how good we are at a sport, no matter how well we're doing, there will come a time when we have an off day, slip into a slump, or are dominated by someone else. And while there's nothing wrong with having ups and downs, and, in fact, it would be unusual if we didn't, it's a lot easier to take if we've been realistic, and gracious, all along about our skills. Even the best athletes stumble occasionally, and to do so with poise is a skill that athletes of all levels should master.

◆

My skills will be on sometimes and off others. I need to remain consistently confident in myself no matter how they may vary.

In previous years I was so fired up at times I made little mistakes. So I kept telling myself to be patient, relax, play like you do in practice. What I've been doing in practice will carry over into the game.
—*Randall Cunningham*

It is not uncommon to have been practicing extremely well all week—making every putt on the golf course, running at a good pace, hitting well in batting practice, and serving winners on the tennis court—only to reach game day too keyed up to perform our best. All of the confidence, calmness, and success we had been experiencing all week in preparation for competition seems to have disappeared, and we are frustrated as we try to find the skills and mental focus that we need to get the job done.

If only we could play as well when it counts as we do when it doesn't. If only we could convince ourselves not to get so fired up in anticipation of competition, but rather to approach a competitive situation as if it were nothing more than a more structured practice session. The fact is, we are no less competent than when we were working out. We haven't lost our touch or our stamina or our talent—our bodies have just been taken over by our minds. We need to approach any game or match or race with as much confidence and as little anxiety as possible. The more we can convince ourselves to think of a competition as a more serious workout, the more apt we are to be able to play the way we do in practice —which can often be quite impressive.

◆

I can encourage myself to approach competitions like workouts
in a relaxed and patient frame of mind.

What I've learned is that you really have to tune into your "denial mechanism" quickly if you want to stay active. In other words, everybody gets to a point where they start to overdo it and break down or get hurt. And almost everybody denies it when it first hits. Staying healthy is a question of how quickly you can get beyond the denial and deal with the reality.

—*Frank Shorter*

*E*veryone has been or will be injured at some point in his athletic career. It may not be too serious—maybe a strained muscle, or shin splints—but it will be debilitating nonetheless, and the sooner we admit we are hurt and take action to treat the injury, the quicker we will be back in top form. It's too easy to "play through the pain" and ignore a nagging ailment, especially if we are in training for a specific goal. To admit our injury would mean having to agree to lay off activity for a period of time—time we may not feel we have to spare. However, neglecting to treat our impairment will, in many cases, only lead to further, often more serious, troubles down the road. An acute condition untreated becomes a chronic condition that seems untreatable.

It's most important to accept the temporary delay caused by an injury and care for it immediately and thoroughly. Too many athletes have had their careers ruined or cut short by trying to mask or ignore pain. The sooner the hurt is cared for, the sooner it will be healed.

◆

While I may be healthy now, I will pay attention to my body and look for signs of pain or injury and treat them immediately and thoroughly. Pain, no gain.

I think any player will tell you that individual accomplishments help your ego,
but if you don't win, it makes for a very, very long season. It counts more
that the team has played well.

—*David Robinson*

*I*f you play on a local softball team, a college intramural basketball team, a tennis doubles team, or in a regular golf foursome, you know that it takes more than just your own personal statistics to make the team successful. Yes, in professional sports there seem to be the occasional superstars who appear to carry their entire team to victory—Michael Jordan, Joe Montana, and Barry Bonds come to mind—however, ultimately the success of any team is really dependent on the combined success of *all* of the individuals.

While playing doubles in tennis the temptation may be to poach, taking some of our partner's shots; or on the soccer field, we may be inclined to hog the ball rather than pass to a teammate. Although our intentions would be for the good of the team, we have to realize and believe in the strengths and skills of our colleagues on the court or field. No matter how well we may be playing, or how impressive our stats are, we are still part of a team, and our priority should be whatever benefits the group. The confidence we exhibit in our teammates will only help boost the confidence they are feeling, which in turn makes for better performances. And when the athletic shoe is on the other foot, we will hope that our partners have the same faith in our abilities.

◆

If I am a member of a team, I am part of a synergistic group that has confidence
in the skills of each member and whose primary concern is the success
of the group as a whole.

> If you've got to remind yourself to concentrate during competition,
> you've got no chance to concentrate.
> —*Bobby Nichols*

Concentration is something we learn over time. It is invaluable to each and every sport we participate in and is something that takes as much practice as learning the skills of the sport. When we work out, we need to work on both the physical and mental part of our games, for even if we never compete at all, we will almost always reach a higher level of performance if we have a focused mind.

Concentration is not something we can call on when we are particularly in need —say in the third and final set of a tennis match, on the green of the eighteenth hole in a round of golf, or the last lap of our 400 Individual Medley swim race. Concentration has to be with us at all times, both in practice and competition— while shooting baskets with a friend, while lifting weights at the gym, and while taking our early morning jog. Even if there's not much of a challenge, or we're not into the game, we still must work to practice good mental fitness, including strong concentration skills. The payoff will be well worth it.

◆

Today's workout will be for both my body and my mind—I'll practice good concentration skills along with my physical ones.

> Don't look back. Something might be gaining on you.
> —*Satchel Paige*

Don't look back. Don't look down. Don't look to the side. Look forward. Concentrate. Don't worry about opponents or compare yourself to others. Play your game. Run your race. Do your thing.

If we work on our own games or skills, never worrying about how we compare to others or what others think, always looking ahead to how we can grow and improve, chances are good that we will succeed. If we spend precious time and energy always looking over our shoulders at the fellow tennis player who is about to pass us on the club ladder, or feeling self-conscious about how we stack up in our exercise class, chances are greater that we will not reach our athletic potential. Participation in sports is about developing our own skills, setting our own goals, and working out at our own pace. It shouldn't matter how well, or how poorly, another athlete is performing. Ultimately it's up to us to do our best, whether competitively or recreationally. Any energy we spend being distracted, worried, self-conscious, or overly concerned is energy that is not being used to pump iron, pedal, and push the limits of our ability.

◆

It doesn't matter how others are playing or what others think; what matters is
that I put all my energy into my own workout or competition.

> When it happens, I want to stop the match and shout, "*That's* what it's all about."
> Because it is. It's not the big prize I'm going to win at the end of the match or
> anything else. It's just having done something that's totally pure and having
> experienced the perfect emotion.
> —*Billie Jean King*

You know it when it happens. It's the powerful zing of a perfect forehand, the thrill of runner's high, the exhilaration of a ski run in fresh powder. It's the point where our bodies perform to their potential—and beyond. Some of the greatest matches, games, and performances in the history of sport have taken place when the athlete or team seems to have been "playing out of their minds."

It's called peak performance, and it's achievable by athletes of all levels and experiences. It happens when your body seems to take control, knowing exactly what to do, and your brain is given the day off. Your muscles just flex and relax, flex and relax, the way they've done hundreds of times before. The long hours of workouts have paid off—you're in the "zone."

Performing at the peak is every athlete's dream. It doesn't happen all the time, but when it does, as Billie Jean King explains, it's worth celebrating.

◆

Next time I reach the zone, I will revel in the thrill of performing at my peak.

I visualize the blood surging through my muscles with every repetition and every set I do. When I pose I've got a mental picture of how I want to look. When you have that in your brain, the physical body just seems to respond. It's important to tell yourself you are good and you look wonderful.
—*Rachel McLish*

Positive affirmations go a long way, and when we can visualize ourselves doing something and then telling ourselves how wonderful we are and how good we look, it's bound to make for success in any endeavor. When we apply this mental-imagery technique to sports, as professional bodybuilder Rachel McLish suggests, it is especially effective.

When we can picture ourselves participating in any athletic activity and doing it well, whether it's our regular fitness class, a tricky chip shot on the golf course, or running up a brutal hill at mile 3 of a five-mile run, we are, in a way, training for the event. The mental workout we are giving ourselves helps to prepare the body for the real thing. The brain absorbs the upcoming challenge and alerts the muscles, putting our bodies through a sort of motionless rehearsal. In addition, the preworkout can be done flawlessly, encouraging us to be self-confident and psyched about doing the real thing. And when we can be self-supportive we are bound to perform better.

◆

I can visualize myself performing at the top of my game and
am proud of my skills.

Everybody has limits. You just have to learn what your own limits are and
deal with them accordingly.
—*Nolan Ryan*

It's difficult to face up to our limitations. Once we have figured out just where our limitations lie we can't run from them or sweep them under the carpet—we have to deal with them. Often we compensate for our weak spots by overdeveloping in other areas. This can be an effective method for coping with our less strong points, but in the long run we won't be helping our overall performance. Discovering our limitations can help us to find the areas that we need to work on and improve. Even when we are assessing our limitations we can never lose sight of our strengths. If we stop to think about it, we will realize that there will probably always be some things that we do better than others.

This principle can also work in choosing what exercise we will do. It is always a good idea to operate from our strengths because we will then be able to achieve our best. Becoming familiar with our limitations isn't an excuse to not try, it is an opportunity to see what we should spend our time on. If we are not runners, we aren't going to get too excited about pounding the pavement. We may be much better off (and happier) swimming or working out with an exercise video at home. Knowing what we can and cannot do can help us exercise better.

◆

I will know my limitations, but I won't be limited by them.

*If behind in the second half because your running game has stalled,
switch to a passing attack.*
—*John William Heisman*

*H*ow many times have we been stalled in our workouts or in competition because our usually successful strategies and game plans seem to be ineffective? Our killer serve and volley game in tennis seems to have disappeared; the pacing in our morning five-mile run seems a little off; and our basketball team's rock solid zone defense is uncharacteristically weak. We try and try, but we just don't seem to be performing up to our caliber. Legendary college football coach John William Heisman wanted his teams to be versatile and be able to move to another plan if they were having trouble executing the first one.

We, too, can apply this strategy to our own athletics. We are not going to be as adept and successful at the same things every day, so we should be able to switch gears and try something else if it seems warranted. If we normally ride for twenty-four minutes on the LifeCycle and then move to the StairMaster at the gym, but if we find we just aren't into riding the bike today, we should be able to consider changing our plan. If today was the day we were to do some interval training at the track, but we're just performing our sprints up to par, maybe we should wait another day. The more flexible we are with our workout programs, the more we'll enjoy them, which naturally makes us work all that much harder and more efficiently.

◆

If today's exercise plan or game strategy doesn't seem to be working, I'll move on to something that will be more successful.

Certainly we're not satisfied with just winning games. We've been playing some pretty good hockey, but we think we can play much better.
—*Mario Lemieux*

For a professional you'd think that winning would be the only thing. However, the attitude that takes a professional a notch above the rest is the attitude that says playing at your best is the ultimate goal. The competitive arena isn't the only place that can inspire us to bring out our best. In order to excel, we have to decide just what it is that we want to accomplish so that we can be successful and know what a winner is on our own terms. Our best can be anything from winning the club golf tournament to completing a five-mile run in eight-minute miles.

We've all had those days when we put in just enough effort to get through our routine. And that's all we are doing—just getting it over with. Our hearts aren't in it, our heads aren't in it, our bodies are just going through the motions. Once in a while it's okay to phone in our performance; after all, it's better than sitting around doing nothing. But it's easy for it to become the norm, and when that happens we may just as well be home. We can get the most from ourselves by striving to do one better than the last time. If we won, great; we'll win bigger next time. We should never be satisfied with all the elements of our game. There's always something that can use a little fine-tuning, and that's where we find the challenges that will make us better.

◆

I will always strive for the next level.

> I've always believed that you can think positive just as well as
> you can think negative.
> —*Sugar Ray Robinson*

Why is it that negative thoughts seem to come up much more easily than positive ones? It may be that we are conditioned to evaluate and criticize everything we do. We may do it because we think it is the best way to learn. But it is really the best way to beat ourselves up. It is *so* easy to psych ourselves out that we sometimes become our own worst enemy. And yet, thinking about ourselves is something that we can totally control. We can't control how our opponents feel about us or what other people think of our workouts, but we can take charge of what we think about ourselves.

Our minds can have a very powerful influence on our attitude, which in turn influences our performance. When those negative thoughts arise we need to counter them with a positive, and more powerful, thought. If we are in the habit of thinking, "I can't do this," we have to turn it around and say, "I can do this, I will do this, I am doing this." Sometimes this means turning the negative into a positive by focusing on our strengths rather than our weaknesses. Positive thoughts can get us psyched up, keep us going through the rough spots, and inspire us to success.

◆

When a negative thought comes up I will replace it with a positive one.

I think of it [base stealing] as an art because when I get out there, I focus. My total concentration is focused on that moment when I'm going. I'm in a zone.
—*Rickey Henderson*

Some of the best athletes in the world report reaching their peak performances while in a "zone." Record base stealers like Rickey Henderson, runners, tennis players, and golfers claim to achieve an athletic nirvana, where body and mind are as one, working together to run faster, play better, feel stronger. And when this incredible mind/body experience takes over on the field, court, course, or track, the athlete is at once exhilarated and relaxed as his performance excites him while keeping him calm and focused.

To call upon this zone at will would be amazing, but, unfortunately, not possible. What we can do, however, is clear our minds of extraneous clutter while working out and competing so that we can encourage the state. The more free we are of anxiety, frustration, and unnecessary distractions the more chance we are giving ourselves to reach a level where mind and body work in tandem and we perform at the top of our game.

◆

Today I will work out with a clear, focused mind—a good way to get into a zone.

The medals don't mean anything and the glory doesn't last. It's all about your happiness. The rewards are going to come, but my happiness is just loving the sport and having fun performing.
—*Jackie Joyner-Kersee*

It's amazing how often the subject of fun comes up when professional athletes talk about the reasons they play. Sure, many people view sports as a means to an end—it is a way to bring home the trophies and awards, gain aerobic fitness, or even improve our bodies by toning them or losing weight. But think of how much more likely we will be to consistently work out if we find something fun to do. If we aren't finding any fun in what we do for exercise we may need to reconsider not only how we are spending our time but why.

Exercise shouldn't be torture. Yes, we sweat a lot, and there are many aches and pains that go with playing hard, but even in a hard-fought battle we can see the love of the game on many athletes' faces as they push themselves to their limits. When we don't have any fun we have to use that much more energy to get ourselves up for exercise. Fun is one of the best by-products of sports, and if we can't find the fun in our sports we are missing an opportunity to bring out the joy in ourselves.

◆

Trophies aren't the goal, having fun is.

When the going gets tough, the tough get going.

—*Anonymous*

We've heard it before, and we'll hear it time and time again. When the pressure is on, the score is tied, time is running out, our opponent is gaining on us, and we're tired and sore, that's the time to really pour on the juice. Even in a workout, when we're in the last minutes of step class, the last mile of our run, or the last few reps of circuit training, the time is right to dig in and go for it down the stretch.

It may be ego. It may be obsession. It may be some inner drive to push our personal limits, but there is something that makes certain athletes really fight to the bitter end, both in competition and in training. It happens to all of us at times. We're completing our last flip turn in our swim workout, entering our last mile in our bike ride, or in the last set of a tennis match, and all of a sudden we get a second (or third or fourth) wind that will propel us through the last lap, to the finish line, or through the final point. Wanting to go down fighting, or really pushing our limits in a workout, is the sign of a true competitor.

◆

The more challenging my workout or competition, the harder I will work.

Every time I go out there I think in my heart I can win. . . . If a horse has four legs,
and I'm riding it, I think I can win.
—*Angel Cordero, Jr.*

While confidence and the will to succeed are no strangers to many professional athletes—after all, it is a long road from sandlot Little League to Major League Baseball, and self-assuredness is practically a must—it's also equally as important that amateurs and fitness enthusiasts maintain the same positive self-image. Hanging in there through a tough high-impact class, winning a club tennis tournament, and beating a targeted 10K time are the result of skill, practice, and a combination of confidence and desire. And while it may seem that an aerobics class at the local health club is a far cry from professional baseball, the specific goal is not necessarily as important as the fact that we have one.

Hall of Fame jockey Angel Cordero, Jr., who amassed more than seven thousand wins in his over thirty-year career, never got on a horse he didn't expect to win with. Regardless of what the bookmakers were saying, Cordero always felt he was riding the favorite. We should approach every workout and competition as if we're going to ace it—and that's not with "attitude," it's with confidence. We should step onto every track, field, court, and course with the deep-down belief that we'll step off a winner.

◆

I believe I will ace my next workout and take my next opponent.

The most prepared are the most dedicated.
—*Raymond Berry*

*T*here is more to commitment than just showing up. We can hit the gym at dawn, but if we are not ready to do some work it won't make any difference that we showed up at all. We can drag ourselves out of bed in the morning, but we may just as well as slept in if we half-heartedly do our morning workout. Preparation is key to following through on our aspirations. We need to get ourselves mentally and physically prepared every time we exercise. We need to develop a routine that can help us to progress and that tests our limits as we are doing it. We need to make a plan for what we are going to do every time we work out. Planning and thoughtful preparation are indicative of a solid, unshakable commitment.

If we are willing to put in the time and effort both at the gym and beforehand we will definitely see results. It can help to write down our goals for every workout. Somehow putting it all down on paper can make the commitment seem more real. We don't have to show it to anyone else—it is for our use only. If we take the time to record our goals as well as our accomplishments then we will have an indisputable record of what we have done. As well as an indisputable record of what we are going to do.

◆

I am prepared to make a commitment.

When I go out on the ice, I just think about my skating. I forget it is a competition.
—Katarina Witt

Whether or not we ever compete in our sports, we can still learn from three-time Olympic gold medal figure skater Katarina Witt. Even if we just work out on a regular basis, we'll find ourselves working harder, more efficiently, and more effectively if we simply concentrate on the task at hand, ignoring the potential outcomes. If we focus on our morning swim workout, not thinking about the clock or how fast the person in the next lane is going, we'll find ourselves enjoying a more rewarding practice. If we take the field in a baseball game and simply do our job, not worrying about the score or making errors, we'll probably be pleasantly surprised at the end of the ninth inning.

It's when we get too caught up in the meaning of our workouts or competitions that we stumble. The stopwatch, the judges, the scoreboard all serve to take away our concentration, making us waste precious energy on worry, anxiety, or even overconfidence. There are far too many variables that may cause us to trip up on the field, court, course, or track—once we step out there we need to have a clear and focused mind so we can ward off distractions and perform to our peaks.

◆

When my workout starts, I am thinking only of it. I will do my best to avoid the distractions that can impede my best performance.

I honestly believed I would make it. I had the desire. A lot of people have the ability,
but they don't put forth the effort.
—Joe Carter

So much of success in sports at both the professional and amateur levels can be attributed to attitude. The combination of skills, practice, and desire is impressive in any forum, and it is only enhanced in sports, where desire is often the one ingredient that makes a good athlete great. Hours of practice and incredible skills can take us only so far. And desire alone, unfortunately, can help only so much. But combine the physical aspects with this inner drive and you have the makings of real success.

Most of us work out and compete because we want the exercise, the exhilaration, and the camaraderie of sports. We practice by setting up a workout schedule, often combining activities in an effort to avoid boredom and injury. We set goals for ourselves so that even if we don't compete we will see improvement as we aim higher and higher.

What we need to remember, however, is the real lift we can give ourselves by improving our attitude. A positive outlook, the desire to do better, and setting and meeting expectations is invaluable in our successful fitness program. It may not produce the sweat, or leave us with the achy muscles that a good physical workout does, but attitude takes us a long way toward our ultimate goal, no matter what that may be.

◆

I have the desire to work out aggressively and improve at my sport.

Resolve never to quit, never to give up, no matter what the situation.
—Jack Nicklaus

As kids we all had dreams of being up to bat, two down, bottom of the ninth, bases loaded, full count, down by one run, and hit a home run; or being down a point and passed the basketball to make the final shot at the buzzer; or coming back from a 5–2 deficit to win game, set, and match. However, the fact is that too many times in these situations, or ones just like them, we don't make the clutch play we dreamed about because we had long since given up hope of winning the game, match, or race.

But, if we are to take perennial PGA champion Jack Nicklaus's advice, we will always consider ourselves still in the game, regardless of the situation. If we decide up front to make this our philosophy, then when faced with a tough position we would have no choice but to keep fighting until the buzzer sounds. As good as this advice is, no one says it's easy, especially when we're down and not feeling particularly confident about our skills. However, in the long run it's a far better feeling to have gone down fighting than to lose having thrown in the towel early.

◆

I will not give up in my daily workout, nor in competition,
no matter how tempting it is.

Everything is practice.
—*Pelé*

Practice, practice, practice. Repeating skills over and over again can be very boring. But everyone, from professional to amateur, needs to spend time and effort on skills and techniques. By repeating certain moves over and over again our bodies will actually remember how to do them right without our minds having to tell us each and every time. The goal is to have many of our moves happen automatically and effortlessly. Investing time in practice is like buying ourselves a guarantee that we will perform in the clutch. Soccer star Pelé rose to world-renowned fame for his skills as a player, and we can be sure that he worked on those skills every opportunity he had. Practicing applies to the basics as well as to the fancy finesse moves. In fact, practicing the basics will enable us to build a solid foundation on which our special moves can be added.

Practicing can seem overwhelming. There may be so many things we want to work on that it's hard to know where to begin. We can't improve our entire game overnight. We have to break it down into parts and take those on one at a time. Whether it's our putting, our serve, or our endurance, we can decide to work on that one thing and we will find that our overall performance will get better also.

◆

I will make a commitment to practice and build my skills.

I think it's the mark of a great player to be confident in tough situations.
—*John McEnroe*

Tough situations can bring out our best. In fact, all of our mental and physical preparation is for these very moments. When we are faced with a difficult task we may find ourselves questioning whether or not we can deal with it. A moment of doubt can spell defeat. Maintaining our confidence will be a challenge sometimes, but we can do it. The best players always have their strengths at the front of their minds and have complete trust in their own abilities.

Having confidence in ourselves can help us to handle the most challenging of opponents or workouts successfully. Knowing that we are prepared and knowing what we can accomplish will support us no matter what we find ourselves up against. Positive self-talk will help our confidence to grow and stay strong. Every time we are successful we will reinforce our belief in our competence. When we are facing a difficult situation, whether it is a moment in a game or a larger goal that we have chosen for ourselves, we have to believe not only that we can get through it but that we can make it through with flying colors. Having healthy confidence is like having our own cheering squad right with us as we play or work out. Confidence always says "Yes, I can," no matter how hard it may seem to keep going.

◆

Confidence will see me through.

It's not who jumps the highest—it's who wants it the most.
—*Buck Williams*

Good news if you're a five-foot three-inch basketball wannabe. However, the implications for all of us are worth noting as well. We aren't all physically perfect for the sports that interest us the most, and, in fact, many times we take up athletics feeling not quite suited for working out at all. Because so much of success in sports is about desire and perseverance, the majority of us who enjoy physical activity, but aren't built like the quintessential athlete, can enjoy a variety of sports and workout programs.

It isn't just being the fastest or strongest or most agile that makes one successful in sport. It's a potent mixture of natural ability, hard work, desire—and, at times, luck. Natural ability is, well, natural, God-given ability. Hard work is putting in long hours of practice. Desire, however, is immeasurable. It's heart. It's the ingredient that makes aching legs sprint the last fifty yards to beat the clock, or quivering abs do ten more sit-ups.

Natural ability and hard work will take you a long way toward your goals— that's no secret. Those attributes plus desire will get you there.

◆

Today I want more in my workout—and will reach a little farther to get it.

I look at victory as milestones on a very long highway.
—Joan Benoit Samuelson

A victory can seem like an end, but it is also a beginning. When we have decided that we want to do something—run a marathon, win a golf game, lose weight—and we reach that goal, we have achieved a victory. But we are not done yet. It's important to celebrate our victories because they are the symbols of the fruition of our efforts and determination. They represent the goals that we have been striving toward whenever we work our exercise program. However, every victory should spawn another goal. We have reached one rung on the ladder and now we need to make a plan for getting to the next level. Just as movement is key in efficient and productive exercise, movement toward our goals is key in our being more efficient and productive.

Exercise and working out are long-term propositions. They do not stop just because we have reached one milestone. One milestone may take us to a point where we can see even more milestones ahead. Every success that we experience has a dual meaning—it is a celebration for what we have done and an inspiration for what we have yet to do. We need to be sure to honor both aspects of these victories. So we can celebrate for now, but we musn't relax too much. Tomorrow we'll be moving toward a new goal.

◆

I will look at every victory as inspiration to keep moving forward.

Games lubricate the body and the mind.
—*Benjamin Franklin*

No matter how frantic we may be at the office, no matter how stressful some relationships can be, no matter whether we're bogged down by paperwork, housework, or schoolwork, we can always benefit from a game of one-on-one, a swim, or a round of golf. Without fail, these brief time-outs in our otherwise hectic schedules really deliver. Our hearts pump, we sweat, our endorphins kick into high gear, and we seem to reach a state that is more relaxed, with a head that is less cluttered and muscles that ache with that "good kind of hurt" feeling.

More than a drink or a smoke, exercise is the most consistent way to "lubricate the body and the mind" and to reach a natural high.

When the pressure is on, our shoulders are tense, our brains are clogged with a million percolating factoids, it's time to lace up those athletic shoes and blow it all out.

◆

With a clear head and relaxed body as a reward, I'm working out today.

Fear can be conquered. I became a better person and a better football player
when I learned that lesson.
—*Roger Craig*

You don't have had to be facing a defensive line of three-hundred-pounders
whose main, let's say *only*, objective is to crush the person with the ball—that
being you—to know what fear is in sports.

Perhaps most relevant to athletes of all levels and sports is fear of failure. Who
among us hasn't choked in a tennis match because we anticipated a tough game
and were then unable to execute? Or what about those of us who avoid competing
in a 10K running race because we're afraid we might not be able to finish, even
though we regularly train at distances that are equal or longer? We intimidate,
even paralyze, ourselves by these usually unfounded fears.

While it is always easier said than done, we need to take a step back when we
find ourselves anxious about performing. What are the facts? Could I be letting
fear get the best of me when, in reality, I should be feeling more confident?
Coping with fear or inadequacy and failure is never easy, but these negative
feelings can be alleviated with a careful, critical look at the circumstances.

◆

Fear of not performing up to a certain level can be debilitating. I need to look
carefully and realistically at my goals so as to feel confident in my ability
to work out and compete.

> In large part, my success against good pitchers was a matter of confidence. And
> my mental edge was knowing that I could hit a good pitcher's best pitch. The thing
> I had on my side was patience.
> —*Hank Aaron*

Patience. Patience. Patience. Not being patient will inevitably lead to frustration, and if we cut ourselves some slack we will feel the benefits both mentally and physically and see the change in our fitness program. It takes time to develop our athletic abilities. We can't transform ourselves into a .400 hitter or an advanced golfer overnight. If we are impatient with our progress we will push ourselves too hard and end up with an injury, or worse, so discouraged that we give up.

We have to trust ourselves. We have to believe that we can accomplish what we have set out to do. We also need to have the patience to wait for the right time. This applies to everything from entering into a competitive situation to moving up to the next hardest level of a workout class to taking on that next half mile in our morning run. Whether we are starting a new sport or working on an old one, we have to have patience to give ourselves enough time to learn the ropes and develop our skills. If we approach our workouts with patience, we will find that we'll enjoy them a lot more and we won't get frustrated or discouraged.

◆

I will look for and take advantage of my opportunities.

> What it comes down to is that anybody can win with the best horse. What makes
> you good is if you can take the second- or third-best horse and win.
> —*Vicky Aragon*

We've all had the experience of doing something we never thought possible: the report we never thought we'd finish on time or that project around the house that seemed hopeless but finally came together after some concentrated effort and work. The thing that propelled us to finish and be successful was determination. Especially the determination to use all of our talents single-mindedly, no matter what the odds.

Impossible tasks remain impossible if we don't attack them and break them down into the possible. That means taking what we have to work with and using it to our best advantage. Let's think back to when we first started exercising. Almost everything we took on looked daunting, and it always seemed as if the odds were stacked against us. But when we put on our game face and put our mind to it, things began to go the way we wanted them to. If we are just starting out and feel as if we are facing the impossible, we should remember that everyone else has felt the same way. The trick is to take what we have been given and make it work for us. With hard work and determination we can prove our abilities to ourselves and to anyone else who happens to be watching.

◆

I will transform the impossible to the possible.

Learn to think like a winner. . . . Think positive and visualize your strengths.
—*Vic Braden*

A winner is confident in her skills and ability and does not overreact when she may not seem to be up to par.

A winner can visualize a winning shot, an effective move, a final stretch sprint, and a game-winning play long before taking the field, court, or track.

A winner has a clear mind—relaxed and focused on the task at hand, whether it's a challenging workout or an important competition.

A winner doesn't give up no matter how desperate the situation may seem to be.

A winner's mind can keep his legs moving even when they can't seem to go another step.

A winner doesn't always come in first but is always up for another game, or match, or challenge.

◆

Today I will think like a winner.

Concentration is why some athletes are better than others. . . . You develop
that concentration in training. You can't be lackadaisical in training and
concentrate in a meet.

—*Edwin Moses*

We play the way we practice.

Even if we work out regularly, day after day running, swimming, or shooting hoops, the results of these hours of practice will only be as good as the effort we put into them. Whether it's endurance, accuracy, strength, or concentration, as Olympic gold medalist Edwin Moses suggests, we have to demand as much of ourselves on the practice field as we do on the playing field.

Skills such as the ability to concentrate while performing are honed during hours and hours of working out. We learn what our weaknesses are and focus on ways to transform them into strengths. We have to expect the best from ourselves in all situations, whether in a short training run or an important race; a tennis lesson with the pro or the club championships. We can't goof off in training, assuming that when it really counts we'll be able to focus and perform to our peak. It's just not likely to work that way. Our minds and bodies learn skills after practice and repetition. It's up to us to prepare for competition and other challenges in a sufficient manner.

◆

It's important that the effort I put in during a workout be my best.

*I'm proof that great things can happen to ordinary people if they
work hard and never give up.*
—*Orel Hershiser*

We can all prove that great things can happen to ordinary people, because hard work and perseverance are incredibly powerful and effective—should we decide to employ them. We all have the potential to be far greater than we can even imagine. We're limited only by our desire, motivation, and drive. And while athletic success may seem to come much easier to some than to others, we must believe that we can take ourselves a long way if we really buckle down and charge ahead.

The fact is, people have different aspirations and goals for themselves in all aspects of their lives. We want to reach a certain level in business, have a particular life-style, and get something out of our athletic abilities. Pitcher Orel Hershiser wanted to reach the Major Leagues. Some of us want to reach a competitive level; others of us are happy to work out recreationally on a fairly regular schedule. No matter what our target is, we're all certainly capable of reaching it. Deciding on what we want from ourselves is half the battle. Once we've set our sights on our achievement, we need to call upon all of the hard work and perseverance that Hershiser advocates. Then, great things will come our way as well.

◆

I can achieve what I set out to in the athletic arena; I simply need to set my sights on a goal and go for it.

What is absolutely indispensable is strict follow-through, effort, and stick-to-itiveness. Don't be frightened if things seem difficult in the beginning. That's only the initial impression. The important thing is not to retreat; you have to master yourself. This ability to conquer oneself is no doubt the most precious of all the things sports bestow on us.

—Olga Korbut

Races that seem too long; step classes that seem too advanced; basketball teams that seem too competitive; swim workouts that seem too ambitious. We have all faced tough workouts that seem to stand like unsurmountable challenges before us. We are intimidated by the difficulty, length, or competition of an exercise class, a workout, a game, or a race. Yet these are the times when it's most important for us to call on our self-confidence and perseverance to take on the challenge.

Most of the time when we do decide to go for it we discover that we are better prepared than we thought. We may find matches that seemed too tough, races that seemed too grueling, and exercise classes that seemed too advanced are doable after all. We're actually in pretty good shape. We, too, can compete out there. We've been working hard and it seems to have paid off. It's incredibly satisfying to face a challenge head-on and come through successfully. It validates our hours of practice and is a great motivator. We're encouraged to stick with our exercise program because at last we see results.

◆

I know I can face the challenges that come my way and handle them successfully.

> We all choke. You're not human if you haven't.
> —*Curtis Strange*

Sometimes it's nerves, sometimes it's fear, sometimes it's being in an unfamiliar situation or playing an untested opponent. Sometimes there is no telling where it comes from. Somehow our brains short-circuit or our bodies don't respond and we make errors we never made before. We miss a shot we've made hundreds of times in practice or we start running at a pace we can't maintain or we falter just as we are about to get to the next level on the StairMaster. For whatever reason, we just can't do today what seemed automatic yesterday. If we do start feeling a little tense or find ourselves making mistakes we don't usually make, we can take a few seconds to regroup, breathe deeply, and get ourselves back in control.

Choking is really the one thing that all athletes, from pro to amateur, have in common. Sooner or later everyone does. It often arises out of an overpowering desire to do our best that backfires. Unless it is chronic, choking isn't a huge problem. The real problem arises when we start worrying about when, and if, it will happen. There are no sure ways to avoid it. But if we start obsessing about it the next thing we'll be doing is choking.

◆

Choking is not the end of the world. If it does happen to me, I'll just shake it off, refocus and keep on playing.

Winning has a joy and discrete purity to it that cannot be replaced by anything else.
Winning is important to any man's or woman's sense of satisfaction and well-being.
Winning is not everything; but it is something powerful, indeed beautiful,
in itself, something as necessary to the strong spirit as striving
is necessary to the healthy character.
—*A. Bartlett Giamatti*

Winning isn't everything, but its importance can't be denied. It can make us feel competent and successful, powerful and effective. It can be something we work toward week after week or something we enjoy for the moment and then move on. Winning can encourage us to continue to practice, work out, and compete. It is a sign of progress and a measure of accomplishment.

What's important for us to remember, however, is that winning is not just coming up with the highest number of points, the lowest handicap, the fastest time, or the best score. Winning is also acing an expert ski run for the first time; it's beating a targeted 5K time; and it's cramming ten more sit-ups. Winning is not just beating an opponent, and it's not just about score—fortunately, winning is about competing against ourselves, the clock, and our goals as well.

While the traditional win in a competitive setting is truly a natural high, it's closely followed by the personal win in a private setting in the form of a best time, an achieved goal, or a peak performance.

◆

Winning comes in a variety of ways—traditional and nontraditional. Today I will
look to "win" in my daily workout.

Everybody in the world thought we couldn't do it. But we did it, dammit.
—*Bill Koch, after winning the America's Cup*

It is terrific to prove people wrong. Knowing that we have can give us an extra boost when we win. When we are the underdog and we prevail we have done more than just win, we have overcome other people's expectations that are intended to keep us down. Sometimes people's low expectations of our abilities can inspire us to go out and show them how wrong they are about us.

It's not always other people's expectations that can relegate us to the underdog position. It's important to pay attention to what we really think about our chances for success. Do we believe that we can win? We should because that is where winning begins—it begins with us. Everyone else, from family to friends to our competitors, may not think we've got what it takes. It is our job to prove them wrong. If we believe, we will be able to overcome all of their doubts. But we have to tackle our own doubts first. Self-doubt is probably the most debilitating injury we can experience. It is an injury because it diminishes our ability to play our best and to battle our hardest. If we doubt ourselves we will not succeed. If we have faith in ourselves, even if nobody in the world is behind us, we can achieve our goals.

◆

I won't let doubts, my own or anyone else's, keep me from doing my best.

I'm trying to do the best I can. I'm not concerned about tomorrow
but with what goes on today.
—*Mark Spitz*

Today is a very important day for fitness:
Today I will exercise.
Today I will get to the gym.
Today I will join that aerobics class.
Today I will challenge myself.
Today I will focus and concentrate on my workout.
Today I will get up and go running.
Today I won't quit.
Today I will do my best.
Today I will do better than I did yesterday.
Today I will put on my sneakers and go.

◆

I won't think about what I will or will not do tomorrow; I will concentrate
on what I can do today.

I believe in rules. Sure I do. If there weren't any rules, how could you break them?
—*Leo Durocher*

Rules *were* meant to be broken, weren't they? Well, certainly within reason, and definitely when it's for our own good and well-being. For example, if one of our own personal rules is to run every Monday, Wednesday, and Friday morning, and we wake up one of those days feeling more like visiting the gym, by all means we should allow ourselves a little leeway. Or if one day before our regularly scheduled tennis games we suddenly don't feel up to playing—we're too sore, or tired, or just not into it—maybe we should consider taking the day off or, at the very least, altering our plans a little.

We should never be so stuck on a plan or an exercise regimen that we can't deal with slight alterations. Yes, we can set up workout rules for ourselves to help us stay motivated—run at least three times a week; bike at least ten miles at a time; improve swim times each workout—but we've got to allow for flexibility. If we stick too rigidly to the fitness guidelines we set up for ourselves, we run the risk of resenting, and ultimately rejecting, the entire idea. Rules are fine to use as motivation and encouragement, but if we find ourselves having trouble sticking to them on a regular basis, perhaps it's time to think about rewriting the exercise bylaws.

◆

Rules about working out *are* made to be broken, especially
if we'll benefit from the change.

> Being the underdog and never having won before was a special moment.
> This time I knew what to expect. But it's very different when you can
> come back and win again.
> —*Bonnie Blair*

When we are the underdog, no one knows what to expect from us (sometimes we don't even know what to expect from ourselves). We can operate anonymously with no pressure to perform in a certain way or at a certain level. But once we have made our mark there will be people gunning for us. It's hard enough to keep our cool and play our best in a standard competitive situation; it is even harder when we are the target for everyone else. It adds even more pressure to what can be a very tense situation already.

When we have been able to meet our exercise goals or win a tournament, it may feel as though we can never get to that level of accomplishment again. What we have to keep in mind is that if we have done it before we can definitely do it again. No matter who is trying to beat us out we will have the strength to prevail. We need to be sure that we don't add ourselves to the list of those trying to beat us. We have to stay strong against the opposition and need to make ourselves our strongest allies. It can be harder to overcome all of the pressure, but we can do it.

◆

Whether I am the underdog or favored to win, I will always give it my best shot.

There are several different ways to make training more fun, and I've come upon some of them by accident. It's easy to get into a routine in which you do the same thing every day. The more you can break out of that, the longer you will stay excited about the sport.

—*Scott Tinley*

Variety *is* the spice of life, and nowhere is that more evident than in athletics. It is a lot easier to keep up a consistent training program when we combine a number of different activities to achieve our fitness goals. It helps us avoid injury, get a more complete total-body workout, and ward off boredom. We will usually put in more time, more enthusiastically, when we can look forward to a change in our workout every once in a while.

If we prefer to use the StairMaster at the gym but are starting to get a little sick of it, we should take some time with the stationary bike and the rowing machine. If our favorite exercise is running but we're feeling a little sore, we should try cycling or swimming for a day or two. If we have a regular tennis game but the weather has prohibited us from playing, maybe it's time to go to the gym and work out in a circuit training class. No matter what our preference, we can always benefit from making a change in our routine.

◆

Today, I'll try something a little different.

I only play well when I'm prepared. If I don't practice the way I should, then I won't play the way that I know I can.
—*Ivan Lendl*

Practice is a testing ground for what we can do in real competition. It isn't just killing time between games, it's a way to test our limits and work on whatever errors we have been making. In a game we really can't take risks because that isn't the time for experimentation. For example, it's safe to try a new serve when we are practicing, or it's safe to try a different running stride when we are working out. It's usually not a good idea to try something new when we are in the heat of a game or a race.

When we practice we are developing and testing our abilities as well as developing good habits and reinforcing what we have learned. It is also a time for us to correct and overcome our weaknesses. It may be a little boring, but repetition is the best way to increase our muscle memory and keep our skills at their best. Practicing the way we should means giving the same amount of time and effort we would to a "real" game. It is also a way to get ready for whatever our opponents may throw our way.

◆

I will treat my practices with the same respect and intensity I bring to my games.

If your body is telling you to slow down, listen to it. If your body is saying you
should keep going . . . then keep going.
—*Lynn Swann*

*L*ike a car sputtering and coughing in need of gas, or one humming and responding with ease after a tune-up, our bodies give us clues about how they
need to be treated. Unfortunately, however, athletes are not always the most
perceptive at picking up and acting on the hints that their bodies send them. We
are at times singularly bent on achieving a goal, improving our game, beating an
opponent, and we ignore anything, including injury, that may distract us.

A blistered hand, a leg cramp, and sore calves are all signs that we need to
slow down, refuel, or lay off altogether. Repeatedly running on shin splints or
adding more reps before recovering from achy back muscles will only do us in in
the long run. We must listen carefully to our bodies and act on problems immediately so we can be back out there as soon as possible.

(If, on the other hand, we find our bodies wanting more exercise, we finish our
workout still brimming with energy, we can also respond accordingly—obviously
within reason.)

◆

I will listen to my body and not push too hard if I'm feeling too sore or tired.

There were a lot of good games, a lot of ups and downs, and I played with intensity and enthusiasm, but most important, I played to win.
—*Carlton Fisk*

Competition—specifically winning—is a great motivator for many athletes. Sure, they love to play the game or run the race, but some people get their greatest high from coming out on top. It's as simple as that. They may get this thrill as a member of a softball or basketball or rugby team that is successful, or it may be as a lone runner competing in local races. The athlete may enjoy the relatively understated victories of winning a round of golf at the club or revel in the excitement of a championship sailing regatta won.

While the heat of battle, the challenge of training, and the fun of the sport itself may come into play, some of us are truly turned on by giving our all and ending up with the fastest time, most points, or best score. We love the thrill of victory—we despise the agony of defeat. What's important to remember, however, is that a perfect record is rare indeed, and no matter how accomplished we are, we are bound to find ourselves facing a loss every now and then. Everyone likes winning. And while it's fine to love to win, it's best if we try to find a balance that helps us accept losses as they come as well.

◆

Winning isn't everything, but it is satisfying.

One way to break up any kind of tension is good deep breathing.
—*Byron Nelson*

When the pressure's on—you're down by a set in the local tennis tournament; you're serving to send the match into the ever-important tie-breaker; you're starting to feel yourself choke—stop and take a long, deep breath.

When you're three-quarters of the way through a long, tough run—the monster hill is just around the corner; you're starting to feel the pain; your water bottle is down to the last drop—slow down and take a few deep, rejuvenating breaths.

When your advanced step class is feeling next to impossible yet the body beautiful next to you seems to be handling it swimmingly—there are still forty-five minutes left in the hour class; if you stop the only way back to the locker room is through the center of the class—hang in there and breathe in deeply to renew that energy.

When all eyes are on you—you're putting for a birdie in the last hole of the club's golf championship; the wind has started to pick up, as has your stress level; your opponent is breathing down your neck—step back, breathe in, relax, and make the shot.

◆

A pause, a deep breath, and another look can help me refocus and psych up to meet a challenge.

> We generally make too much of winning. Let's face it, someone
> always has to win; that is the nature of competition. But the mere fact of winning
> doesn't make you great.
> —*Wilt Chamberlain*

We all put a lot of emphasis on winning. It starts when we're little and playing in the playground or playing in Little League. It continues in high school and college sports. The first question people ask after a game is, "Who won?" Nobody asks who played well or who had the most fun or showed the most improvement. It's no wonder that we always feel like we have to be winning or it isn't worth playing at all. There are many people who try to make every event into competition. An afternoon bowl turns into a contest to see who can beat whom. Sometimes the focus on winning saps all the fun out of playing.

We should try and relax our absolute focus on winning. Especially on winning at all costs. Wilt is right, there will always be a winner and a loser in any competition. Even the best players lose once in a while. And they don't give up because of a loss, they keep on going. That is where greatness lies. You're not great just because you won. Greatness lies in truly giving it your best shot. When we focus only on winning we miss the lessons we can learn from competition. If winning is the only thing, a loss means that we have gained nothing from the experience.

◆

Winning doesn't make me great; the way I play makes me great.

I know what it takes to get through the Open, although I don't think I've mastered it to perfection—you have to block everything out, be extremely focused, and be relaxed and mellow, too.
—*Jennifer Capriati*

There is a fine line to walk between being totally focused and keeping loose. If we try too hard to be intense we may find that we are always on edge and really nervous. When we are too keyed up we will find ourselves making unforced errors. Too mellow and we can lose our intensity altogether. A lax attitude can keep us from performing our best.

We all have our own version of the U.S. Open. It may be the club tournament, the weekend 10K, or that killer step aerobics class. In all cases we need to find the middle ground between focus and freedom that will bring out our best. We are really the only ones who can determine how to achieve that balance as well as what totally psyched and totally mellow are for us. We will find our individual levels and balances by practicing and determining what works best for us. We may also discover that the balance may vary from event to event. When we want something badly enough, it is pretty easy to get totally psyched up for it. It is much harder to keep ourselves relaxed. We need to remember to take a deep breath or two and play our best.

◆

I will find that balance between intensity and relaxation.

People who enjoy what they are doing invariably do it well.
—*Joe Gibbs*

*E*ver notice that you often do your best, most productive workout or have the most success in competition when you're particularly enjoying what you're doing? When you can let go of any outside stresses and are not anxious about performing, you seem more apt to hit a personal best, beat a tough opponent, or become incredibly exhilarated by your usual exercises. It is a wonderful feeling and is really the height of sports participation.

Team members who get along, are supportive of one another, and are in the groove are far more successful than those whose strategy involves blame and selfishness. Individual athletes who are having fun are more apt to get into the zone of peak performance. It doesn't matter if you're a professional basketball player or a weekend softball player, a competitive tennis player or a casual jogger, the attitude that you bring to the field, court, or track will do wonders for your performance.

◆

Today I'm going to have fun out there.

*I worked very hard. I felt I could play the game. The only thing
that could stop me was myself.*
—*Jim Abbott*

Professional baseball player Jim Abbott overcame amazing adversity. Born with a malformed right arm, he taught himself to pitch and catch a baseball by switching his glove on and off his left hand, and became a successful Major League pitcher. Abbott attributed his achievement to always believing in himself and his ability. And, although everyone's personal challenges are different, we can learn from someone like Abbott.

We all get in our own way every once in a while, especially when it comes to athletics. However, once we realize this, as Abbott did, we can probably take a step toward being a lot happier and going a lot farther. We need to understand that competence at any sport takes hard work and practice, with a large dose of self-confidence. We need to remember that our most important and influential fan should be ourselves. No one has more control over what we can and cannot do, and no one has more riding on whether or not we can do it. When it hurts to run one more mile or it feels as if our backhand has disappeared, when the last rep on a tough machine seems like an impossibility, or we can't seem to connect at the plate, that's when we need to believe the most.

◆

I believe in my ability—I know I can do it.

Sport is singularly able to give us peak experiences where we feel completely one with the world and transcend all conflicts as we finally become our own potential.
—*George A. Sheehan, M.D.*

In other words, participating in athletics, no matter at what level, is just plain great. We are strengthened both physically and mentally—while playing at something that is, we hope, fun most of the time. We have the potential to reach incredible peaks while working out, to achieve "runner's high," or get into the "zone." We are able to put aside the problems and issues we face at home or at the office and become simply a runner, a golfer, a tennis player, a weight lifter, or a cyclist. The only thing that's in front of us is the challenge that awaits around the corner, in the next set, or on the next hole.

Sports encourage us to set goals, raise our expectations, and accept challenges that are at once intimidating and exciting. We are limited only by our own attitude, and are encouraged or discouraged only by the amount of confidence in ourselves. We needn't wear the uniform of a professional team or carry the membership card of an exclusive club to reap the tremendous rewards of a regular fitness program. Every athlete of every level has the same chance to experience the thrill and the pain, the success and the failure. We just need to play hard and persevere, and the peaks will come.

◆

Today I will give myself an extra push to reach closer to my potential.

There's always the motivation of wanting to win. Everybody has that. But a champion needs, in his attitude, a motivation above and beyond winning.
—*Pat Riley*

Winning isn't everything. It is a lot of fun and a great motivator, but it isn't the only thing that can drive us to being champions. A champion isn't just someone who wins trophies. We can be champions even if we never enter a single competition. We can achieve our personal bests in our individual workouts if we maintain the right perspective. A true champion has the right attitude. Part of that attitude is the desire to improve and to meet and overcome challenges. When we win a competition we have overcome an opponent by using superior drive and skill. We can also bring this into play when there is no competition in sight. If we approach our workouts with a winning attitude, we will be a winner in our own personal arena.

If we play only to win, we will be missing something—the joy and fun of being able to exercise and get our bodies moving the way we want them to move. Playing at our best can be the payoff for the days and weeks that we devote to exercising. Don't eclipse the fun by thinking only about the win. Playing beyond winning is playing to learn more and to enjoy ourselves more.

◆

I won't only play to win, I will play for the sake of playing.

When I look at hockey, I think the mental aspect is about 60 percent of the game.
If you think you can do it, you can.
—*Eric Lindros*

*E*very game has a mental aspect. In team sports or individual competition the mind has to be working *with* the body for success. If two equal competitors meet and one is mentally sharper than the other, chances are the one who's thinking will win the game.

Getting the mind involved can also help build confidence and hone skills. A game can be won mentally throught anticipation, visualization, and psych long before the players take the field. When an athlete concentrates on what he is capable of and thinks about what he aspires to do, he can add an extra boost to his physical edge.

When the mind and the body are working together, there is an almost constant exchange between the mental and the physical. Mental preparation involves thinking about what needs to get done. What's the best approach to running up that hill? Where should that volley be returned? Visualization can help anticipate what will happen and what our reaction will be. Mental psych involves positive self-talk and bolsters our confidence in our abilities. On the court, on the road, or in the gym the mind can be our biggest ally.

◆

I will make the effort to make my mind work as well as my body and
believe in what I can do.

If I play my best, I can win anywhere in the world against anybody.
—*Ray Floyd*

*T*here are a lot of things that can get in the way of our working out. We all have busy schedules, but just because we are away from our usual routine it doesn't mean that we can't make some time for fitness. We should make it a habit to include our workout gear when we pack our bags for some time away from home. We never know when we may suddenly find ourselves with some extra time for exercise. Or we may be in a hotel that has gym facilities. If we are prepared, we may not have to give up on our exercise. When we are away we may not be able to fit in our usual workout, but whatever we do—some sit-ups while watching the news, a brisk walk between meetings—can help us feel as though we aren't completely neglecting our fitness program.

It can be hard to work out when we are away from home, but it's not impossible. A little creativity can go a long way toward keeping us on track.

◆

No matter where I am, I will try and get in a workout.

I can't concern myself with what's going on with the club or what the media is writing. If you pay attention to those things, that's when you get yourself in trouble.
—*Don Mattingly*

Keeping focused on the job at hand will help us to succeed. When we are working out our minds should be on working out. No more, no less. Once we have on our workout gear we shouldn't be thinking about our jobs or our relationships or errands we need to take care of. We need to pay attention only to the things that are important to our exercise and what we are working on now. There will be plenty of time to worry about the other stuff after we have completed our exercise routine.

With this type of intensity and focus we can also keep ourselves from being bored or distracted, which isn't always easy. There are too many people around, or not enough, or we start wondering about someone else's workout: How do they do that? How long have they been working out? What kind of shoes are those? Am I in better shape? Am I fatter than her? When our minds wander we are not putting in maximum effort. And without maximum effort we won't keep moving forward and achieving our goals. We must focus on what we are doing or we will undoubtedly lose our way.

◆

I will focus on my workouts and block out everything else.

Practice without improvement is meaningless.
—Chuck Knox

*I*deally, every time we step onto the field or into the gym to work out, we should see improvement in our skills. Every morning run should be just that much better than the one the day before. Today's circuit training session is more productive than yesterday's. Our 1,500 meter swim this afternoon will be an improvement over the one we did the other day. While this constant progress from day to day may seem unlikely, and even unrealistic, it should be a goal for us. There's no reason we can't go into our workout every day with the intention of having our best day yet. And, in fact, this positive approach will do wonders toward that end.

However, even if we don't seem to show the great strides on a day-to-day basis that we had hoped for, we can be sure that there have been at least a few baby steps of progress. The fact that we get out on the court or course or track or to the gym or the pool on a regular basis is valuable in and of itself. We are staying motivated and sharp while maintaining our cardiovascular health and coordination. If we approach every practice with the *intention* of performing our best and improving our skills, we can feel confident that all of our hours of sweat are not in vain—they are, in fact, invaluable.

◆

I approach every practice intending to improve on what I did the day before.

> It's not over till it's over.
> —*Yogi Berra*

We've all seen surprising endings to sports contests—the three-pointer at the buzzer that wins the championship or the grand slam in the bottom of the ninth that wins the pennant. Stories are legion about fans leaving before a game is over thinking that their team has lost only to hear about an amazing rally to win at the last second.

This philosophy doesn't apply only to team competition, it works for individuals as well. We can bring a premature end to our workouts by giving in to what seems to be inevitable. We may feel we can't pump our legs anymore in our weekend bike ride, or that we want to give up after two miles of our regular five-mile run, but if we pause for a moment and keep pushing we will find that we have it in us to keep going. We have to keep in mind that the apparent outcome doesn't necessarily have to be so. An aerobics class or a run may be going badly, but there is almost always time to pull it out at the end and transform what looked like a decided failure into a success.

◆

I will follow through to the very end no matter what the outcome appears to be.

> I am confidence. I never give up.
> —*Arantxa Sánchez Vicario*

*T*enacity backed with faith in ourselves is an almost unbeatable combination and is the ideal ingredient in the formula for success. Our belief in what we can accomplish will take us to a certain level of performance, and it will help us to continue to improve and grow. Add in a "never say die'" attitude and we will be consistently well armed for victory.

There are countless times when giving up or giving in seems to be the only sensible option. In the face of a strong competitor or seemingly insurmountable odds we've all thrown in the towel. Unfortunately, we have probably sold ourselves short in the process. We haven't allowed ourselves to try everything we are capable of to keep on going. We have cheated ourselves because we have given up on ourselves. Sometimes we quit because we have a shaky hold on how confident we can be about ourselves. But it's at those times that we should dig in and fight even harder. Failure can become a self-fulfilling prophecy. The next time we will think, "Well, I couldn't do it last time, so I won't be able to do it now," further diminishing our confidence. Our willingness to keep fighting will help our confidence to grow. As our confidence grows it will bolster our desire to keep on going. In other words, the more we fight, the stronger the fight in us will be.

◆

Never say die.

The taste of defeat has a richness of experience all its own.
—Bill Bradley

Remember "The thrill of victory . . . and the agony of defeat"? For years sports television viewers who watched the "ABC Wide World of Sports" introduction witnessed the fate of the wayward ski jumper as the announcer intoned, ". . . the agony of defeat." While most of us have never experienced a loss quite so dramatic, we have all experienced defeat in one way or another, and it often smarts, if not physically at least psychologically.

Defeat is not limited to what we experience when we lose in competition. Defeat is also not completing a training session as successfully as we had hoped, not running as fast or as far in our morning jog, or falling short of a number of workouts per week goal. All of these occurrences may make for discouragement; however, fortunately, these feelings shouldn't last, and once we get over the initial disappointment we should be able to use what we've just experienced as a learning tool for the next time. The sooner we can process the loss, and then get over it, the sooner we can move forward toward improvement.

An off-day on the basketball court, a run where our legs feel like lead, or a real wimp-out at the gym are all likely to happen once in a while. It's important to take from these experiences only what we need, throw out the rest, and move on.

◆

A poor performance happens every once in a while. I will learn what I can from this experience and quickly move on.

Whenever I get to a low point, I go back to the basics. I ask myself, "Why am I doing this?" It comes down to passion.
—*Lyn St. James*

We've all reached low levels of energy and motivation, when we question our participation in athletics because we're bored, in a slump, or are just not enjoying ourselves. The thing about sports, however, is that they should be fun. They should challenge us, yet be a positive overall experience. Sports and fitness should teach discipline and perseverance, yet should also be a healthy outlet for extra energy and activities we look forward to.

Even professional athletes, and maybe *especially* professional athletes because of the huge time demand, go through periods of discouragement, boredom, and frustration. But as top race car driver Lyn St. James says, that's the time to take a close look at what motivates us. Hopefully it's the love of the sport, or the exhilaration from the exercise, not a negative factor like peer pressure or obsession with our weight. It's the greatest feeling to be working out at our peak and thoroughly enjoying ourselves in the process. When this is not the case much of the time, it's important to examine our motivation and be sure we are doing the right activity for the right reason.

◆

Why I exercise is as important as whether I do it at all. Today I'll look at the reasons why I work out and make sure they are positively motivated.

I know it [the final round of the 1993 U.S. Open] will be tough. I'm just going to go out there like I did today and give eighteen holes of the best concentration and effort I can.
—*Lee Janzen*

*T*he times when we're faced with the toughest challenges—the squash opponent we've never beaten, the hill we've never run all the way up, or the time we've never beaten—are the times when we really have to hunker down and go for it, calling on all of our mettle and muscle. We have to focus our energies, clear our minds, and psych ourselves up to meet the challenges head on.

When the obnoxious buzz of the 6:30 A.M. alarm clock can barely get us to move, let alone wake us for a morning run; when the cold, damp weather forecast makes us want to bag our round of golf; and when the thought of going to the gym on our lunch break is about as appealing as sitting through a budget meeting, we need to dig down deep for the motivation to give us the jump-start we need. Many times these tough situations bring out the best performances and, ultimately, the most satisfaction. We just have to heighten our confidence and put out the best effort that we can at the time.

◆

When the going gets tough, I get going.

You have to set the goals that are almost out of reach. If you set a goal that is attainable without much work or thought, you are stuck with something below your true talent and potential.
—*Steve Garvey*

*S*etting goals can be a very tricky business. Too high and we will never reach them. Too low and we will get there but we really haven't challenged ourselves. So how do we figure out where our next goal should be? Sometimes it involves a lot of trial and error and a little common sense. If we can comfortably run three miles, our next goal should be to run four. If our racquetball partner beats us every game, we can try a new strategy and see if we can edge up on her. We may want to beat her the next time we play, but that may not be realistic for now. We need to start somewhere because we can't do it all at once. Starting somewhere could also involve taking a lesson or a class that can help us to put our dreams into action. It's also important to keep moving those goals up. When we hit one then we can move on to the next one. Beware of goals that are a cinch to meet. The ones that we can do easily usually aren't a test of what we can really do. We need to be sure to reassess our goals often and keep striving for whatever is just out of reach.

◆

My goals will be ones that I can work toward and that will really make me work.

> I always felt that my greatest asset was not my physical ability,
> it was my mental ability.
> —*Bruce Jenner*

*T*hat's pretty surprising, since after winning the 1976 Olympic decathlon Bruce Jenner was considered the best athlete in the world, and one would expect an athlete of his caliber to feel especially confident of his physical strengths. Obviously for Jenner his success was a combination of physical and mental skills that worked exceptionally well together.

Every athlete has physical and mental abilities, yet rarely does an athlete receive accolades for good mental fitness. It may be acknowledged, but it doesn't appear to be as valuable as good old-fashioned muscle.

However, the closer we look, the more we uncover about the value of good psychological fitness both in training and in competition. It may be the simple act of visualizing ourselves running a race or successfully making a shot that is challenging. Or it may be repeating an affirmation that gives us the confidence to perform or even meditating before we step out onto the field, track, or court. No matter what the technique, our skills will be greatly enhanced by working out both our muscles and our minds as we pursue our athletic endeavors. There's more to athletic success than just *physical* fitness.

◆

Today I will work out my mind in ways that will enhance my body's performance.

Any time you try to win everything, you must be willing to lose everything.
—*Larry Csonka*

It's no fun to play if we are always playing it safe. There are definitely times when we need to be a little conservative, to not take a flyer or a big risk, but we can't be that way all of the time. If we are not willing to risk, we will not be getting any big rewards in return.

If we always hold something in reserve, we will never really know what we are capable of. What are we waiting for? Every day is an opportunity to test our limits and find out how much we can gain. It's easy to be content with the same old routine, but we will never stretch and grow if we don't test those limits.

If we find ourselves turning in consistent, solid performances, that's the time we should shake things up by taking a risk or two. Let's say we have worked up to a certain number of miles each day when we bike. We could continue to do that particular distance at that particular pace for the rest of our lives. Or we could be willing to challenge ourselves and to try to do it a little faster or to extend the mileage. By taking these chances we will not only make our workouts more interesting, we will get our bodies working harder or differently and give our fitness program a little lift.

◆

Today, I will be willing to go for more.

In sport, mental imagery is used primarily to help you get the best out of yourself in training and competition. The developing athletes who make the fastest progress and those who ultimately become their best make extensive use of mental imagery. They use it daily as a means of directing what will happen in training, and as a way of pre-experiencing their best competition performances.

—*Terry Orlick, author of* In Pursuit of Excellence

We can all benefit from using mental imagery in our training and competing, regardless of our skill level. By mentally running through our workouts beforehand, seeing every shot on the tennis court, every hill on our bike ride, and every curve on our run, we are, in effect, practicing in advance. In so doing, we are preparing our bodies and minds for what may lie ahead and perhaps even figuring out how best to handle certain challenges.

Professional athletes often use mental imagery before competing to anticipate the course of a tennis match, running race, or basketball game. By visualizing potential moves by our opponents, we are then able to rehearse our own responses. Likewise, if we have a certain strategy in mind, we can try and guess the various ways our opponents might react and develop an effective defense.

Even though we might not physically lift a finger while mentally practicing, we are, in fact, giving our minds a terrific preworkout that almost always translates to success on the field, court, course, or track.

◆

I will visualize success in today's workout.

> When you're riding, only the race in which you're riding is important.
> —*Bill Shoemaker*

Now is the only thing that counts in sports. Whether you're working out or competing, the only thing that matters is what is happening at the moment. If you're in a 10K footrace or a step aerobics class, a tennis match or a basketball scrimmage, that's where your mind should be, and there only. Hall of Fame jockey Bill Shoemaker would race in several races a day, yet each race was an individual event for him. He would focus on the current race only—not the one he just won, nor the next one on the card.

A relief pitcher who loses a game one night and is called upon the next day to save a win for his team cannot be thinking about what went wrong the night before; he's got to deal with the task at hand. For the tennis player who must meet an opponent she recently lost badly to, spending time reliving that loss in the current match would surely be detrimental. Or, finally, the runner who is facing a killer hill that in the past has meant stopping to walk can't think about the last time—every approach should be a new challenge.

Every competition or workout is a brand-new chance to improve and learn. It's important to approach the starting line, first serve, or tee off with a clear and focused mind.

◆

Today's workout or competition is the most important—
I will concentrate on it only.

I don't consider myself a home-run hitter. But when I'm seeing the ball and
hitting it hard, it will go out of the park.
—Ken Griffey, Jr.

*I*t's funny how we sometimes don't see our own abilities clearly. Or how we resist labeling ourselves just in case we can't live up to the advance billing. How many times have we said, "Well, I'm not an athlete, but I run and swim and work out and . . . "? We have to remember not to sell ourselves short and to acknowledge our accomplishments, because we have spent long hours and hard work earning them. Do we think of ourselves as beginners when we are really intermediates? Do we consistently run eight-minute miles, yet label ourselves a ten-minute miler? It is worthwhile periodically to examine how we refer to our level of performance. When we take a close look, we may be surprised to find that we are stronger and more accomplished than we thought.

In many cases, before we can feel comfortable saying we have certain skills, we need to work up to a level of play. There may be some days when we deserve to be called a "home-run hitter" and other days when we fall short. But we have the ingredients to hit that mark. We know how to see our goals and put our power behind whatever we want to be.

◆

I will rethink my opinion of my abilities.

I've been in a lot of trouble and come out of it. I think it shows a lot of good character.
—Stefan Edberg

It takes a lot of strength to come back from being in a losing situation. It can feel like the easiest thing to do is to give up, believing that we can't overcome. It is easier to quit, but quitting makes it much harder for us to ever be able to win. Yet, if we can suck it up and get back on track, we will be able to recover. It is easy to have strength of character when we are being successful. It is much harder to keep ourselves psyched and believing in ourselves when we are down. When we don't make the effort to come back, we are conceding the win before the game has been played out. In this situation we haven't been beaten, we have beaten ourselves.

In many cases we set ourselves up for a loss before we ever begin. We don't think we could ever run that far, lose that weight, or learn to play that game. The minute we run into a little trouble we are the first to say, "See, I told you I couldn't do it." It takes guts to dig in our heels and refuse to be beaten or at least to go down giving it our best shot. The good ones may get knocked down, but they don't stay down for long.

◆

I will have the courage to dig in and fight back from being down.

When I was young, I never wanted to leave the court until I got things exactly
correct. My dream was to become a pro.
—*Larry Bird*

Larry Bird's dream became a reality. He didn't get to the pros by just sitting
around dreaming—he supported that dream with action and perseverance. And
once he achieved that dream he continued to dream, as well as to reach higher
and higher to become a superstar basketball player.

Dreaming is an excellent way of setting goals for ourselves. When we tap into
our hearts' desire, we have created a powerful goal to strive for. However,
having a dream isn't enough, because dreaming alone won't make it happen. Our
dreams need to be fed with conscientious practice and hard work. When we set
our sights on a goal, we are making a commitment to do whatever it takes to
make that dream come true. That commitment has to be followed up by daily
attention. This doesn't mean that we have to spend every waking hour working
out or thinking about our goal—that would be impossible and we'd burn out very
quickly. It does mean that when we are working on that goal all our energy
should be focused in that direction. We also need to make the time to work on
our dreams and not give up because we don't feel like working. A solid short
workout is better than a long, lazy, distracted workout any day.

◆

My dreams are important and I will give them the attention they deserve.

Forget the past. Workouts done years ago bear no relevance to what you can do today—and can be a cause of injury if you try to duplicate them without your past level of fitness.

—Hal Higdon, author of Run Fast

Who hasn't been through the routine of laying off from exercise for a while, whether for an injury or just being in need of a break, and then trying to jump right back in where we left off? We then are unable to run at the same pace for the same distance, shoot as many consecutive free throws, throw the softball as accurately, or swim as efficiently, and get upset and frustrated with ourselves because of our mediocre performance. "Gee," we say, "I used to be able to run five miles," "My arm has always been so accurate, I wonder what the problem is," or, "I'm so out of shape—what's the matter?"

Basically what has happened is that we have discovered we can't take time off from working out or competing and expect to come back at exactly the same level we left off at. What we forget is that it took us a while to get to the previous level in the first place, and when we take a break we have to allow for a catch-up period. For those who work out regularly and are forced to take time off, this is especially frustrating. We need to keep reminding ourselves that we will return to our previous level in time, and rushing to be there too soon can only result in disappointment and possibly injury.

◆

What I've done in the past is not as relevant as what I'm doing now and not as important as what I'll do in the future.

I didn't play my best golf. But I won because I played a little bit better than everyone else.
—*Patty Sheehan*

Your best isn't always what is needed to be successful. In many cases your success will depend on who or what your opposition is and how you match up against them. You don't have to be a hundred times better than your opponent or even 50 percent better. Sometimes all it takes is a small margin to win. Some of the most exciting games come out of evenly matched contests where one player has just that little bit of an edge over her opponent that allows her to pull ahead. If you are consistent in the way you play (including practice), your best will always be at a higher level than anyone else's. That way, even if you play slightly below your absolute best, you will, in most cases, be successful.

It's not always the flashiest player who wins. More often than not it is someone who can judge the competition and adjust her play to that of her opponent. It's not necessary to blow your opponent out of the water to be the winner. It is a bona-fide win no matter if it is by a landslide or a tiny margin.

◆

I will always play a little better than my opponents.

My father taught me that the only way you can make good at anything is to practice and then practice some more. It's easy to practice something you're good at, and that's what most people do. What's tough is to go out and work hard on things you don't do very well.

—Pete Rose

It is so much more fun to practice the things we are adept at. There is a lot of satisfaction in sinking that putt that we do so well or effortlessly making turns down the ski slope. It's also natural that we are drawn to what we can do with relative ease. But it doesn't necessarily challenge us or give us an opportunity for improvement.

It is much harder to work on the things that are not automatic or comfortable. When we try to correct our weaknesses it may feel like it's a constant reminder of what we can't do well. Try thinking of it as becoming much more balanced. It is also a great way to discover some of our hidden talents. There may be some things we haven't attempted because we just assumed we couldn't do them. By taking on some of the things that we don't do well we will undoubtedly surprise ourselves. The hard work we put into improving ourselves will eventually get results. We will become more balanced players, we will build our confidence, and we will definitely improve our overall performance.

◆

I will take on some of the things I don't do well.

With confidence, you can reach truly amazing heights; without confidence, even the simplest accomplishments are beyond your grasp.
—*Jim Loehr, author of* Mental Toughness Training for Sports

With confidence we can run faster and farther. We're more coordinated. We're stronger, calmer, more focused and effective. Our jump shots go through the hoop without touching the rim. Our backhands go down the alley without being touched by our opponent. Killer exercise classes are not a problem; nor are brutal hills on a bicycle. Confidence gives us the mental and physical edge we need to perform to peak.

On those days when confidence seems to be lacking, so do our skills. We feel discombobulated, spastic, ineffective, and just plain out of sorts. Maybe our confidence is down because we're tired or have had a bad day in other aspects of life. Or maybe we recently lost badly to an opponent. Or maybe we're tackling a new exercise or move and are having trouble mastering it. No matter what the source, this unwelcome ebb in confidence level is disconcerting and discouraging.

It's important to keep our confidence on the rise—positive affirmations are one way. We know we can get the job done, and with an upbeat outlook, we're more likely to do it.

◆

I'm confident in my athletic ability, and today I will work out or compete with that positive outlook.

Every time—all the time—I'm a perfectionist. I feel I should never lose.
—Chris Evert

This attitude got Chris Evert to the top of the world of women's tennis, kept her there, and made her a legend. But in all her years of tennis, she did lose, more than once. There is a fine line between having confidence ("I am a winner") and being too much of a perfectionist ("I will never lose"). Losing isn't something that we have to like, but it is something that we have to face. If we give too much power to losing, we can find ourselves permanently beaten instead of just temporarily beaten. If we strive only for perfection, we are demanding too much from ourselves.

If we can never accept that we may make mistakes or fail, we are ignoring a fundamental part of the game. Perfection, even for a professional athlete, is too much to ask. It cannot be achieved. If we demand perfection of ourselves every day, every workout, every time, we will be disappointed. And when we get disappointed in ourselves we will become discouraged and give up—then we will be perfectly unhappy.

We need to be wary of demanding too much from ourselves and trying for unreachable goals. We will not only become discouraged but we will miss all the great things we are doing now—slightly less than perfectly.

◆

Perfection is an illusion—I will not be misled by it.

You've got to love what you're doing. If you love it, you can overcome any handicap or the soreness or all the aches and pains, and continue to play for a long, long time.
—Gordie Howe

There is a huge difference between playing a game because we love it and playing it because we feel we have to. When we love a sport, it adds another dimension to the way we play. When our hearts are in it, we bring all of ourselves into the game. If our love for the sport or competition or for simply working hard is activated, we are on the top of the world. Sometimes it's easy to forget what we love about exercise because we get caught up in what it is doing for us. It's easy to observe the difference in other people. The ones who have a true love of exercise are easy to spot—they are the ones with smiles on their faces. The smile doesn't necessarily come from winning, either. You'd be surprised, however, at the correlation between those who play with their hearts and those who win.

Having heart and love of our sports can get us through some difficult challenges. Sometimes heart keeps us driving when the physical and mental odds seem stacked against us. No matter what our situation, love of sports keeps us forever finding ways to challenge ourselves, either by reaching new heights in what we are already doing or by looking for new arenas in which to expand our abilities.

◆

I will find what I love and do it.

When someone tells me there is only one way to do things, it always lights a fire under my butt. My instant reaction is, "I'm gonna prove you wrong."
—*Picabo Street*

Inspiration can come from many different angles. Proving someone wrong can be a powerful way to get ourselves going. But that's not the only reason to work out. There isn't one right way to do anything. There are some standard practices —such as the way you put on or use your equipment—but from there on out it's anybody's game.

The way we play our best is to find our own style. No two tennis champions serve exactly the same way. The mechanics may be similar, but through practice and experimentation they have found what works best for them and have put their personal touch into how they play. This doesn't mean we can't learn from someone or follow someone else's example. One of the best ways to learn is to have someone show us how she does it. Remember that it's only an example, not a blueprint. Under certain conditions or circumstances we may want to respond differently or try a different tactic. It's impossible to play exactly like anyone else. We can have a similar style or form, but no matter what, we'll still be ourselves. And there is nothing wrong with that. One of the most rewarding experiences we can have is to discover and develop our own style.

◆

I will find the way that's best for me.

Besides pride, loyalty, discipline, heart, and mind, confidence is the key
to all the locks.
—Joe Paterno

*W*hile there are many traits that contribute to success—in business, academics, or athletics—none seems to come up more often and carry as much weight as self-confidence. The executive who's preparing for an important presentation, the student who's preparing for an oral exam, and the athlete who's preparing for a tough workout or match all need self-confidence to help them perform to the best of their abilities.

No matter how well we did in our last practice, no matter how sharp our skills are, and no matter how pumped we are to compete, if we step out onto the field or floor or court with less than optimum confidence, we could be in for disappointment. It's sometimes astonishing how much attitude can affect performance—from the boardroom to the ball field, we can almost count on a good showing if we can face our challenges with a positive outlook.

◆

I will tackle today's workout with self-confidence and make it a good one.

When I am on a streak, I'm confident and . . . I could stand on my head and [get a] hit. When a player's going bad, he thinks too much and gets himself out.
—*Gary Carter*

Feeling as if we can do no wrong is an unbelievable experience. No matter what happens, things seem to go our way. This "luck" is often the culmination of lots of practice and hard work and is the dream of every athlete.

When we are on a streak we will do anything to stay on it (some people even resort to lucky charms or particular warm-up rituals to keep themselves on a streak). Paradoxically, many people fall off a winning streak when they start trying too hard to stay on. Sometimes thinking too much can be a dangerous thing. When we start thinking about every move we make and how important our continued success is to us, we may soon find ourselves making unforced errors. Overthinking or overanalyzing our performance isn't helpful. Yes, it is good to reflect on what we have done in the past and plan what we want to do in the future, but if we spend too much time thinking, we won't be able simply to react. Part of the confidence that leads to getting on a streak is trusting in our own abilities to respond to any given situation. If we take the time to think about it, we will miss our opportunity.

◆

I won't think myself out of a winning streak.

> I got where I am with sufficient talent and then simply by wanting it more and
> working harder to get it. And to keep it.
> —Dennis Conner

It's not always the best athlete who wins. We've all been intimidated by the skills and abilities of our opponents that we can't ever imagine ourselves attaining. Having talent helps, but that talent needs to be backed up with desire and hard work.

We've all known that "go for it" athlete. She's not the best player on the team, but she gives 100 percent every time and makes an invaluable contribution. She's always a contributor because she gives her all in every practice and every game. She doesn't get discouraged because she isn't as talented as some of the other players. She knows her strengths and she plays them to her advantage by using her head. She thinks more and works harder.

Wanting to improve or win should be an important part of our athletic endeavors. We may never play in competition, but we can still use that desire to our advantage. We may not have natural abilities, but by working hard we can accomplish a lot.

◆

I know that I want it and I'm willing to work hard to get it.

Losing doesn't eat at me like it used to. I just get ready for the next play, the next game, or the next season.
—*Troy Aikman*

No one likes to lose. Not NFL quarterback Troy Aikman, not the player in the local tennis tournament, not the neighborhood Little League team, not the weekend golfer. Fortunately, most of us don't have to worry about losing in front of thousands of spectators as Aikman does. However, we all do lose occasionally, and are forced to find a way to deal with it. And facing a loss can be difficult and can hinder future successful performances if not handled properly.

In a perfect world, whenever we suffered a loss, we'd learn from it, leave the loss behind, and move on. Unfortunately, that's not so easy to do. Too often we get hung up on thinking about our mistakes and missed opportunities and don't spend time looking forward to our next workout or competition and how we can succeed then. Instead we continue to look back, distracted, and not perform to our potential. We need to do an about-face. Any loss or failure to meet a goal is just that, and should be used not to self-deprecate but to psych us up to do better next time.

◆

When I fail to meet a workout goal or suffer a loss in competition, I will try to learn from the experience and then move on, looking forward to my next chance to work on my skills.

> Guys around the league make jokes about how hard we practice. And sometimes, in the middle of four or five hours of running, you're thinking, "Yeesch, this is ridiculous."
>
> —*Doc Rivers*

But NBA players don't make jokes when Doc Rivers's team, the New York Knicks, beats them for a spot in the basketball playoffs. And the Knicks themselves probably don't think that all that practicing is ridiculous when it pays off. Professionals don't let up. They have to practice harder than the rest of us because they are doing it for a living—not just for recreation. The recreational athlete isn't getting paid to exercise, but she is getting other, very valuable rewards. Exercise is an unbeatable tension reliever, and there is nothing better for the heart and lungs and muscles. But it doesn't work unless we do.

Hard work will get us a measurable return on our investment of our time and energy. We may have days when we think, "Why am I doing this?" It's a valid question to ask ourselves. The answer can help us determine just how much work we need to do. Then we can adjust our workouts to meet our goals. When we raise our aspirations, we will also need to increase the intensity and duration of our workouts. "Four or five hours of running" is unrealistic for the average athlete. If a sport is not our job, we do not need to spend that much time at it. Overkill is just going to exhaust us or injure us.

◆

Hard work gets me where I want to go, but I have to match
my workouts to my goals.

Great works are done when [one] is not calculating and thinking.
—*Zen master D. T. Suzuki*

While a lot can be said about the problem-solving powers of active endorphins, and while it is true that countless brilliant ideas have been born as a result of adrenaline pumping, peak athletic performance usually occurs when the mind is clear and still—a clean slate, at once taking in everything and nothing. We're not using the brain to figure out a tough situation at the office, nor is it overthinking a personal issue. We simply allow it to enjoy the freedom of few intellectual demands, and we benefit from the extra physical boost we seem to get by doing so.

Struggling with a difficult problem while exercising may be helpful for brain-storming solutions; however, it may hinder athletic performance by taking up a lot of our energy. That's not to say that using exercise time to figure things out is a bad idea—in fact, it can be quite beneficial—it's just that every once in a while it's good to work out with a clear mind, giving ourselves the potential to perform at a higher level. It's during these exercise sessions that we're most apt to see and be encouraged by marked improvement.

◆

Today I will allow myself to work out with a clear mind, not one clogged with problems to solve and issues to address.

I don't care how good you play, you can find somebody who can beat you, and I don't care how bad you play, you can find somebody you can beat.
—*Harvey Penick*

Well, now there's an eye-opener. But how true it is, and how well we can use it to our advantage.

Have you ever felt unbeatable, the best, at the top of your sport, only to be unexpectedly felled by a hungry competitor or even a challenging workout? Maybe you had let your workouts slip a little, or maybe you were distracted and not fully participating. There's nothing like an unexpected defeat to shake you up and get you back on track.

The same can be said for a hard-earned victory. Sometimes it feels as if all the practice and concentration will never pay off, until finally we have a big win, either over an opponent, a coach, or a stopwatch. It gives us a big lift. We have made progress. We are improving. We want to get out there tomorrow and continue working.

◆

Today I will work hard on my skills, knowing that there are opponents of all levels out there. I'm not the best, and I'm not the worst, but I'm a good athlete who will continue to look for challenges as I improve.

Winning isn't everything, but wanting to win is.
—*Vince Lombardi*

We can't win every single time. No one ever has, no one ever will. For every undefeated season or championship year there are plenty of games lost. We can, however, always want to win. Part of wanting to win is deciding just what a victory is. Obviously in team or individual competition winning is determined by the final score on the scoreboard—or is it? Sometimes the final score doesn't tell the whole story. A team may not have won the game, but one of the players may have achieved a personal best performance. Or it may have been the first time the team got to that level of competition. They may have won on an entirely different level than that of numbers or score.

Wanting to win doesn't just apply to team or one-on-one competition. Often we can be our own best competitors. Victories can come in all different forms. We can win by beating our best time for our usual run, increasing our reps on the Nautilus machine, or by simply making it through a tough aerobics class. Wanting to win can get us over the hump to success on our own terms.

There may have been times when we really wanted to win and didn't come out on top. It does happen. If we have wanted something and it didn't turn out exactly the way we wanted it to, we should take another look. We may well have scored a victory on another level.

◆

I will always want to win but will recognize that the final score doesn't always tell the whole story.

I've always got such high expectations for myself. I'm aware of them,
but I can't relax them.
—*Mary Decker Slaney*

*T*he demands we put on ourselves can break us down mentally and physically. Even if we are mentally tough, we may put ourselves at physical risk if we push ourselves beyond our endurance. It is one thing to dig into our guts to pull out a last-minute rush; it is quite another to force ourselves to play when we are injured or unwell. Expectations can be tricky things. If we don't demand enough of ourselves, we will not perform well. If we demand too much of ourselves, we will not perform well, either.

Are your goals realistic? Or are you driving yourself to do something that is clearly beyond your reach? Do you need to exercise a little patience with yourself? Are you trying to attain a goal that realistically needs more time to complete than you are allowing yourself? While it is important to keep reaching for higher and higher goals, you can ensure that you will never reach them if you try to do too much too fast. When you examine your expectations, you need to evaluate them objectively. Are they actually preventing you from doing your best by keeping you constantly discouraged? If you give yourself some slack, you may find that you will do better than you ever did when you were driving yourself to achieve.

◆

I will develop realistic expectations for myself so that I can develop my abilities.

Most games are lost, not won.
—*Casey Stengel*

If you've ever won a squash game and perhaps felt you weren't playing your best; or your softball team beat another squad despite not working all that well together; or you won a running race that another runner seemed to have in the bag, then you know what Casey Stengel is talking about. While your or your team's performance may have been good, it was probably far from flawless, yet you still triumphed. Unfortunately, this was probably due more to your opponent's errors than your dominance. But don't get complacent, because chances are next time the shoe will be on the other foot.

There isn't an athlete alive who has ever escaped this predicament, so the best we can do is be aware of it and hope to head it off. (The next best thing we can do is jump in there and take advantage of an opponent when it strikes his game.) Because so much of athletics is mental, our heads are often what mess us up the most. Choking, loss of confidence, lack of concentration, psyching out, and low motivation are just a few of the perils that face us. If we pay as much attention to our mental fitness as we do to our physical fitness, we won't fall as often into the trap that Stengel describes.

◆

I will not win games for my opponent.

The best and fastest way to learn a sport is to watch and imitate a champion.
—*Jean-Claude Killy*

*F*rom childhood on, we use imitation as a way to develop athletic and other skills. From table manners to hitting a baseball, we have our very first lessons from those we consider "experts in the field." As adults, however, we sometimes forget the importance and effectiveness of imitation in learning.

Sometimes we can improve our skills by simply watching a pro or instructor or other talented athlete, either on television, on tape, or in person. He may give us a model of form or strategy that has been lacking in our game, stroke, or shot.

Whether it's a new dance move in exercise class, a tough tennis shot, advanced ski maneuvers, or footwork on the basketball court, it's remarkable how the brain records the moves we are seeing and then alerts the rest of the body as to what parts they will play in creating this new and improved skill.

◆

I'll watch another athlete perform my sport or exercise and try to learn something from him.

Nobody does it [climbs mountains] for scientific reasons. Science is used to raise money for the expeditions, but you really climb for the hell of it.
—*Sir Edmund Hillary*

We can never know exactly why people exercise or compete or pit themselves against the elements or enormous challenges. We may think they are doing it to gain knowledge or achieve glory, but looks can be deceiving.

Next time we are working out we should take a look around us. We will probably see people of all ages, shapes, and sizes who are working with everything from lazy inattention to incredible intensity. If we went around and asked them why they are exercising, we would get a wide range of answers. Many people go to the gym or run or exercise to lose weight or keep their hearts healthy. While they come to the gym with different intentions, they are all working hard to achieve a particular goal. They could be trying to get thin for an event or have been put on a workout schedule at their doctor's recommendation. No matter what inspired them to work out in the first place, the ones who will get the most out of their exercise are the ones who can't imagine *not* working out and who have a hell of a good time doing it. Sometimes the best reason for working out is "Just because . . ."

◆

Today I will do it just for the hell of it.

Now when I lose a match, I know I lose on the court—not in life.
—Gabriela Sabatini

It's hard not to let a loss affect our perspective on ourselves. We may feel that we've lost or failed when we don't make it all the way through an aerobics class or finish our run in a certain amount of time or at a certain distance. Well, we may not have achieved our goals for that particular performance on that particular day, but that doesn't mean we won't make our goals tomorrow or the next day. Beating up on ourselves won't get us around the track any faster. If anything, we will probably start believing that we won't be able to accomplish what we want to.

It's important to leave our losses on the court or at the gym. We should think of losing as something that happened at a particular time and in a particular place —it's not going to be with us forever. If we carry it around with us, it will undoubtedly affect our future games. It can also make us unsure of ourselves and make us lose confidence. However irrational, that mistrust of ourselves can creep into other areas of our life ("No wonder I can't get ahead—I can't even run three miles"). The best way to rebuild our confidence is to acknowledge the loss and learn from it. We don't have to give in it.

◆

A loss is never permanent unless I allow it to be.

> Baseball is fun. I love it.
> —*Wade Boggs*

*E*ven professionals play at their best when they enjoy what they are doing. When it is not fun anymore, it is time to quit. It is the same for the nonprofessional. If we are not having fun, then we are going to give up. Remember, however, that it isn't going to be fun every single minute. Workouts should be hard and challenging, which is actually part of the fun. Think of how great it is to be at the end of a particularly difficult workout, or how much fun it is to master a skill or achieve a goal that we have been working on for weeks. It's fun because it brings a smile to our faces along with a well-deserved sense of accomplishment.

No matter what our attitude, workouts and fun don't always seem to go together. Sometimes we turn our exercise routine into an inflexible, demanding regimen that doesn't allow us to enjoy ourselves while we are exercising. Remember when we were kids and we imagined that every at-bat was the bottom of the ninth in the World Series? Or that laps in the pool got us across the English Channel? Or that the fans went wild as we sunk a basket from way outside? Just because we are grown up doesn't mean we can't engage in a little creative daydreaming. It may be just what we need to smile, relax, and keep on working.

◆

I will remember to have fun even when I am "working" out.

You play the way you practice.
—*Pop Warner*

*T*here's a reason your football coach, swimming instructor, or tennis pro harped on you to practice, practice, practice. And there's an explanation for why he or she got on you for dogging it on the field, in the pool, or on the court. The effort that we put forth in our workouts translates into our performance in a competitive situation. In other words: Practice like a winner, play like a winner; work out below potential, compete below potential.

Regardless of our skill level, or whether we ever compete at all, we can benefit from always trying to give 100 percent in practice. If competition to us is a weekly softball game, 10K race, or round of golf, the workouts leading up to that day are best spent concentrating on honing skills and developing stamina. If, in fact, we never go one-on-one at all—our only opponents being ourselves or the clock—we'll still find value in workouts that are productive, effective, and effortful. Yes, sometimes it's hard to get motivated to work out at all, let alone to psych up for that extra umph, but, as football coach Pop Warner reminds us, the practice is as important as the play.

◆

Every effort should be 100 percent effort. Today's workout gets my full energy and attention.

I have no regrets because I know I did my best—all I could do.
—Midori Ito

Giving it your best shot is all that really counts. It doesn't matter if you are competing in a big race or match or working out at the gym. If you give your all you will never be disappointed. You may wish that the end result were different, but if you can ask yourself, "Did I try my hardest?" and answer "Yes," then you have done all that you can do. Winning or being the best isn't the only goal to strive for. If you can honestly say that you have made a 100 percent effort, then no matter what the outcome you can be proud of yourself.

There is nothing worse than walking away from a workout or a game wondering "what if?" You sell yourself short when you don't follow through all the way and push yourself to your limit. Sometimes when you feel you can't keep going you really need to dig in and not give up. Afterward you can pat yourself on the back for going the extra distance instead of beating yourself up for quitting. It may be that giving it your best shot isn't enough to win or be a success this time. However, you will discover that if you continually make your maximum contribution you will soon be rewarded.

♦

If I don't give up or give in, I'll have no regrets because I will have given my all.

You can get tired just doing one sport all the time.
The body loves variety. . . . It likes change.
—*Priscilla Welch*

Most of us have always switched around our workout activities if not day to day, then at least every once in a while. This sports rotation has a name—it's called cross-training, and everybody's doing it. No more do we feel the pressure to run seven days a week, play tennis day after day, or swim lap after lap without a time-out. Now we're encouraged to pursue different interests for more well-rounded, total body fitness, to help prevent injuries, to alleviate boredom, and to have more fun.

With cross-training we can run, bike, and swim, or we can take a funk class, karate lessons, and use the StairMaster. What you do is purely personal, although the idea is to combine sports or activities that work different parts of the body. A rigorous lower-body workout should be balanced with one for the upper body. A tough run should be followed by a turn on the rowing machine or a swim.

When our legs ache from too much cycling, or we're so sick of step class we could scream, it's time to add a little variety to the mix. It'll put the energy and motivation back into our workout programs.

◆

Variety is the spice of life, and cross-training is the variety my fitness regimen needs. Today I'll work out in a different way.

Concentration, Confidence, Competitive Urge, Capacity for Enjoyment
—Arnold Palmer's "4 C's of playing a better golf game"

When one of the most successful, if not *the* most successful, golfer of all time offers advice on playing a better game, it's certainly worth a moment of our time. Especially when his words of wisdom are transferable to all sports and to athletes of all levels.

Concentration: It's the ability to focus on the task at hand without being distracted by irrelevant stimuli. The better we can do this, the better we can do our workouts.

Confidence: The more comfortable we are with our skills and our ability to call on them as needed, the more confident we are. The more confidence we have, the more likely we will be able to play our game successfully.

Competitive Urge: Regardless of whether or not we actually formally compete, the competitive urge is a valuable trait that helps us grow and improve in skills and strategy. It's the desire to better ourselves as we go head-to-head with the clock, an opponent, or yesterday's workout.

Capacity for Enjoyment: Perhaps most important of all, this should be every athlete's goal as he or she works out or competes. When the activity is fun, we're bound to do better, and the better we do, the more we enjoy it. Exercise should not be drudgery—we should always try and make it a positive part of our lives.

◆

Today I'll look for all "4 C's"—concentration, confidence, competitive urge, and capacity for enjoyment—when I work out.

I start toward the plate, and I imagine myself putting the "sweet spot" in the hitting
area just as the ball is getting there. I see a line drive going to center field. It's
important to me to see myself putting that bat there and not swinging it. When I
visualize, I feel my approach and the contact.
—*Reggie Jackson*

Visualization is a great aid to achievement. It allows us to test our abilities
before they are being challenged for real. It also lets us plan our approach,
decide what we'll do in different situations, and reinforce the image and idea of
performing at our best. Visualizing can apply to all aspects of our workouts. We
can see ourselves flawlessly executing a perfect putt or a textbook dive, or we
can envision ourselves successful at the completion of our workout. We can imagine how good we will feel to have the hard work behind us. Seeing something in
our mind's eye will give us something to strive for.

Our minds and our imaginations are very powerful allies in every workout,
whether it's practice or the big game or if we are only doing it for ourselves.
When we picture ourselves breaking the tape at the end of a race, acing our
serve, or being ten pounds lighter, we are adding a strong influence to our
physical performance. Sometimes we have to do something in our minds before
we can do it in the gym.

◆

I will see it and I will do it.

To succeed at the level I want to . . . you have to be focused and serious.
You have to take a no-bulls*** attitude.
—Kent Steffes

To be the best at anything takes time, practice, and perseverance. To succeed in sports is no different. Professional athletes tell of hours of shooting hoops, serving tennis balls, running, or putting on their way to the top. There don't seem to be any shortcuts. Yes, some athletes are born with incredible gifts of coordination, strength, speed, and stamina, but they, too, work hard to maintain and improve in the never-ending quest to reach a peak.

Priorities, desires, and dreams are different for everyone, and are what make us individuals. No aspiration is more important or valid than any other, as long as it is pursued with an all-out effort. Whether we, too, hope to compete professionally or want to maintain a three-day-a-week gym schedule, run in weekly races, or lose a few pounds, we have to approach our goals with a tough-as-nails attitude if we really want to succeed.

◆

My fitness goals are important to me, and I will put in
an all-out effort to reach them.

> Only a man who knows what it is like to be defeated can reach down to the bottom of his soul and come up with the extra ounce of power it takes to win when the match is even.
> —*Muhammad Ali*

*L*osing isn't easy, but it can teach us some valuable lessons. Being defeated can teach us that we are capable of losing gracefully. It can also teach us that we want to do everything in our power not to be in the losing position again. When we have tasted defeat, we will know just what we need to do to avoid losing. Yes, there will always be someone who wins and someone who loses, but in any competitive situation there is nothing wrong with trying our best, and working our hardest, to be the one who is the winner.

Unfortunately, there are times when we will be fighting our hardest just not to lose. It's at these times that we will need to dig deep for that little extra that will carry us through to triumph. Sometimes it takes that extra challenge to bring out our best performance. When we are battling back from the brink of losing against someone who is our equal, we will do it because we know that a tie is unsatisfactory. When we know what has caused us to lose in the past, we will be able to find something within us that will take us to victory.

◆

I will dig deep and create a win from a loss.

Luck is what happens when preparation meets opportunity.
—*Darrell Royal*

Ever have one of those days when everything seems to go right? Athletic ability is at a high, and you feel coordinated, strong, quick, and effective. Whether you're competing or just doing your regular workout, it just seems effortless and enjoyable. It feels like your lucky day.

Chances are, we all experience this athletic euphoria every once in a while. All of our hours of practice and preparation finally seem to pay off in a single afternoon. Coach Royal explains it as the perfect meeting of preparation and opportunity. We have worked and worked on our skills and strategies and finally we are given the chance to let them show. The hours of tennis lessons pay off in winning a tough match against a previously unbeatable opponent. The miles of cycling show their importance in our finally making it to the end of our most challenging ride without stopping. The days of team practices seem worth it when we handily put away our opponents on the basketball court.

It's a wonderfully satisfying feeling to put in a good performance and get good results. It makes the preparation worthwhile and the need to watch for and seize opportunities obvious.

◆

Achievements will follow if I continue to practice hard and take advantage of opportunities that present themselves.

If you set a goal for yourself and are able to achieve it, you have won your race. Your goal can be to come in first, to improve your performance, or just to finish the race—it's up to you.
—*Dave Scott*

It's important to set goals for ourselves in all aspects of our lives. A level of achievement in our career, a resolution to eat better, or a challenge to lose or gain weight are all possible targets to aim for in day-to-day life. In sports, too, goals are extremely valuable as they help us chart our growth and accomplishments on a regular basis. Because goals are so personal, we should be in complete control of setting and aiming for them. And because we know our own abilities so well, we should be able to set appropriate and obtainable goals that provide a challenge but are not too far out of reach.

We should approach every workout and competition with a goal in mind. Not only will it serve to motivate us but it will also help us keep track of our progress. As professional triathlete Dave Scott implies, a goal can be anything from completing a workout without stopping to beating a time; outplaying an opponent to improving a stroke, shot, or serve. And when we meet these demands on a regular basis, we will feel more confident and be more apt to reach farther next time.

◆

I will set a goal for today's workout that is appropriately challenging and reasonably achievable.

It's not that all of us have to dedicate our life to our sport; rather, we can dedicate our sport to our life—approaching our training as a way of life which enhances virtually all the endeavors we undertake.
—*Dan Millman, author of* The Warrior Athlete

Athletics should be but a part of our full and well-balanced lives. Even professional athletes have to do their best to maintain other interests and fulfill other responsibilities. None of us should become obsessed with competing or working out, no matter what our skill or commitment level. Author and former Olympic gymnast Dan Millman has the right idea when he suggests we use sports as a way to enhance our lives—applying the benefits of fitness and competition toward some of life's other challenges.

The lessons we learn on the court, the field, the course, or the track can help us with issues we face at home, in the office, with friends, and with family. The challenges that arise in business or in pleasure can often be solved with the help of skills we have learned on the playing field. By making sports an important but not an all-encompassing part of our lives, we can achieve the greatest balance and reap the most reward.

◆

Working out is important to me, but I must remember to stay balanced, not letting any one thing dominate my life.

> I've never had to cheat. I get 'em with what I got.
> —*Dave Winfield*

Having confidence in our abilities allows us to trust that we can get the job done. Cheating is only for people who aren't good enough to win by their own merits and abilities. Any victory that is gained by cheating is only an illusion—it's not a real win.

Cheating isn't just about bending the rules to beat an opponent. We can cheat ourselves, too. Every time we don't put enough time and effort into our workouts we are cheating ourselves. Every time we question or doubt our abilities we are cheating ourselves. Every time we avoid working out we are cheating ourselves.

Cheating or even just cutting corners deprives us of an opportunity to learn just what we are capable of. If we give in to the impulse to cheat, we will soon find that we will rely on cheating instead of counting on our skills and experience to keep us going. We need to know that our abilities can make us successful in any situation we encounter. Cheating can't really get us ahead of anyone else or even of ourselves. Sooner or later it will catch up to us.

◆

I know that I've got what it takes and I don't need to take any shortcuts.

If you're not a little bit nervous before a match, you probably don't have the
expectations of yourself that you should have.
—*Hale Irwin*

Everyone gets the jitters now and then, and not just before a big game or
match. We feel nervous before giving a big presentation at the office. We get the
shakes before going out on a date or meeting someone new. Sometimes we worry
about starting a new job, taking a test, or delivering bad news. In most circumstances where we have a challenge facing us, and aspirations to perform to a
certain level, we will feel nervous and uncertain about how things will go. And
while we may exhibit various manifestations of being nervous in these situations,
usually the nervousness is not detrimental to our performance.

The same seems to hold true for preathletic nervousness. We approach each
and every match or workout with a goal in mind. We want to win two out of three
tennis sets, we want to swim for a personal record. We want to run faster,
jump higher, score more, and play more effectively. By putting this pressure on
ourselves we are saying, "I expect to perform to this level out there today. It
may be tough, but this is where I'm aiming." We're giving ourselves a target that
is a challenge and causes us a bit of initial anxiety. Yet it's important to keep our
expectations of ourselves high. It keeps us motivated and sufficiently on our toes.
It's when we don't feel those butterflies before a match that we should worry—
that could mean we're not pushing ourselves toward improvement as hard as we
could be.

◆

It's okay to be nervous before a big game or tough workout. It means I have set
a goal for myself that will be a challenge to reach.

> You can't just rely on talent to win.
> —*Scott Young*

We can be the most talented and skilled players or athletes in the world, but if we don't work at it, neither we nor anyone else will ever know how good we are. Talent that isn't shaped and forged by practice and training is talent that is wasted.

If we just rely on our natural abilities, we won't get very far. We have to go beyond our talents and draw on the other things we are made of—spirit, heart, and brains. When we play beyond our talent we will tap into those extra reservoirs that can take us over the top.

If we are talented, we owe it to ourselves to go as far as we can. The only way to do that is to challenge ourselves. Sometimes the best challenges to our abilities come from within. We are the only ones who can know how hard we are striving and how much of what we are doing comes from talent and how much comes from the pure adrenaline of really going for it.

◆

I will strive to play beyond my talent.

You learn you can do your best even when it's hard, even when you're tired and maybe hurting a little bit. It feels good to show some courage.
—*Joe Namath*

We don't often equate athletics with courage. But think about it—it takes courage to keep working out when we are tired and sweating and our muscles are aching and we can think of nothing we'd rather do than stop. It takes courage to take on new challenges and to keep improving, whether it's adding laps to our swim or lifting more weights or trying a new way of working out. It takes courage to make the decision to devote some time to our health and to improving our bodies. It takes courage to play a game against someone who is more skilled or more experienced than we are. It takes courage to keep going when we don't feel as if we are making any progress. It takes courage to admit when we need help or instruction or a break. It takes courage to win, and it takes courage to lose and then go out and play again.

Every day that we work out is an opportunity to recognize and build our courage. It will feel great to meet the challenges of working out, and it will feel even better to know that we can meet them head-on with no holding back. We possess the secret to success: courage.

◆

Even when it's hard (especially when it's hard), I will show my courage and keep on going.

I know that I'm never as good or bad as any single performance. I've never believed my critics or my worshippers, and I've always been able to leave the game at the arena.
—*Charles Barkley*

If we quit the first time we lose, we will never know if we are capable of winning. If we quit the first time we win, we will never know if we are capable of learning more about the game. One game doesn't determine who will win in the long run, and we can't learn everything there is to know about our abilities or our potential from one day's work.

There will be people who will praise us to the hilt and people who will never be happy with the way we play. The danger lies in taking one or the other extreme to heart. Listening too intently to our detractors may lead us to lose faith in ourselves. While it's great to hear encouragement from our supporters, it is helpful to take their praise with a grain of salt. If we begin to believe that we are "the best" and "the greatest," we may be tempted to not work as hard. When that happens we will almost surely lose. No matter the outcome of any contest—victory or defeat—we will be coming back another day, and it won't matter what happened the last time—today's game is the only one that counts.

◆

I will keep a level head when it comes to listening to my critics or my fans.

I've learned that you don't have to win first place to win.
—*Kim Zmeskal*

The biggest winners aren't always the ones with the blue ribbons and the gold medals. The biggest winners are the ones who make a commitment to improve and follow up on that commitment with action—consistent, positive action. The real winners are the ones with heart who give their all and work their best. They are the ones who take on every challenge with determination and spirit. True winners welcome the opportunity to learn something new, and they know that there is always something new to learn, no matter how long they have been exercising. Winners are always willing to share what they know with others.

Winners know their strengths and limitations and when to take a break and when to push ahead. Winners know that there can be lessons found in losing and that losing isn't the end of the world. Winners know that a loss is the risk they take for playing and are willing to take that risk—again and again. Winners are measured by the effort they make, not by the trophies they win. Winners never give up, no matter how hard it is to keep going. Winners may not be first in the standings, but if they are first in spirit and effort, they will never be losers.

◆

I am a winner.

It is better to throw a theoretically poorer pitch wholeheartedly, than to throw the so-called right pitch with feelings of doubt—doubt that it's right, or doubt that you can make it behave well at that moment. You've got to feel sure you're doing the right thing—sure you want to throw the pitch you want to throw.
—*Sandy Koufax*

Doubt has a way of creeping in without our noticing it. Suddenly, when we are doing something we have done hundreds of times before, we find ourselves thinking, "What if I can't do it this time?" "What if I don't do it right?" "I can't do this, can I?" Never mind that we really *do* know that we can. That flicker of doubt can throw us off enough to add a negative performance to our day. Confidence can help us to power through some of those doubts. Confidence can even wipe doubts out of the picture entirely. It can also help us to give 100 percent all of the time.

We can be successful if we put all our mental and physical effort behind whatever we play or however we exercise. If we hold back, even a little, we are cheating ourselves out of a potential maximum performance. Sometimes it's not so important what we do, it's how we do it and the attitude we have while we are doing it. If we know we can do it, we won't hold back because of doubt and fear.

◆

I know that I can do it right.

Visualization lets you concentrate on all the positive aspects of your game. It also bolsters your confidence and helps you focus on executing, not on thoughts that could distract you.

—*Curtis Strange*

Visualization is an effective and valuable training tool for athletes of all skill levels. We can obviously all benefit from any extra workouts we can get, and visualization is a great way to practice without ever having to lace up our shoes. Whether we play weekend golf, are an avid runner, or make a living as a professional ball player, we can use this mind/body technique to "see" ourselves performing our sport before we actually take to the field, course, track, or court. By using our "mind's eye" to work through a textbook move, we're actually practicing without even moving. Working on a tennis serve that has been a little off, a putt that is inconsistent, or the moves for an aerobics class that tend to challenge us is as easy as closing our eyes and seeing ourselves execute to perfection.

If we compete, we can anticipate and visualize our opponents' moves and our responses. How will we defend against an outside shot on the basketball court? At what point should we make our move in the 5K race? What is the best strategy for playing a serve-and-volley tennis player? Visualization is the rehearsal—competition is opening night.

◆

Before I work out today, I will visualize myself performing to the best of my ability—and then I will try to do the same.

> You always have to give 100 percent, because if you don't, someone, someplace,
> *will* give 100 percent and will beat you when you meet.
> —*Ed Macauley*

Even if we rarely compete, basketball great Ed Macauley's advice is worth heeding, for in order to continue improving and becoming more and more fit we need to keep challenging ourselves. And that means putting out a maximum effort while training as well as in the heat of competition.

It's clear that if we play in tennis or golf tournaments; run, cycle, or sail in races; or are part of a softball, basketball, or volleyball team, we need to keep up our motivation level and give our best effort so that we can perform to our maximum potential against opponents. What's not as clear is that even if we go head-to-head with other athletes infrequently, it's important to stay sharp, strong, and focused for those occasions when we do, as well as for those times when we challenge ourselves with a stopwatch or a goal.

◆

No matter how competitive I am, it's important to keep my game sharp, my skills
honed, and my energy high.

I had no idea what to expect. All I knew was I was going for the gold medal.
That was the dream.
—*Pablo Morales*

When we are going for our dreams we have to keep everything else in the background. Sometimes it is better not to speculate about what obstacles may stand in our way or what the competition may be thinking or doing. If we worry too much about the other guy, we can easily psych ourselves out. If we keep focused on the end result, everything we do should be geared toward that goal. If it is important enough to be a goal, it is important enough to work for. Sometimes we can't completely scope out the situation or anticipate everything that will happen. But single-minded focus will help us to overcome any unpreparedness we may feel.

In some cases not knowing what to expect can work to our advantage. Instead of thinking about other factors, we can just think about ourselves and the contribution we have to make to ensure that our dreams will come true. If we don't know exactly what to expect, we can prepare ourselves as best we can for any eventuality. If we enter into a competition prepared for anything, we will not be surprised by whatever our opponents throw our way.

◆

I will keep my focus on my dream and be prepared to do anything
to make it come true.

Losing is no disgrace if you've given your best.
—*Jim Palmer*

If you can walk off the tennis court, the baseball field, the track, or get out of the pool and feel confident that the performance you just exhibited was the absolute best you could have done, whether or not you came home with the trophy, you can be very proud of yourself. If after working out with weights, jogging a few miles, practicing your tennis serve, or hitting at the driving range you are sure that you just gave 110 percent to your workout, whether or not you achieved a personal best, you should feel good about your exercise program.

So much of fitness and participation in sports is about motivation and perseverance. We all deserve much more credit than we give ourselves for just getting out there and doing it in the first place. Just getting ourselves to work out on a regular basis, putting forth our best effort all the time, is a major achievement. And if we compete in our sport, every time we play and do our best we are truly experiencing what makes athletics so exciting and rewarding. Not everyone can bring home a prize or work out flawlessly all the time, but everyone can really go for it every time she hits the court, course, field, or track.

◆

I can be proud of myself every time I give my best.

The more I train, the more I realize I have more speed in me.
—*Leroy Burrell*

We won't know what we are capable of accomplishing unless we are willing to test our limits. Many of us hit a certain level and then believe we have gone as far as we can go and are content to accept our place. But complacency will not get us to achieve at our maximum potential.

Do you ever find yourself saying, "I could never . . ."? Well, you never will unless you try. Dare to set your sights a little higher. Be brave enough to make yourself work a little harder. Try taking on another workout partner or opponent who seems to be at a more advanced level than you. Take on the challenge of improving yourself. You may be surprised to find that you are much more capable than you first thought.

You may not have been making progress because you have hit your personal wall in that particular activity. Change things around a little bit and try something new. Work a new event or exercise into your regular fitness regimen. Change the way you work out or the order in which you do your training. Add an extra half hour or an extra day to your usual workout week. By pushing yourself a little harder or being a little more creative in the way you play you may discover some untapped talent.

◆

The more I put into my workouts, the more I will get out of them.

You can't tell someone to "Go for it," to be whatever they care to be, and at the same time be careful. If we all ride the safe road, who will we look up to?
—*Julie Krone*

We all have to take a turn in the fast lane and take some risks. If we just stay on the same old trail, we won't ever discover what fun we can have doing something other than our usual routine. In order for our workouts to pay off we have to spend some time working on our fitness program and our sport. Boredom can be very detrimental to an exercise routine. To keep things interesting it is important to try something new or to go out on a limb. The risk can be relative—for some it may mean taking up a new game, for others it could be entering a road race or other competition, for still others it could mean going from a beginner to an intermediate class. The important thing to remember is, even if you are not an example for someone else, you are the best example for yourself.

If you are constantly testing your limits, you will soon discover that they are always changing, and you will always need to adjust to keep up with yourself. You really are your own best competitor because you can set interesting, achievable goals and then pump yourself up to go for it.

◆

I will try the unbeaten path and take a risk.

To give yourself the best possible chance of playing to your potential, you must
prepare for every eventuality. . . . That means practice. . . . There are no shortcuts.
You must lay the proper foundation.
—*Seve Ballesteros*

Practice. Practice. Practice. It's so monotonous. Is there no way to avoid it? Maybe if I skip today I can catch up tomorrow. I don't really need to practice for my next opponent, I've beaten him before. I'll just take it easy in my workout so I can save my energy for when it really counts.

How many times have we heard ourselves bemoaning the need to practice? Sometimes it seems so boring. And so repetitive. Why can't we just go right to the real thing? Well, as professional golfer Seve Ballesteros implies, one can never get enough practice, especially if one wants to reach his potential in a sport. No matter how well we think we are returning serves on the squash court, there will always be someone who can whip the ball past us. No matter how many times we have practiced fielding grounders on the softball field, there will always be that occasional one-hopper that ties us up. No matter how many putts we have sunk from ten feet out, there will always be unforeseen conditions that may throw us for a loop.

We can never hit enough practice serves, do enough wind sprints, shoot enough free throws, or take enough batting practice if we really want to reach our peaks. It's long, hard work, but doubtless it's worth it.

◆

Practice, although draining at times, is invaluable in my quest
for reaching my peak.

I've always felt the pressure to win, but most of that pressure is from within.
—John Elway

Sometimes we set impossibly high standards for ourselves. We seem to apply more pressure to achieve on ourselves than we would on anyone else. At times we can be so tough that if someone else was telling us to do what we were telling ourselves we would think she was being unfair and unrealistic. Are you treating yourself fairly? Do you demand perfection? Do you allow yourself to make mistakes? Do you beat yourself up for falling short of the very high standards you have set? Pressure of that kind can destroy you. It can push you down so far that you can never rise above it.

Pressure isn't all bad, however. We sometimes need to lean on ourselves to get moving or get psyched to draw out our best possible performance. A little pressure can give us just the push we need to get off our butts and get moving. It is when the pressure crosses the line and gets to be too much that it can actually prevent us from playing our best. We must be careful to keep the amount of pressure we put on ourselves in check so that we can get the most out of our workouts and competition.

♦

I will be careful not to put too much pressure on myself.

I honestly believe it helps a pitcher not to let people know he's upset. To me, it would give the batter an advantage. If I never change my expression, he doesn't know if I feel good or bad.

—*Jimmy Key*

There are times when we are competing when we feel like crying in frustration, cursing in anger, or confronting our opponents. Then there are other times when we want to jump for joy, gesticulate to pump ourselves up, or yell out in excitement. Sometimes, however, the best strategy is to curb these outbursts, to keep ourselves calm and our opponents guessing. By maintaining composure in the toughest and most triumphant moments we will be able to stay on an even keel and not lose our concentration to any emotion, whether positive or negative.

When we're winning a game and playing extremely well, it's sometimes tempting to celebrate victory too early. Not only can this make us lose focus but it may serve to fire up the other team to get its act together. On the other hand, when we're in the unfortunate position of losing a game, a race or other match-up, we may have a tendency, consciously or unconsciously, to give up too soon, which is demoralizing for us and a signal to our opponents to move in for the kill.

Keeping our emotions in check while competing is usually a good strategy. It works in our favor, to the consternation of our opponents.

◆

When the heat is on, I will keep a calm, cool attitude.

Keep your mouth shut and let your racquet do the talking.
—*Rod Laver*

*T*he best way to prove our skills to ourselves or anyone else is not by "saying" but by "doing." Whether we run competitively, play recreational softball, or are a weekend tennis enthusiast, we'll receive a lot more respect from our colleagues by quietly and modestly performing at our best. A service ace, a personal-best time, and a solid double go a long way toward establishing our competence in our own minds as well as in those of competitors and workout partners.

We've all been annoyed by other athletes who constantly talk a good game but regularly fail to deliver. They trash-talk, they chatter, they embellish details of previous workouts and competitions. We find it distracting and irritating, especially when they can't seem to "put their money where their mouths are." A poised, self-confident, and modest athlete is usually a more successful athlete in the long run. He is also a more appealing and more sought-after opponent.

◆

I'm confident in my athletic ability and will let it prove itself.

No matter how good you are, there's a lot of luck involved.
—*Reggie Miller*

*S*ometimes it seems as though things are really going our way in our athletic endeavors. When we run we feel light and quick and efficient; on the tennis court we're nimble and agile and accurate; and while circuit training we have extra strength, endurance, and coordination. On the other hand, there are days when we feel we probably shouldn't have gotten out of bed, let alone laced up our athletic shoes and attempted a workout. We get a cramp in step class, are repeatedly off target on the golf course, and get a sideache while power walking. It seems like it's just not our day, and, in fact, it's probably not.

Regardless of our skill level or experience, on some days luck is with us, on some days it's not. Even top professional athletes go through spells of bad luck, when they are plagued by injuries, slumps, and bad breaks, as well as periods of extreme good fortune—whether as a result of favorable officiating, weather conditions, or any number of variables. Like the pros, amateur and weekend athletes of all sports face these same challenges and get these same opportunities.

We need to acknowledge that we cannot control the luck factor in both working out and competing, but we can enjoy the good fortune when it's around, while coping with, but not blaming ourselves for, the tough luck.

◆

There are certain things I can't control, and if today's not my lucky day, maybe tomorrow will be.

I succeed on my own personal motivation, dedication, and commitment. . . . My
mind-set is: If I'm not out there training, someone else is.
—*Lynn Jennings*

*T*he fact is, if you're not a professional or college athlete with a coach breathing
down your neck at practice every day, it's really up to you to motivate and train
yourself. And if it seems too cold to run, too wet to cycle, or too late for a round
of golf, you're the one who can make the decision to follow through or suffer the
consequences on game day.

It's not easy to force yourself to go to the gym after a long day at the office, or
to serve a couple of baskets of tennis balls when other options are more inviting,
or to get up in the morning to run when the thermometer is barely hovering
above freezing, but ultimately, you're the only coach you have, and the discipline,
dedication, and motivation have to come from within.

If it takes Lynn Jennings's approach of keeping in mind the fact that your
opponent is probably out there braving the cold, the dark, and the exhaustion,
then use that as the subtle kick in the pants you might need. Even if you're not a
regular competitor, you can still use the anticipation of future events to get you
out there.

◆

If I want to compete in my sport, I need to be practiced and prepared—since
chances are my opponents will be.

It's great to win, but it's also great fun just to be in the thick of any truly well and hard-fought contest against opponents you respect, whatever the outcome.
—*Jack Nicklaus*

*T*here is nothing quite like performing at our maximum. We will most often play our best when we are working to win against stiff competition. Playing against someone who isn't as good as we are can lead to victory, but it's a little hollow if we haven't had to fight for it.

It's easy to get completely lost in a hard-fought contest. Time goes by so quickly that the game may seem to end in a blink of an eye. The game seems to take on a time and personality of its own. When we are playing against someone and we are evenly matched, every point can be a joy—no matter if we win or our opponent wins. We can even take pleasure in her winning especially when we are playing at our hardest.

Sometimes a game can be such an even battle that it seems like we are both winning. And, in fact we both are when we are challenging each other, playing with intensity, and learning from each other.

◆

I will look for contests that will challenge me because the fun lies in the challenge not just in the winning.

I have always adhered to two principles. The first one is to train hard and get into
the best possible physical condition. The second is to forget all about the other
fellow until you face him in the ring and the bell sounds for the fight.

—*Rocky Marciano*

*H*ow many times have we lost a game or match before we've even begun?
Choked in a race before the starting gun has even been fired? Unfortunately,
most of us have probably had these experiences at least once. And if we think
back, we've probably had them because, unbeknownst to us at the time, we did
not adhere to at least one of boxing great Rocky Marciano's principles of success.

Principle 1: Train hard and get in the best possible physical condition. Well,
maybe we took our workouts a little for granted, didn't take our practice sessions
as seriously as we might have.

Principle 2: Forget about your opponent until the word "Go." Maybe we were
either overconfident or psyched out by our upcoming competition; either under-
practicing or getting so mentally worked up as to virtually paralyze ourselves.

No one is immune to losing, but preparation and proper focus will put the odds
more in our favor.

◆

My body should be prepared and my mind should be focused
to achieve my best performance.

*It's unbelievable how much you don't know about the game
you've been playing all your life.*
—*Mickey Mantle*

Sometimes the best time to take lessons is after we have been playing a sport for a while. There are a lot of things we may have missed when we were first learning the basics. We were probably so eager to get ahead and to be better that we may have skipped, or not completely understood, some valuable techniques, strategies, or concepts. When we revisit some of the fundamentals, because we are now an advanced/experienced player, we can take a lot more away from the lesson than we could when we were beginning. Taking a few lessons can also give us a new perspective on how much we do know about our activity.

We don't have to get into a formal instruction situation or commit ourselves to an entire series of classes. We can learn from playing with a different partner or opponent; we can change or add to our routine; we can read a book, rent a video tape, or simply watch other people do our sport. Teachers can come in all forms and formats; it's just a matter of finding the one that works best for us.

◆

There is always something to learn. I will try to learn one new thing today.

I always want to do the best that I can with the opportunities that God has given me. The only way that you can do that is to give yourself the chance to go as high as you possibly can. If you don't have the confidence in yourself and you don't have the desire to compete and move ahead, then you start to get stagnant. . . . If I fall a little bit short, then I'm still further ahead than if I hadn't reached at all.

—Don Shula

*I*n other words, better to have tried and failed than never to have tried at all. We all have potential in whatever we attempt, and not to push ourselves as far as we possibly can is to waste the talents and opportunities we've been given.

We should take full advantage of the chances we have to put forth our best effort. Every workout should bring out the best we can possibly do at the time—our best run, swim, ski run, tennis game, or weight-training session. Every competition should be the same, plus some. We're so fortunate to be able to do the things we can do that it's important we show our gratitude by doing our best each and every time we take the field.

◆

I'm thankful for the talent I've been given—I'll use it to its fullest every time I work out or compete.

> Forget about style; worry about results.
> —*Bobby Orr*

Sometimes we get too hung up about how we look in our aerobics class or on the tennis court; we worry about our running style and our golf swing; we fret over our technique on the soccer field and our efficiency while circuit training. We're concerned about what people think, how they're evaluating us, what they're saying. Basically, we're wasting a lot of valuable energy on issues that really make very little difference as to how effective we actually are.

While style and form are definitely relevant, especially as we're learning and trying to improve in a sport, it is far more important and encouraging to look at our progress. There have been dozens of highly effective professional athletes who have had rather nontraditional styles. Tennis player Bjorn Borg's strokes were not the picture-perfect smooth strokes that most of us are taught, yet he went on to be the top player in the world. Professional basketball player Rick Barry shot every foul shot from between his legs, yet had one of the best free-throw shooting percentages in the NBA. What if these two top athletes had been deterred by their unconventional playing styles?

If we are experiencing success with our game as is, we should be less concerned with how we look and concentrate more on how well we are doing or how we can improve.

◆

Today I'll think less about how I look in my workout and more about how well I do.

> When an athlete is injured, she must allow time to heal and
> then recondition and rebuild.
> —*Tracy Austin*

*W*hen we're injured our bodies are trying to tell us something, and it's very important to pay attention. Sometimes an energetic workout or a new routine will make our muscles feel sore. This is just our bodies getting used to a new level of activity or adjusting to using different muscles. It's a sign that we're working hard. At other times it's a sign that we have overworked ourselves and that we need to take a break. Sometimes a rest of a day or two will do the trick. Seeking medical attention can also help us to find out if we have a serious injury and, more important, what we can do to recover.

There are athletes who play hurt, but they aren't doing themselves any favors. Many of them, including tennis player Tracy Austin, had to learn the hard way about ignoring injuries. Coming back too soon after an injury may seriously limit the amount of time we can stay back. After being hurt we really need to take the time to protect ourselves from being injured again. We need to listen to our bodies—let them tell us how to work up, gradually, to what we were doing before we were hurt. It can be frustrating, but if we take it slow, we won't regret it in the long run.

◆

If injured, I'll take the time to allow myself to heal.

Don't try to perform beyond your abilities—but never perform below them.
—*Frank Robinson*

Do your best, but don't overdo it. We've all heard that advice. We're encouraged to perform to our potential—on the baseball field, the volleyball court, in our high-impact class, and in the pool—reaching as far as we can based on our skill level. We're told to set realistic goals and reach for them. Coaches, friends, and teammates tell us to "Go for it." We strive to play our best, run our fastest, get our best scores, and perform at our peaks. We're careful to stretch to our limits but not overdo it for fear of injury or exhaustion.

We should always take to the court, course, gym, or field with the intention of giving our best effort. A competitive event is more successful and a workout more fruitful when we have truly performed to the best of our abilities. We have set goals and aimed for them, and if we have fallen short, it's not for lack of trying. It simply means we must work that much harder the next time. Participation in sports is an ongoing challenge to us. We work hard to improve on a regular basis, while being careful to stay within the range of our skills. It's a learning process that relies on our own motivation and direction to make it work.

◆

Every effort is my best effort.

Competition is the spice of sports, but if you make spice the whole meal
you'll be sick.
—*George Leonard, author of* The Ultimate Athlete

Competition is a fun way to test ourselves. For many people, competition is the culmination of all of their training, practice, and workouts. But we can't compete all the time. When we compete we need to be at a high level of intensity. If we keep at that high level over a long period of time, we will burn out. We just can't keep that up for too long. Even professional athletes—who live to compete—know the value of taking some time out once in a while.

Balance between competing and working out can be maintained, and if it is, it will help us to become stronger athletes. It is entirely possible never to compete in any type of organized activity. Being dedicated to exercising doesn't mean that we have to enter races or join a team. Traditional competition is not essential for progress. We can improve and learn without going head-to-head with someone else. In fact, we can compete with ourselves or a clock or someone else's record. It isn't something we have to do, but adding a little competitive edge to our workouts may help us to perform better and we may even enjoy it more. Don't overdo, because too much is just as bad as not enough.

◆

I will add a little spice of competition to my workouts.

What's the worst thing that can happen to a quarterback? He loses his confidence.
—Terry Bradshaw

Losing confidence is probably the worst thing that can happen to any athlete. When we have lost our confidence we have lost the foundation that supports all of our endeavors. We can only get so far on pure abilities, because even if we have the potential we will not be able to fulfill that potential unless we firmly believe that we can. It is faith and belief in ourselves that can carry us through the toughest workouts or the most grueling contests.

When we lose our confidence we will be constantly questioning and second-guessing every move we make. We will be so caught up in trying to figure out if we can do something that we will not be able to function. Many a race has been lost because confidence disappeared at the last minute. To keep confidence as our constant companion, it must be nurtured and built up carefully over time. Taking on increasingly difficult challenges is the best way to get and keep our confidence solid. Confidence can't be built up with false accomplishments or even by the support of friends and teammates. Support from others is great, but our belief in ourselves is the only thing that we can always rely on to carry us through.

◆

Confidence is my constant companion while I work out.

You're not a bad person just because you shoot a bad score. You just need to keep plugging and realize that there will be better days. . . . I know there's more to life than just golf. I can put it in perspective.

—*Dawn Coe-Jones*

It's not the end of the world if we have a bad day on the golf course, or make an error on the softball field, or can't finish an aerobics class. We needn't feel like failures if we don't beat a racquetball opponent whom we usually whip, or we do only part of our swim workout, or foul out of our basketball game. Everyone is entitled to be a little off every once in a while, and the less of a deal we make of it, the sooner we'll return to our true form. It's when we wallow in our mistakes that we are doing ourselves a great disservice.

No one is perfect, and very few are even close, so we must be sure to keep our expectations in check and our participation in sports in perspective.

◆

Sports should be only part of my well-balanced life.

Once you establish an aggressive mental attitude, you can turn your attention to correct technique.
—*Tony Gwynn*

Sometimes the best way to make progress in athletics is to put the technical aspects aside temporarily and concentrate on mental fitness. Often the one thing we need to lift us up to the next level is not another lesson, a longer practice, or a more challenging opponent but a little "attitude." And with that new outlook, we may suddenly find the rest of our skills coming into place.

We've all been stalled at a certain plateau where, try as we might, we just can't take the next step. If it's our golf game we're working on, we may spend hours on the driving range hoping to hone our skills, only to end up frustrated and sore. Our swim workouts may be just as annoying. Formerly our best event, now our breaststroke seems to be floundering. We practice longer, ask for coaching, even watch videos of accomplished swimmers, all to no avail. It is at these times that we may want to consider putting technique aside for the moment and get a little mental tune-up. Baseball great Tony Gwynn suggests an aggressive attitude. What works for us may be a more focused mind or more self-confidence.

Ultimately the specifics don't matter as much as the idea of taking a break on the physical and putting our heads to work. Attitude is a vital part of athletics— we can't progress on skills alone.

◆

Today's workout will concentrate on both aptitude and attitude.

This game . . . it's a big wheel. It goes around in a circle. Sometimes you're at the
top. Sometimes you're in the middle. Sometimes you're at the bottom.
Sometimes you stay a little too much at the bottom. But you know you're going to
be at the top again. Everybody will have his opportunities.

—*Jose Santos*

*T*he game jockey Jose Santos is speaking of is horse racing, though it could just
as well be any sport, as we've all experienced these same ups and downs. There
are days when we are at our peaks, the sport seems effortless, and nothing seems
to distract or hinder us. We can't seem to miss a shot on the basketball court, we
could ride the LifeCycle forever, and it just seems as if we were born to swim
butterfly. Then there are the days when it feels as if we don't have an athletic
bone in our bodies. Our golf clubs feel foreign in our hands, we have absolutely
no footwork in aerobics class, and running three miles may as well be running a
marathon for how slow we're going.

The good news is, these bad spells never last. The bad news is, neither do the
outrageously good streaks. Luckily, though, most of us find some sort of a happy
medium that we gravitate toward on a regular basis. The important thing, then,
is to keep it all in perspective—to maintain a positive attitude when we seem to
be slumping and to stay in touch with reality when we're performing out of our
minds. We all go through these athletic peaks and valleys—we just have to learn
to hang on and enjoy the ride.

◆

Sports are filled with ups and downs—many of which I have no control over. The
best I can do is stick with it and make the best of the situation.

Fear is probably the thing that limits performance more than anything—the fear of not doing well, of what people will say. You've got to acknowledge those fears, then release them.
—*Mark Allen*

Ever felt self-conscious about entering a race, joining a team, or participating in a fitness class? We all have. Maybe we were worried about not performing up to par and perhaps embarrassing ourselves. Maybe it was, as triathlete Mark Allen says, fear—fear of how others would judge us. We all have periods of self-doubt and discouragement about ourselves, ranging from lack of confidence in our skills to discomfort with our fitness level or the shape our bodies are in. The problem is, these fears don't motivate, they paralyze us, keeping us from attempting the challenge at hand.

Only by recognizing and understanding these fears can we overcome their negative effects on our training or performance. We need to think about how they originate and how realistic they are. Will we be judged harshly if we do not win a match or perform to a top level? Probably not. Most of the time, we are our own toughest critics. Once we recognize that, it becomes a lot easier to release our fears.

◆

Today I will acknowledge my fears and try to work through them.

I enjoy winning, but there are benefits in losing, too. Before you can be a winner,
you have to learn to lose.
—*Isiah Thomas*

No one really likes to lose. Losing can be uncomfortable, even embarrassing, and can make us feel like never competing again. However, there are lessons that can be learned from losing. The mistakes that caused us to lose can be overcome and transformed into victory. Saying, "I stink" isn't going to change much the next time; however, saying, "I'm having trouble getting my first serve in" gives us a goal to work toward. If we can see the reason that we lost, it can become the focus of our training and may even become the reason we win in the future.

Learning to lose with grace is also difficult. It takes something away from our credibility and poise if we throw a tantrum every time we lose. It's not that we should be completely accepting of losing—it's best to fight against it as much as possible—but that we have to realize it is part of the game. You can't win every time, nor can every contest end in a tie. Losing can also be an excellent motivator. Most winners will often rest on their laurels, but the losers will practice even harder for the next time. Losing can feed desire as nothing else can.

◆

When I lose, I will take a close look at the reasons why and work on them.

If you have confidence, you have patience. Confidence, that is everything.
—Ilie Nastase

Confidence can take us a long way. If we are confident in ourselves and our abilities, we will know that we are capable of whatever we set out to do. Confidence is the fuel that can keep us moving through opposition. It won't matter if that opposition is mental or physical or another individual. When we have faith in our skills we won't force our accomplishments, we will know that they will happen, that we will succeed. Confidence can surround us and protect us from making foolish mistakes and losing our game.

Building confidence is very important. It takes time, but the time will be well spent because it is an investment in ourselves. Building confidence means not taking on too much too soon and learning to pace ourselves. If we try to overreach our developing abilities, we will get discouraged. When we master one skill at a time we will build our confidence level consistently and create a solid foundation for whatever activities we choose to take on.

◆

I will concentrate on increasing my confidence because that is one of the building blocks to becoming a better athlete.

Football success is desire and speed and intelligence—and desire is 85 percent of it.
—Bud Wilkinson

Desire is so much a part of every sport and physical-fitness activity. No one but ourselves can motivate us to get up early and run five miles, go to the gym during our lunch hour, work out to lose ten pounds, or train for a triathlon. We have to want it. We have to crave the high that we get as we pound the pavement in the wee hours of the morning. We have to need the break from the office to go pump iron and sweat. We have to want the terrific sense of accomplishment we get when we are able to drop those extra pounds, and we have to be excited by the opportunity to compete in activities we have become proficient in.

Whether we work out at home to an aerobics video or with a team for a basketball league; we exercise a few times a week or a few hours a day, we are all pushed along by the desire to achieve a goal. Desire is the ultimate motivator —greater than a workout partner, a coach, or a teacher. With desire we feel driven in a positive way to reach an end, give our best, and stick with our program. Desire is not negative. It is not desperation or fear or obsession. It is the purest form of motivation, something no one else can give us—we can only find it within ourselves.

◆

Desire is my motivator. It is what gets me to work out on a regular basis and give my best effort.

It used to be I wanted everything to be perfect. Now I can take the good with the bad. Because I realize now that I'm going to get another at-bat, another chance.
—*Albert Belle*

We can't always enjoy a perfectly played game or a flawless practice. Nor should we expect to. As with all other aspects of our lives, we have our ups and downs, our good days and our bad days. And while it's everyone's hope always to work out at a top level and compete to our full potential, we have to be ready to accept, and ultimately learn from, an off performance.

Luckily, if we do go through a slump, there's always another chance for us to redeem ourselves. We can work out again tomorrow. We can schedule a round of golf for next weekend. And we can sign up for the next tennis tournament. Even top professional athletes like Major League Baseball home-run king Albert Belle realize that they, too, will get another at-bat. This is not to say that because we get another chance we are not as driven and focused as we can be as we compete or work out; this only means that in the event we don't perform to our potential, we are able to learn from the experience and not stew over it. No one likes to find herself in a softball game, a 10K race, or a step class where she is just not getting the best from herself. It's incredibly frustrating to know we could be doing better. But rather than torture ourselves over it, we have to accept it as part of being an athlete and look forward to our next chance.

◆

I always want to do my best, but in case I have a bad day, I need to remember that I'll always get another chance to do better.

You can learn little from victory. You can learn everything from defeat.
—*Christy Mathewson*

*U*nfortunately, it's true. We do learn a lot more when we have suffered a disappointment on the court, in the pool, or at the track. When we win, we revel in the excitement and feel proud and encouraged to work harder and do more. When we are defeated, however, we are forced to examine our performance closely, wondering what went wrong and why.

We consider our practices: Did we not do enough? Did we work too hard? Were we concentrating on the wrong things? We look at our off-the-field preparations: Maybe we didn't get enough sleep? Ate the wrong thing? We examine the event itself: In a tennis match, did we rush the net too much? In a swim meet, did we start too fast and lose energy at the end? In a rowing regatta, did we not get into the right rhythm? In a basketball game, did we play selfishly or conservatively?

The questions will come fast and furious. What we have to be careful to do, however, is not use them to get down on ourselves for failing but rather use them as a way to study for the future. There will always be another game, match, or race that we can begin to prepare for, and what better way than to build on the skills, talent, and strategy we already have?

◆

Disappointments in both competitions and practices should be carefully examined
—their lessons used in a positive way in the future.

I've swum for my country, I've swum for my coaches and my schools and my teams.
I decided this time I was going to swim for me.
—Janet Evans

And when Janet Evans swims for herself it is an impressive sight to see. She is focused and determined and she clearly enjoys what she is doing. All of us are most efficient and effective when we are working for ourselves and for our own satisfaction. Other types of motivation can be inspirational, but when we are working for our own reasons we will be working as strongly and as smartly as possible. It's not enough to decide to do something because someone else tells you to or thinks it is what you should do. You have to decide what is best for you and what your own personal approach will be. All the coaching in the world won't make an athlete out of someone who doesn't want to be an athlete. The desire and motivation have to come from within. You are your own best motivator/coach/cheerleader.

There is something very special about successes that come from our own hard work and determination. We can take intense and well-deserved pride in accomplishments that come from doing things our way—especially if we have found the way that works best for us. It's okay, sometimes, to let our egos take the front seat and put ourselves first.

◆

Whatever I choose to do I will choose to do it for myself.

Of the mental hazards, being scared is the worst. When you get scared,
you get tense.
—*Sam Snead*

*F*ear comes in different shapes and sizes: fear of winning, fear of losing, fear of looking foolish, fear of letting people down, fear of injury. The list could go on and on. No matter what we fear, it can paralyze us so that we can't do anything. It can make us forget just how good we are. It can make us forget everything we know. When we are scared we need to slow down, take a deep breath, and regroup. It is also important to determine where the fear is coming from. Is it something that has been lurking around for some time or is it something that has appeared out of nowhere? Sometimes we can talk ourselves into being scared, and if we can talk ourselves into it, we can talk ourselves out of it.

It is completely understandable to have a little fear when we are facing an outstanding opponent or trying something new. Fear goes hand in hand with taking risks—but letting fear get out of hand will sink you. Being a little scared or nervous is not all bad. That feeling of butterflies can just as easily get us psyched up as make us too nervous to do well. Fear needs to be tamed and channeled so that it isn't debilitating.

◆

I will have no fear.

What I loved most about track was that it was me against everybody else.
—*Dave Wottle*

*T*here's a certain excitement when we compete as an individual that is unique. We feel the anxiety about being completely responsible for the performance, no matter how successful or disappointing, and the exhilaration of being solely in control of the outcome. We don't have the luxury of teammates to lean on to help us win, nor do we have to worry about teammates who may bring us down if they are having a bad day. We are in charge of our own destiny.

While some athletes don't care for the pressure of being out there alone, left to win a running race, or a tennis match, or golf tournament without the support of a partner, others prefer the autonomy and freedom that comes with participation in an individual sport. We are singularly able to reach our goals, or feel the pain of defeat. Either way we have the satisfaction of knowing that it was we alone that achieved that end. There's no one to share the blame with, but on the other hand the joy is *all* ours. It's truly our own achievement.

◆

It's a great feeling to reach a goal on our own power and perseverance.

Show me a guy who's afraid to look bad, and I'll show you a guy
you can beat every time.
—*Lou Brock*

Any athlete who's concerned with anything other than competing or working out to the best of his or her ability is wasting valuable energy that is better spent on the task at hand. Whether motivated by fear, intimidation, or even ego, an athlete who is more concerned with how he or she looks while exercising is missing the point.

An athlete's main concern should be having a clean, clear mind, and executing to his or her potential. A golfer more concerned with stroke style than stroke effectiveness is using his skills and training ineffectively. A runner who avoids longer races because she is afraid of not doing well is impeding her own chance of improvement. A tennis player who doesn't challenge up on the ladder is motivated by fear of losing a match instead of the challenge of possible advancement.

It's not easy being confident enough in our skills to avoid ever falling into these traps. However, we should be on the lookout for motivation that is based on fear of or concern for what others will think.

◆

I am not concerned with what others think about how I work out or compete.

There are no winners, only survivors.
—Frank Gifford

Gifford is talking about professional football, but this comment could apply to any intense no-holds-barred contest where everyone is giving his all. Have you ever just collapsed, exhausted, after running a race or playing a game and it didn't really matter who the winner was? You gave all you had to give and you can walk away physically drained but mentally elated because you really put yourself on the line. You brought out the best in your opposition and they brought out the best in you.

Winning really is relative. You can be a winner by simply playing your best and trying your hardest. You can be a winner by being able to learn from your mistakes and being willing to come back another day. Sometimes simply surviving is winning. If you held your own against a tough opponent and made her work for her victory then you have held up your end of the contest. If you hung in there and didn't quit, you are also a winner. Especially if you are participating in some form of athletics that doesn't keep score. You are a winner if you survive that advanced aerobics class, or tack on that extra mile to your weekend run. If you see something you have started through to the end, you can call yourself a winner.

◆

I will not quit. I will survive. I will be a winner.

Even though circumstances may cause interruptions and delays, never lose sight of your goal. Instead, prepare yourself in every way you can by increasing your knowledge and adding to your experience, so that you can make the most of opportunity when it occurs.
—Mario Andretti

We may not be able to physically work toward our goals every day, but if we keep them in our minds and in our thoughts, it can help get us what we want. When our workout routine is interrupted we can still keep ourselves on track by preparing ourselves in other ways. This may mean reading books on technique or watching tapes of other athletes or of our own performances. Preparation is the key. We have to be ready, both mentally and physically, for anything. It's also important to prepare ourselves for every contest—not just the big ones. Never take any competition for granted because we can learn from all of our experiences—win, lose, or draw. Every time we work out we have the opportunity to learn a little more about ourselves and what we are made of.

When we get sidetracked due to illness or injury or time constraints, we can still keep our goals in sight by planning how we will get there and knowing what we need to do when we can work out again. Having a solid, and workable, plan in place is essential if we are going to be able to get what we want.

◆

I will always keep my eyes on what I want to accomplish.

I truly believe I can win every race I enter. Of course I know in my mind I *won't* win every one, but I believe in my heart that it is not impossible.
—*Julie Parisien*

Our hearts and minds sometimes seem to be in opposition. Logic would seem to say that most of the athletic accomplishments that we all look up to and celebrate really shouldn't happen. A triple axel? A fifty-point game? For the nonprofessional these accomplishments could be out of reach primarily because we have not made the decision to devote our lives to our sports. No matter what level of working out we engage in, we have to determine what our personal best would be.

Once we know what we want, we have to go out and get it. Sometimes this means ignoring our logical minds and giving ourselves over to what we desire in our hearts. What is in our hearts is very powerful. When our wishes are planted firmly there and we truly believe, we will soon see those dreams come true at the gym or on the court or on the track. What our heads say may be technically true, but sometimes our hearts are smarter than our heads. We need to take the time to shut out the mind chatter that tells us what is likely or possible and carefully listen to a voice that tells us that anything is possible if we only believe.

◆

I believe in my heart that anything is possible.

Success is the person who year after year reaches the highest limits in his field.
—*Sparky Anderson*

*E*veryone has his own definition of success. But consistency has a huge impact on whether or not we are successful. It's not enough to just go out and succeed once. One victory may mean that we have been lucky or got a break. It's not really possible to define ourselves as a success until we have had a repeat performance. That repeat performance doesn't necessarily have to be coming in first or winning the championship—it can simply be attaining the highest level of performance we are capable of.

Consistency is also important in establishing the way we play, when we play, and how much we will improve. We can't just go out once in a while and expect to perform well. It's unrealistic to expect quality from ourselves when we don't invest some quality time in our workouts. In fact, the more time we put into our workouts, the more we will get out of them.

Success isn't something that can happen all the time, and it doesn't happen overnight. Devoting time and energy, day after day, will get us playing at the top of our game.

◆

I will perform my best as often as possible.

One thing I know is that the world will not allow me to just play tennis. It will not allow me to be Number 15 in the world. So I do it right or I don't do it at all.
—*Boris Becker*

It is very difficult to live with expectations, whether we have created them for ourselves or they are placed on us by others. High expectations can be debilitating and can end up making us play worse or give up entirely because of the pressure. However, when used in a positive way, expectations should motivate us, not discourage us.

Expectations that are too high can take all the fun out of our sport or exercise. Setting goals is important, but we need to be realistic about those goals. If we set the hurdle too high, we may never get over it. If expectations are preventing us from playing because we are afraid of not achieving them or living up to some impossibly high standard, we need to reassess our desires. No one can be perfect, and if we expect ourselves to do it right every time, no matter what, we are setting ourselves up for disappointment. Perfection is very rare. We can, however, strive for having a perfect record in being willing to keep working for our goals.

◆

I will be sure my expectations motivate me, not discourage me.

Every man's got to figure to get beat sometime.
—Joe Louis

In other words, "You can't win 'em all." No matter how accomplished we are, how much we practice, or how well we're coached, there will come a time, or two, or three, when we will be done in by an opponent who is just that much more accomplished, more practiced, or better coached. Even the greatest athletes in the world fail occasionally, and it doesn't matter if it happens in the fifth set at Wimbledon, or the third set at the local park, it still smarts.

No amount of training ever really prepares us for a loss, especially one that is extremely tough or unexpected. And it often takes all of our energy to handle it in the gracious manner that is appropriate.

We don't have to like losing, but we do have to deal with it on occasion, so it's best to be prepared to cope with any possible outcome so as not to be ashamed of our behavior later.

◆

Sometimes I win, sometimes I lose, so I should always be ready to handle either situation with grace and aplomb.

> Durability is part of what makes a great athlete.
> —*Bill Russell*

Not everyone can be as quick and agile as Michael Jordan, as powerful as Martina Navratilova, as steady as Jack Nicklaus, or as versatile as Jackie Joyner-Kersee. Most of us, in fact, don't even come close. However, most of us can become and continue to be good, reliable athletes regardless of our particular skill level.

Basketball great Bill Russell attributes part of his success to what he refers to as durability. By being a consistent, flexible, go-anywhere, do-anything athlete, Russell was a major asset to his team. For the rest of us, durability means maintaining our strength, reliability, and taking care of ourselves so we can be active and healthy for a long time. There's no need to get out there and kill ourselves every time we compete, or overdo every workout until it hurts.

Consistency in practice will mean consistency, and longevity, in performance. The smarter we are in pacing ourselves and in appropriately setting our challenges, the more durable athletes we will become.

◆

Smart workouts lead to good performances and long, healthy athletic careers.

None of us really pushes hard enough. People always talk about playing over your head when you are up against someone really good. Maybe you don't play over your head at all. Maybe it's just potential you never knew you had.

—*Fran Tarkenton*

Sometimes we can only live up to our potential when we are pushed from the outside. Unfortunately, if we learn to rely on that push from someone else, we will never be as demanding of our own performance as we should be. If we can play well only in clutch situations, then we won't be able to be consistent or turn in a solid game under average circumstances. If we challenge ourselves in noncompetitive situations, we will become more familiar with the limits and, more important, the expanse of our abilities.

Knowing what we are capable of will allow us to adapt our game to a wide variety of opponents and situations. If we know that we can dig in and come up with a second wind in the last mile or in that last set of tennis, we won't be trying to conserve energy in the beginning so that we will make it through to the end.

◆

I will be sure that I am always playing up to my potential.

When I'm in this state everything is pure, vividly clear. I'm in a cocoon of concentration. And if I can put myself into that cocoon, I'm invincible.
—Tony Jacklin

Many athletes tell of being in a "zone" or, as British golfer Tony Jacklin refers to it, "a cocoon of concentration," where all thoughts are on the game and a peak performance is well within reach. It's as if we can do no wrong; our bodies and our minds are as one, the synergy between them incredibly powerful.

Unfortunately, not all of us are able to reach this state of pure mind and flawless motion on demand, if at all. It takes an amazing amount of discipline to be able to focus so intently on our sport that all other distractions fall by the wayside. We must take the field or the court or the course with a clear mind and a goal in sight. Even in noncompetitive situations we can reach this ultimate state with similar results—a workout that is close to perfect, a run that nears a personal best, a ski run that is the best of the day, a golf lesson that is incredibly productive.

With focus and concentration we can reach this zone of perfection, where body and mind are in sync to great results.

◆

I can reach a peak performance by focusing my mind on the task at hand.

There's only so much physical energy and resilience in the body. If you go beyond a certain point, you're in trouble.
—*Bill Rodgers*

No pain, no gain—no way. While there are a handful of athletes who still subscribe to the masochists' school of physical fitness, thankfully most of us have realized the ineffectiveness, and even danger, of overtraining. While we may push ourselves to the limits of our strength and stamina at times, for the most part we have learned to recognize these limits and work within them. It's not that we're skimping on workouts, or taking it easy; on the contrary, we are targeting our potential and pushing ourselves to reach it.

When we have unreasonable expectations of ourselves, we tend to work out to excess, and therefore are apt to suffer the consequences: typically injury, exhaustion, and poor performance. Our bodies have limits, and while we can seem to overdo it on occasion with no adverse effects, it's when we are constantly trying too hard that we chance trouble. It may start with a little pain here, a strain there, but eventually we find not only a performance that suffers but the possibility of an injury that could sideline us for weeks.

Being in tune with our bodies is vitally important to athletes of all skill levels. While we want to stretch our limits with challenging workouts, we don't want to push our luck with downright stupidity.

◆

While improving is important to me, so is a strong, healthy body, so I need to be aware of my limits and work within them.

Perhaps the greatest satisfaction in cycling has been to discover that there are few things you can't do as long as you're willing to apply yourself.
—Greg LeMond

Sometimes our limitations are all in our heads. Although we seem to have certain physical limitations, they can hold us back only as much as we let them. While a basketball player who is six feet eleven inches will usually have an advantage over someone shorter, that shorter person may be able to use his other assets to succeed on the court. That player knows that he can't excel with height so he applies himself to other parts of his game, such as phenomenal speed or incredible shooting accuracy. Instead of accepting his apparent disadvantage, he has compensated for it so that he can stay in the game. When we say that we can't do something because we have made assumptions of what we are capable of achieving, we are denying ourselves an opportunity to learn. On the other hand, it is tough to just jump right in and tackle something new. That's why we need to spend some time preparing first and then applying ourselves later.

Knowing what it is that we want to do and knowing how we can do it are important for figuring out our game plan. We have to be willing to take the time to investigate the best approach and spend time to truly develop our unique abilities so that we can take on those challenges.

◆

If I make the time, I can make my goals.

If you ask a fifty-goal scorer what the goalie looks like, he'll say the goalie's just a blur. But if you ask a five-goal scorer, he'll say the goalie looks like a huge glob of pads. A five-goal scorer can tell you the brand name of the pad of every goalie in the league. I'm seeing the net, he's seeing the pad.
—*Wayne Gretzky*

It's very easy to see only the obstacles that stand in the way of working out— time, family commitments, work. But we need to assess these obstacles objectively and see how big they really are. Can we at least see a glimpse of our goals, or are they blocked completely from view? Can we do something to move the obstacle or make it a little smaller?

We also have to be aware of when we create obstacles for ourselves. Is it *really* too cold to run? Or is that just an excuse? Could we modify our goals to fit with the current situation? Would a twenty-minute workout instead of the usual hour allow for some level of exercise and some movement toward what we want to accomplish? Sometimes obstacles are only as big as we choose to make them. With focus and concentration we can make them become a blur instead of a blockade.

◆

I will shift my focus from the obstacles to my goal.

No matter how long you have been playing, you still get butterflies
before the big ones.
—*Pee Wee Reese*

Whether we're competing in the World Series, or the playoffs of the corporate softball league; running the 1,500 in the Olympics, or the local two-mile fun run; putting to win the British Open, or our Sunday foursome, we all experience some sort of nervousness before important competitions. Even the most seasoned athletes admit to butterflies and jitters before they are called upon to perform in "the big ones." And for those of us who don't compete regularly it's that much more likely that the challenge of competition will make us uneasy.

The good news is nervousness, if channeled the right way, can be helpful in tough situations. It needn't be detrimental to our performances on the softball field, the track, or the golf course if we try to refocus the anxious energy into our game. Harnessing our nervous energy and transforming it into strength and speed we can use in competition keeps us focused and prevents us from wasting this valuable energy on useless worrying.

It's okay to be nervous before a big game, tough match, or even a challenging workout—it certainly happens to the top athletes. It's just important for us to be able to acknowledge this state of mind and try to put it to better use.

◆

The best athletes get nervous every once in a while. When I feel this way I need to make better use of this extra, misplaced energy.

An hour of hard practice is worth five hours of foot-dragging.
—*Pancho Segura*

*H*ow many times have we finished a long, involved workout only to feel we didn't do that much at all? A three-hour tennis match, a two-hour bike ride, or an evening at the gym may have seemed like good, solid periods of exercise. Except that when we were finished, we didn't have the healthy exhaustion and sense of accomplishment that usually follow an aggressive, hard, productive workout. What we've probably done is put in twice as much time for half the results.

A workout that is approached in a lazy, low-energy way is obviously not as effective as one where we really go all out. A workout where we are concentrating, fired up, and truly giving our best effort is ultimately more valuable to our fitness program and much more satisfying.

There will always be days when we just don't feel like pushing ourselves to run, swim, go to the gym, or take an exercise class. Those might be days when we should consider taking a day off from working out. If we can make a deal with ourselves to rest one day and work extra hard the next, we'll probably make more progress in the long run.

◆

Workouts are most effective when I give my best effort. If I don't have that to give today, maybe I should consider taking a day off and working harder tomorrow.

If you trust your nerve as well as your skill, you're capable of a lot more than you can imagine. I never felt that if I didn't win the gold medal, I was nothing. I just had to give it my best shot.
—*Debi Thomas*

*T*hat's really what sports and exercise are all about—giving it our best shot. Whether we are part of a team, competing on our own, or working out individually, we will get the most out of our abilities if we give our all the first time and every time. We have to be willing to give an all-out effort because without it we may fall short. Belief in what we can do is what really allows us to excel at our sport. Striving for the top doesn't mean that we have to be miserable about a less than perfect performance. There will be plenty of times when we won't come out on top, but this is nothing to be discouraged about. We need to take the time to assess where we began and what we have accomplished. If we have truly given it our heart and soul, we have nothing to be ashamed of if the results don't match our goals. We will just know better what we have to do next time.

Even if we have been disappointed, we can focus on our strengths and be successful the next time. Believing in ourselves can carry us farther than any victory.

◆

I will give it my best.

Each sport or training regimen determines what the athlete's body will be like. But the process can be aided by suggestion, visualization, and other mental techniques.
—Michael Murphy, author of Golf in the Kingdom

We may be tall and wiry like a basketball player, or sturdy and strong like a power lifter, lean and light like a distance runner, or agile and quick like a soccer player. Our bodies come in all shapes and sizes, making us better suited for different athletic endeavors. Our continued workouts and training in these areas further increase our strength, speed, flexibility, or coordination, honing our skills for our particular sports.

However, we can always improve our performances, or even train ourselves in a new skill, by using not just physical workouts but mental ones as well. Mental fitness is extremely important to athletes of all levels—professionals and amateurs alike swear by the success of a training regimen that combines the usual physical workout with visualization, meditation, relaxation, and other tools that bring mind and body together.

The body is extremely susceptible to the power of suggestion—what our minds can create, our bodies will try to imitate. Obviously, no one will achieve greatness without skills and training, but mental workouts in combination with the physical make for impressive mind/body synergy.

◆

What I can achieve with physical training alone, I can improve upon
with good mental fitness.

I thought about my first camp, when I was just trying to make the team. Just get
back to basics. Keep it simple and have fun.
—*Dwight Gooden*

We all forget about the fun part. Fun seems to be the last thing on the agenda
when we are dragging ourselves off to the gym, pounding the pavement, or
sweating it out in step aerobics class. We complicate our workouts with unrealistic goals and the fun-depleting mantra of "gotta, gotta, gotta" as in "gotta do it,
gotta lose weight, gotta build those muscles." Somehow fun is never a factor.

Remember when we were kids and we would run or jump just because we
could run or jump? We didn't think about how fast or how far we ran; we just did
it because we felt like it. That was the way to experience the pure fun and joy of
being alive. We didn't do it because we were trying to accomplish something or
we had a distant goal in mind. Sometimes we sap all the fun out of our exercise
by making it an obligation or work. If we can find the fun in our workouts we'll
be much more likely to keep going.

◆

Today I will leave my stopwatch, goals, and work ethic at home and try to
recapture the fun that is in exercise.

How you respond to the challenge in the second half will determine what you become after the game, whether you are a winner or a loser.

—*Lou Holtz*

We are always getting challenged. On the court, on the road, in the gym. It is what drives us to improve. We can't always be consistently great, so sometimes we need a second chance in order to prove what we are made of. How you start out isn't nearly as important as how you finish. You can start slowly, but if you finish strong you can always walk away a winner.

If we never enter into competition, we may find it difficult to think of our workouts in terms of winning and losing. However, if we think of ourselves as our own best competition, our personal wins and losses will be easy to calculate. Think of it this way: If we accomplish our goals we will have added one to the win column. If we slack off and don't maintain our intensity, we can't claim that as a victory.

No matter if we are working out as individuals for individual goals or are part of a team or entering into competition, we should be looking for a challenge that will bring out our best. If we remain unchallenged and are never tested, we won't know what it is to feel like a winner.

◆

I will respond to every challenge as if it is the last half of a championship game.

When you feel good about yourself, others will feel good about you, too.
—Jake ("Body by Jake") Steinfeld

*T*here's nothing better than that postworkout feeling where your heart is pumping, endorphins are racing, skin is glowing, and your energy is high. It's a wonderful feeling of accomplishment when you take the last few pedals in a long bike ride, pump the last few reps in a circuit training session, or let it all out in the last few strides of a power walk. And in that instant when we have that sense of exhilaration—sometimes hand in hand with exhaustion—we also feel good and positive about ourselves, about what we've done and what we can do.

We should hold on to these feelings as long as possible, because as we radiate this energy and health, others around us feel it and are attracted by it. The better we are feeling about ourselves and what we've accomplished, the more the positive energy rubs off on those around us. As hard as it might be to get ourselves to exercise sometimes, if we can just keep in mind this satisfying, afterworkout state of mind, the motivation should come a lot easier for us, as will the good feelings from others.

◆

Exercise makes me feel good about myself—and I want everyone to know it.

If I lose, I'll walk away and never feel bad because I did all I could. There was
nothing more to do.
—Joe Frazier

It's never easy to walk away from a loss. As a matter of fact, it's one of the hardest things an athlete can do. We all want to win, but we can't win all the time. What is sometimes even harder to do is to walk away from a loss with a winning attitude. However, maintaining a winning attitude will be invaluable when it comes time to compete again. There are plenty of times when our own performance isn't at fault—in fact, it's quite good—and we lose anyway. This isn't a time to blame the loss on the crummy court or on our equipment. Blame isn't going to get us anywhere. Knowing that we worked really hard and did our best will help to get us to our next game.

If we have honestly done everything we could, there is honor in defeat. No matter who we are, there will always be someone out there who can beat us. They may take a while to catch up to us but sooner or later they'll show up. And when they do, if we play our hardest and fight for a victory and they still come out on top, we can find comfort in knowing that we played to the best of our abilities.

◆

If you have to lose it's better to go down swinging and knowing that
you've done your best.

Age is a question of mind over matter. If you don't mind, age don't matter.
—Satchel Paige

Claiming the age handicap can be a handy excuse to get out of exercising. After all we all know of sports where athletes in their mid-twenties can be considered close to retirement. We are also inundated with advertising that features young, hard bodies working out. It's no wonder that we feel over the hill long before we should even think of giving up healthy exercise. But we shouldn't give in to that way of thinking. Sure, our bodies may not be able to do everything we used to do, but that's natural. As we age we may lose a little flexibility or endurance, but if we keep on working we can still perform at a high level. We may have to make adjustments to our exercise routines, but we don't have to abandon them. Keeping exercise in our lives can help us stay fit and can battle some of the negative effects of aging. There are plenty of forms of exercise that anyone of any age can do. In fact, giving up on exercise because of our age doesn't make much sense at all. If we do, we are giving up on our health, our hearts, our bodies, and fun. It's not really age that keeps us from working out, our perception of age is what prevents us from working out.

◆

I won't let my age stand in the way of exercise.

You have to want to win and expect that you are going to win. Top players have that edge. Even if they're down a few games, they know they're going to toughen up and come up with what it takes to win.

—Martina Navratilova

Attitude is an important piece of the puzzle. A positive attitude keeps us headed in the right direction and can give us the all important edge we need to come out on top. We have to enter every endeavor knowing, beyond a shadow of a doubt, that we will be successful. If we don't have any expectations for ourselves, we won't achieve up to our potential.

Knowing what we are capable of can help us to reenergize. We have to come back and say, "Yes, I can." We will be able to do this if we have prepared for every event physically and if we have our heads in the right place. It's that firm belief in ourselves that propels us to the top. It's important for us to believe that we are going to win. Our opponents don't believe it—in fact, they are doing everything in their power to make sure we don't win. It doesn't matter if our friends or family think we can win. What really matters is what we think. We have to not only know that we can do it but we have to be the main believer.

◆

I know that I can win.

> World records are only borrowed.
> —*Sebastian Coe*

*T*here are few records that last forever. Even when Roger Bannister ran a mile in less than four minutes, it was only six weeks later that his record was broken by John Landy. Sometimes setting a record just paves the way for someone else. A personal best, however, can last a long time. Our record doesn't have to be enshrined forever in the history books or the Hall of Fame for it to count. It can be enshrined in our hearts. Even then, we will always be looking for ways to beat that record. We always want to test ourselves against a new set of expectations because that is the only way we can improve and grow.

Whenever there is a record, especially a new one, people in that field will set their sights on beating it. No matter how outstanding or seemingly insurmountable that record is, it is only a matter of time before it falls. Striving to beat those records can create new heroes, new expectations, and new records. The legacy of an old record can live on and is the foundation on which new records are built. We probably wouldn't have Hank Aaron if it weren't for Babe Ruth. So any record that you make or break is fuel for the fire of another outstanding performance by you or someone else.

◆

I will always strive for my personal best and break and
set my own records along the way.

The reason I was able to block those shots off the board was because most guys took one look at me and thought, "This kid is too skinny. He can't jump that high."

—*Jerry West*

*F*or those of us who have ever felt discouraged about pursuing a sport or activity because we didn't feel we had the physique for it, famed Los Angeles Laker Jerry West offers us inspiration. Maybe you are interested in running, but are not rail thin. Or perhaps, like West, basketball is your game, but you're not all that tall or filled out. You like to swim, but don't have the shoulders; you enjoy aerobics, but don't feel all that comfortable in a leotard.

Professional sports are full of athletes who, on the surface, didn't seem to fit the bill. In addition to West, basketball has pint-sized guard Mugsy Bogues. And what about female athletes like jockey Julie Krone, who has succeeded tremendously in the male-dominated sport of horse racing? Or pitcher Nolan Ryan who, at the ripe old age of forty-six was still going strong in the Major Leagues? These athletes and many others might have been discouraged by their age, size, sex, or shape from pursuing their sports. Thankfully they weren't.

For the rest of us who might hesitate before taking up or taking a sport seriously, we need to be reminded that we are limited only by a combination of our ability and desire.

◆

I can pursue any sport I set my mind on pursuing. I needn't be put off by perceived limitations on height, weight, or anything else.

I feel that the most important step in any major accomplishment is setting a specific goal. This enables you to keep your mind focused on your goal and off the many obstacles that will arise when you're striving to do your best.

—*Kurt Thomas*

A goal should be a target that is just over the horizon. It is something that is just beyond our grasp and it becomes the thing that keeps us going. Every time we hit the gym, the track or the court we should keep our goals in mind and work out accordingly. Unfortunately, there will always be things that will come up that will turn us away from striving toward our goals—other commitments, responsibilities, and distractions. But if we have the goal in our sights, we will not be deterred.

Setting a specific goal will help us stay on track. The more specific the goal, the more precise we can be about deciding how we will go about achieving it. Being too general in our aspirations will only keep us unfocused, not progressing. Only specific steps can lead us directly to our specific goals. Setting goals will help us to keep working our best and our hardest. Every time we meet any of our goals we will feel great and we will be one step closer to our ultimate goals.

♦

When I work out I will have my goal firmly in sight and in mind.

My motto was always to keep swinging. Whether I was in a slump or feeling badly or having trouble off the field, the only thing to do was keep swinging.
—*Hank Aaron*

This is the attitude that firmly planted Hank Aaron in the record books and the Hall of Fame. It's an attitude that works whether we are trying to break Babe Ruth's home-run record or trying to break our own personal records, or the club record, or whatever goal we have set up for ourselves.

That old cliché about try, try again has lots of truth in it. There are no sure ways to succeed, but a sure way to fail is to give up. Keeping at it can also help take our minds off of other problems. Focusing on something other than what's troubling us can be very liberating and rewarding. Often the focus of working out or being in competition can help to change our attitude or perspective and help us see a new solution to our problem. By persevering we will help ourselves to get what we want. We can get there by keeping our eye on our goals and working, no matter what the circumstances.

◆

I'll leave all other problems aside when I focus on my workout goals.

The most interesting thing about this sport, at least to me, is the activity of preparation—any aspect of preparation for the games. The thrill isn't in the winning, it's in the doing.
—*Chuck Noll*

For those of us who compete in our sports, regardless at what level, we can appreciate what NFL coach Chuck Noll is implying. All those hours of practice, the hundreds of drills, the sweat, the pain, the frustration, and the accomplishments that we endure as we work toward a goal are often more satisfying than the competition itself. Whether it's a running race, a tennis tournament, a volleyball game, or a rowing regatta, we put in long, hard hours of preparation either alone or with coaches and teammates for what may amount to but minutes in a competitive event.

The groundwork we lay is what we can be proudest of because it is what allows us to compete at all. Sticking with it takes the most motivation. It takes our time and our energy as it can be both encouraging and discouraging from day to day. The practice sessions are where we can plan strategies, work on specific skills, and psych ourselves mentally. If we can remember the importance of our daily workouts, their value to our overall fitness plan, and try to enjoy them as well as endure them, we'll get a lot more out of the process of preparing to compete.

◆

I can be proud of, and encouraged by, all the preparation I do
to compete in my sport.

> I do whatever it takes. Whatever it takes to stop the other guy.
> Whatever it takes to win.
> —*Ulf Samuelsson*

*T*here are those who will say that hockey player Ulf Samuelsson takes this attitude a little too far. It certainly is possible to let that "win at any cost" attitude have a negative effect on you and your competitors. But there is something to be said for working extremely hard and playing with desire. It's important for the nonprofessional athlete to figure out just what it will take to win as well as what constitutes winning for them.

The nonprofessional athletes aren't playing for the Stanley Cup, but they are playing for a new seed on the health club tournament ladder or a better time in the mile or the marathon. You know what winning is for you and you also know what it will take to get you there. Usually more practice is involved, but it could also help to get more coaching, lessons, or increase the quantity or quality of your workout. Ulf Samuelsson has a lot of determination and desire, but he backs it up with many, many hours of working out and lots of time on the ice.

◆

I'll figure out whatever it will take to win, and I will go out and do it.

I began to feel what my skis were doing in conjunction with my feet and legs, and I began to understand what different movements did to the ski. The whole experience just made me really confident.
—A J Kitt

Paying attention to the subtle things can make a big difference when we exercise, work out, or play. When we reach a certain level of performance it sometimes feels as if the basics are behind us. We've been there and we've done it and we never want to have to do it again. Well, sometimes it helps a great deal to be reminded of the basics and how they work.

Simplifying our workouts can do wonders for our overall performance. There are probably a lot of things that we do automatically that could use some thinking about. For example, we may have learned to serve the tennis ball in a particular way because we needed to compensate for a lack of strength. Over time we have developed our muscles and now we may need to rethink the mechanics of our serve. Going back to basics and focusing on skill building can be done at any time. Often when we examine the basics, and we bring to that examination our well-developed experience and knowledge, we may be surprised to discover that we can improve on our base skills, which in turn will improve how we perform overall.

◆

Getting back to basics isn't a step backward, it's a new way to move forward.

The only way to overcome is to hang in. Even *I'm* starting to believe that.
—*Dan O'Brien*

Remember Dan and Dave and the Reebok Olympic decathlon competition? Well, Dan didn't make it to the Olympics. And if anyone could have disappeared off the face of the earth (or wanted to) it's Dan O'Brien. It would have been very easy for him to give up and never compete again. A lot of people would have understood. But he didn't. He's out there working hard and practicing and doing what he loves to do.

If he had given up, he would always be the guy who didn't make it. No matter what other successes he had, he would have that disappointment hanging over his head for the rest of his life. Okay, so the expectations for our activities aren't broadcast all over the TV, and if we don't do well no one will really know but us. However, the only way to overcome a loss, an error, or a performance not turning out the way we planned is to get in there and try again. We really don't get anywhere from quitting. It's the easy route, but we will always be wondering what would have happened if we had kept at it and worked harder or better. The payoff for staying in the game can be huge—the only thing we get from quitting is losing.

◆

I will keep on plugging because giving up means sure defeat.

> Winners never quit and quitters never win.
> —*Anonymous*

Sometimes it's easy to get discouraged about our seemingly nonimproving tennis game, our progress, or lack thereof, in our weight-training program, or hitting the wall in our morning run. However, it's important that we have the confidence to stick with a fitness program that challenges us, even when it feels like we're going nowhere. While it may seem simpler to give up, or at least ease off a bit, when we seem to be waging an uphill battle, that's the time for us to really dig in our heels and stick with our programs. Just hanging in there through a tough period will make the ultimate breakthrough a lot more satisfying.

How many times has a championship performance on the tennis court followed a period of seemingly never-ending double faults and unforced errors? What about a personal-best mile time? More times than not the personal record will follow a stretch of discouraging workouts. Quitting or cutting back in training would probably have impeded the final success. No matter how depressed we might be by our lack of progress on the court, course, track, or field, we must make it our policy to stick with our workout regimen. It will always get better with time, and the wait will always be worth it.

◆

I'll stick with my workout program, no matter how tough it may seem at times. The end result will be well worth it.

I've always felt it was not up to anyone else to make me give my best.
—*Akeem Olajuwon*

Ultimately we're the only ones who can get ourselves to work out and perform to our potential. No motivational coach, encouraging parent, gung-ho teammate, psyched-up workout partner, or guilt-inspiring commercial can consistently get us to give our best. Sure, they might get us going in the short term, but we have to be our own best motivator on a regular basis to be as effective as we can be.

We can use our goals to encourage ourselves to work harder and longer; we can use our scales to remind us of our target weight; and we can use friends and teachers to get us going when we're not in the mood. There's nothing wrong with using others to help us keep up our exercise program. However, we cannot rely on these outside influences day after day. Eventually the desire to get fit, lose weight, and win must come from within. We must call upon our own willpower to keep us going when the temptation is to quit. We must dig deep for the energy to work out when we're inclined not to. We must be able to encourage ourselves to persevere when we may not be playing our best. We must be our own best coach, cheerleader, and trainer.

◆

I'm my own best motivator.

This is the payoff for all the tears, the pain, the frustration.
—Summer Sanders

Summer Sanders is talking about making the United States Olympic swim team. But we don't have to be Olympic athletes to understand what she is talking about. We all have our own version of an "Olympic" payoff. It is usually a cherished goal that we have been dreaming about and planning for. It is the carrot on the stick that keeps us working hard, enduring the pain, and making sacrifices.

We always need to keep striving for that payoff. It can be big or small, but all that matters is that it is important to us. It also doesn't have to be the be-all, end-all super achievement. It is possible for a payoff to be a mini-goal that takes us closer to our larger aspirations. An Olympic athlete's first hurdle may be to make the team, her next would be to go for the gold.

If we have goals, we will be able to mark off the milestones that let us know we are making progress. It can be boring to work out and sweat if we don't have something specific in mind to be striving for. Before we start a workout or exercise program, we have to decide what the payoff is going to be. Then we have to start working toward it.

◆

The only way to get to my payoff will be if I keep working toward it.

> When I try to hit home runs, my swing goes to pot.
> —*Dean Palmer*

*T*here is definitely such a thing as trying too hard. If we want something very badly we can put so much pressure on ourselves that we are incapable of doing what is necessary to achieve our goals. We start thinking too much, worrying if we can do it right, and let our nerves take over our play. When we are tense and nervous we will not perform our best. This doesn't apply only to competitive sports. We can put enormous pressure on ourselves when we are running or lifting weights or doing any other solitary, noncompetitive workout.

When we are trying hard to achieve something, it can completely take over our thoughts and actions. The more we think and obsess about what we want to do, the more energy we take away from how we are going to do it. When it comes to attempting something important, the best thing we can do is relax. Tension is the enemy of working well. Ironically, sometimes taking our intense focus off our goals can help. If a goal is looming large, it can put a huge weight on our shoulders and hinder our usually stellar performance. It is not that we need to forget about our goals, it's just that we can't let them control us.

◆

I will remember that trying too hard is just as much of a problem
as not trying hard enough.

I think I've always had the shots. But in the past, I've suffered too many mental lapses. Now, I'm starting to get away from that and my mental discipline and commitment to the game are much better. I think I'm really taking a good look at the big picture. That's the difference between being around for the final or watching the final from my sofa at home.

—*Andre Agassi*

When we are trying to get better at a specific exercise or sport, it is easy to miss the big picture. We get so focused on what we want to improve or on what we do best that we are missing the big picture. Part of that big picture is commitment. Think about it, are we committed to improving our backhand or to winning the set? Are we committed to maintaining mileage on our exercise bike or to losing weight? It's true that commitment to the small stuff leads you to the big stuff, but we need to keep it all in perspective. Knowing our ultimate goal can keep us on target. And our mental tenacity can keep us moving steadily toward that target.

Sometimes it's hard to prevent those mental breakdowns. There will be days when it will seem that everything conspires against our keeping our mind on the game. We have to resist the temptation and keep focused. What we want to achieve is important, and the mental time and energy that we put into our efforts will help us to succeed.

◆

I will keep my mind on the big picture.

I can tell you one thing. I've done this my way. I don't have anybody to blame for this win but me, and I love it.
—*John Daly*

It's important to develop our own way of doing things. After all, we are ultimately responsible for how we play and the outcome. Win or lose, good or bad, we are the one. A bad sport blames the coach, the weather, the conditions, or her opponent when her own performance is lacking. When we rely on ourselves we can claim every victory as our own. Of course, that also means that we will have to take full responsibility for our losses too. Just remember that losses or disappointments come with the territory.

It is a fantastic feeling to know that our successes have been accomplished through our own hard work and dedication. This doesn't mean that we don't have to listen to advice or be able to get valuable input from trainers or coaches or other players. After all, relying on ourselves doesn't make us the instant expert or know-it-all—everyone can use some help sometime. But we need to take that assistance and use it to our best advantage. We can never play exactly like anyone else or be anyone else but ourselves, and the best way to do that is to develop our own style.

◆

I am 100 percent responsible for my performance, win or lose.

There's no such thing as coulda, shoulda, and woulda. If you shoulda and coulda, you woulda done it.
—*Pat Riley*

As another year comes to an end and we prepare our resolutions or goals for the one to come, we'll probably look back over the past months and evaluate various aspects of our lives—our careers, our weight, our relationships, and, particularly, our fitness program. Maybe we had started the year hoping to increase our days at the gym each week. Maybe we had planned to lengthen our daily runs on a regular basis. Or maybe we had hoped to defeat previously unbeatable golf opponents by taking more lessons and practicing religiously. Rarely do we reach the end of a year without these minor regrets or unreached goals. However, the good news is, tomorrow is another day. In fact, tomorrow begins a new year—time to make new plans and set new targets.

While looking back at how we may have failed to keep up our exercise programs in the past is tempting, and almost impossible to avoid, we do need to realize that what we did accomplish in the last year was the best that we were able to do at the time. We worked out as hard as we could. We cycled as far as our legs would take us. We played as many tennis tournaments as we could muster the enthusiasm for. And now, as we look at once backward and forward, at the last year of fitness and the one to come, we can aspire to higher goals based on what we know we can do and what we know we want to do. We have done a lot already. We can do more in the future.

◆

I can, I shall, and I will continue to work out.

Alcott, Amy, with Don Wade. *Amy Alcott's Guide to Women's Golf*. New York: Plume, 1991.

Beilenson, Peter. *The Sports Pages*. White Plains, N.Y.: Peter Pauper Press, Inc., 1989.

Benoit, Joan, with Sally Baker. *Running Tide*. New York: Knopf, 1987.

Braden, Vic. *Tennis for the Future*. New York: Little, Brown & Co., 1977.

Conny, Beth Mende. *Winning Women*. White Plains, N.Y.: Peter Pauper Press, Inc., 1993.

Ditka, Mike, with Don Pierson. *Ditka: An Autobiography*. Chicago: Bonus Books, 1986.

Dorfman, H. A., and Karl Kuel. *The Mental Game of Baseball: A Guide to Peak Performance*. South Bend, Ind.: Diamond Communications, Inc., 1989.

Ferguson, Howard. *The Edge*. Cleveland, Ohio: Great Lakes Lithograph Co., 1986.

Garfield, Charles A., with Hal Zina Bennett. *Peak Performance: Mental Training Techniques of the World's Greatest Athletes*. New York: Warner Books, 1985.

Gibbs, Joe, with Jerry Jenkins. *Joe Gibbs Fourth and One*. Nashville: Thomas Nelson Publishers, 1991.

Green, Lee. *Sportswit*. New York: Fawcett Crest, 1984.

Holtz, Lou. *The Fighting Spirit*. New York: Pocket Books, 1989.

Killy, Jean-Claude. *Situation Skiing*. New York: Doubleday, 1978.

Lebow, Fred, Gloria Averbuch, and Friends. *The New York Road Runners Club Complete Book of Running*. New York: Random House, 1992.

Leonard, George. *The Ultimate Athlete*. Berkeley: North Atlantic Books, 1974, 1990.

Liebman, Glen. *Sports Shorts*. Chicago: Contemporary Books, 1993.

Loehr, James E. *The Mental Game: Winning at Pressure Tennis*. New York: The Stephen Greene Press, 1990.

Lott, Ronnie, with Jill Lieber. *Total Impact*. New York: Doubleday, 1991.

Lynberg, Michael, compiled and edited by. *Winning! Great Coaches and Athletes Share Their Secrets of Success*. New York: Main Street Books/Doubleday, 1993.

Maikovick, Andrew J. *Sports Quotations: Maxims, Quips, and Pronouncements for Writers and Fans*. Jefferson, N.C.: McFarland & Co., Inc., Publishers, 1987.

Millman, Dan. *The Warrior Athlete*. Walpole, N.H.: Stillpoint Publishing, 1979.

Namath, Joe, created and produced with Bob Oates, Jr. *Football*. New York: Simon & Schuster, 1986.

Norman, Greg, with George Peper. *Shark Attack! Greg Norman's Guide to Aggressive Golf*. New York: Fireside/Simon & Schuster, 1988.

Orlick, Terry. *In Pursuit of Excellence*. Champaign, Ill.: Leisure Press, 1980, 1990.

Parietti, Jeff. *The Greatest Sports Excuses, Alibis, and Explanations*. Chicago: Contemporary Books, 1990.

Plaut, David, editor. *Speaking of Baseball*. Philadelphia: Running Press, 1993.

Pluto, Terry. *Tall Tales: The Glory Years of the NBA, in the Words of the Men Who Played, Coached, and Built Pro Basketball*. New York: Simon & Schuster, 1992.

Riley, Pat. *Showtime: Inside the Lakers' Breakthrough Season*. New York: Warner Books, 1988.

Rote, Kyle, Jr., with Basil Kane. *Kyle Rote Jr.'s Complete Book of Soccer*. New York: Simon & Schuster, 1978.

Scott, Dave. *Dave Scott's Triathlon Training*, New York: Fireside/Simon & Schuster, 1986.

Steinfeld, Jake. *Don't Quit!* New York: Warner Books, 1993.

Stern, David, introduction by. *NBA Jam Session*, New York: NBA Publishing, 1993.

Thomas, Isiah. *Bad Boys!* Grand Rapids, Mich.: Masters Press, 1989.

Turner, Ted, and Gary Jobson. *The Racing Edge*. New York: Simon & Schuster, A Rutledge Book, 1979.

Tutko, Thomas, and Umberto Tosi. *Sports Psyching: Playing Your Best Game All of the Time*. New York: Tarcher/Perigee, 1976.

Vecchione, Joseph J., editor. *The New York Times Book of Sports Legends*. New York: Times Books, 1991.

Walton, Gary M. *Beyond Winning: The Timeless Wisdom of Great Philosopher Coaches*. Champaign, Ill.: Leisure Press, 1992.

Kara Leverte Farley is a New York–based book editor who specializes in the areas of sports, health, and fitness, and is an avid athlete and sports fan.

Sheila M. Curry sails competitively, runs, bikes, rollerblades, and has recently taken up racquetball. A book editor whose areas of interest include health, self-help, and psychology, she lives in New York City.

◆